Better Homes and Gardens®

Quilting
PIECES OF THE PAST

175 YEARS OF INSPIRATIONAL QUILTING

Meredith® Books • Des Moines, Iowa

Quilting
PIECES OF THE PAST

Editor: Carol Field Dahlstrom
Contributing Technical Editors: Judy Bailey,
Susan M. Banker, Cathy Long,
Mary Helen Schiltz, Jan Temeyer
Contributing Writer: Carol McGarvey
Designer: Angie Haupert Hoogensen
Copy Chief: Terri Fredrickson
Publishing Operations Manager: Karen Schirm
Edit and Design Production Coordinator:
Mary Lee Gavin
Book Production Managers: Pam Kvitne, Marjorie J.
Schenkelberg, Rick von Holdt, Mark Weaver
Contributing Copy Editor: Margaret Smith
Contributing Proofreaders: Julie Cahalan,
Carolyn Hogan, Pam Wright
Technical Illustrator: Chris Neubauer Graphics, Inc.
Editorial Assistant: Cheryl Eckert

MEREDITH® BOOKS
Editor in Chief: Linda Raglan Cunningham
Design Director: Matt Strelecki
Managing Editor: Gregory H. Kayko
Executive Editor: Jennifer Dorland Darling

Publisher: James D. Blume
Executive Director, Marketing: Jeffrey Myers
Executive Director, New Business Development:
Todd M. Davis
Executive Director, Sales: Ken Zagor
Director, Operations: George A. Susral
Director, Production: Douglas M. Johnston
Business Director: Jim Leonard

Vice President and General Manager:
Douglas J. Guendel

Better Homes and Gardens® Magazine
Editor in Chief: Karol DeWulf Nickell

MEREDITH PUBLISHING GROUP
President, Publishing Group: Stephen M. Lacy
Vice President-Publishing Director: Bob Mate

MEREDITH CORPORATION
Chairman and Chief Executive Officer: William T. Kerr

In Memoriam: E.T. Meredith III (1933–2003)

All of us at Meredith® Books are dedicated to providing
you with information and ideas to create beautiful and
useful projects. We welcome your comments and
suggestions. Write to us at: Meredith Books, Crafts
Editorial Department, 1716 Locust Street—LN120, Des
Moines, IA 50309-3023.

If you would like to purchase any of our crafts, cooking,
gardening, home improvement, or home decorating
and design books, check wherever quality books are
sold. Or visit us at: bhgbooks.com

For information on visiting the International Quilt
Study Center, please contact them at:
The University of Nebraska-Lincoln International
  Quilt Study Center
234 Home Economics Building
Lincoln, NE 68583-0838
402-472-6549

QUILTING For All Time

Quilting isn't just a craft—it is a passion. It is not just sewing, or choosing fabric, or even the piecing and quilting. It is much more than that. Quilting is a response to a time and a place. It is a record of what an artist created for a particular time using her talent to fit the pieces of her life into a handmade quilt.

From the early 1800s until today, each quilt reflects the spirit of the time and the women who made them. Whether the quilts were made from scraps to keep a pioneer family warm, from wool coatings for the men in the Civil War, with patriotic colors during the centennial of 1876, from floral prints and velvets during the Victorian times, or from feed sacks in the 1930s, each quilter had a passion for making that particular quilt.

In this book you'll find exquisite quilts created during the last 175 years. You'll read about the history of the time and why women chose to make the quilts that they did. We've given you the patterns, the instructions, and hopefully, some of the passion that was stitched into these glorious pieces of the past.

As you enjoy this book, think of the women who have shared their love for quilting throughout time. And whether you are making your quilt to keep, to give, or to represent a special event or time in your life, you, too, are sharing your talent and the pieces of your life that fit together to make your unique quilt for all time.

Carol Field Dahlstrom

TABLE OF contents

"I made quilts as fast as I could to keep my family warm, and as pretty as I could to keep my heart from breaking." —A PIONEER WOMAN'S DIARY

1830–1860

Pioneer women of the mid-1800s created lovely patchwork, pieced, and appliquéd quilts as necessity items as well as expressions of personal artistry. This chapter focuses on the quilt history and fabric creations of the early settlers.

1860-1890

During the Civil War, women created warm quilts for the men fighting during this difficult time. In the late 1800s, the quilting style transitioned to elaborate crazy quilts, a reflection of Queen Victoria's love of embellishment.

1890–1920

This era of transition is represented by quilts that make use of a variety of techniques, depending on the economic and social status of the makers. Two-color and Amish quilts are among the representations from this time.

1920–1950

Reflecting the prosperity of the 1920s, quilts from this era used a wider palette of color. As women became liberated, they also renewed their interest in quilting, using pretty pastel designs—even during the Great Depression when feed sacks made their way into the art.

1950–present

Over the past 50 plus years, quilting surfaced as an artistic hobby, utilizing the enormous variety of available fabrics. Traditional as well as contemporary designs are pieced, appliquéd, and quilted to reflect past and current eras.

ALSO IN THIS BOOK

about this book

Quilting Through the Years

This book presents a collection of quilts and history of quilters, fabrics, and designs from the 1830s to the present.

To find such inspiring works we searched for quilts that accurately and exquisitely exemplified the last 175 years. We visited museums and universities and located collectors who graciously shared their enthusiasm and expertise with us. A special thanks goes to the staff of the International Quilt Study Center at the University of Nebraska-Lincoln, who shared many of their vintage quilts with us. See *page 2* for information about visiting the collection at the University of Nebraska-Lincoln.

These collections, along with quilts from individual collectors, served as the inspiration for the 54 projects in this book. Each of the featured quilts tells a story—about a period in history, about the quilters' labors, and about the fabrics, styles, colors, and popular motifs of each era.

HEXAGON MOSAIC c. 1860

Each chapter offers glorious quilt examples, the approximate dates they were made, and any available history. Courtesy: University of Nebraska-Lincoln, No. 1997.007.0145

The Fabrics

For each time period, information is provided about the fabrics that quilters used. Along with photographs of vintage fabrics, you'll discover which fabrics, colors, and prints were popular and readily available during a specified time period.

For historical interest, photographs of such items as magazines, quilt designers, and patterns from various time periods are shown.

JACK-IN-THE-BEANSTALK C. 1941

Making the Quilts

From elaborate appliqué to intricate pieced works, the selection of quilts in this book will inspire quilters to new heights. Quilts are arranged by time periods: 1830–1860, 1860–1890, 1890–1920, 1920–1950, and 1950–present.

Full-size patterns are provided as well as complete instructions and helpful diagrams. Fabric quantities specified are for 44/45-inch-wide, 100-percent-cotton fabrics. All measurements include a 1/4-inch seam allowance. Sew with right sides together unless otherwise stated. If a piece is reversed, it is labeled with an "r" after the corresponding pattern piece letter.

Assembly diagrams illustrate how quilt blocks are joined—showing sashing strips, setting squares, and details.

Throughout, assembly diagrams and measurements for various size quilts are also provided. If a different size is desired, add or delete blocks, sashings, or borders. This flexibility adds personal creativity to the finished quilt.

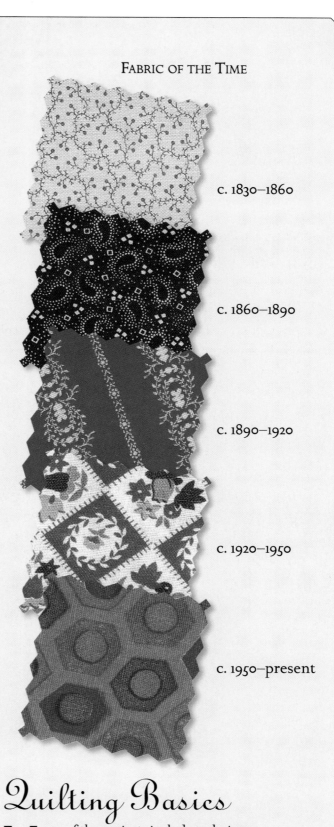

c. 1830–1860

c. 1860–1890

c. 1890–1920

c. 1920–1950

c. 1950–present

Quilting Basics

Many of the projects include techniques such as creating and adding binding. Quilter's Workshop, *pages 280–287*, provides these common quilting basics with step-by-step instructions and detailed illustrations.

1830–1860

Quilting prevailed during this time period. Pieced and appliquéd quilts became increasingly popular, with patchwork quilts replacing wholecloth coverlets. The availability of new fabrics enabled quilters to express themselves through stitching, color, and more design than ever before.

As settlers faced hardships of moving westward across America, they carried with them great promises for the future. When they stopped to form communities, women used quilting to help establish homes and friendships. Over time the technique of wholecloth quilting brought from Europe gave way to pieced and appliquéd blocks.

In Europe, affluent women often made quilts using the technique "broderie perse" or Persian embroidery, by appliquéing chintz cutouts onto plain backgrounds. Before 1800, elegant quilts were

made of wool, silk, linen, or chintz. A woman's needlework skills were showcased in fine handwork of fancy flowers and feathering.

By the early 1800s, medallion quilts—central designs surrounded by a series of borders—became popular. From that technique evolved early patchwork designs, fashioned from squares and right triangles.

The Fabric Boom

By the mid-1800s, upturned economic conditions and new fabrics increased the popularity of quilting. With a growing textile industry—the first cotton textile plant opened at Pawtucket, Rhode Island, in 1790—inexpensive and washable cottons became readily available, and quilters were caught up in creative frenzy.

Patchwork came into its own as one of the most significant phenomena in quilting history. At its heart it is a purely American technique. Making blocks one at a time and joining them together fed quiltmakers' needs for order and beauty. There were no cell phones or e-mails with attachments, so quilters exchanged techniques and ideas by gathering in small groups called quilting bees. There they exchanged patterns, which spread as settlers traveled.

Certain designs became standards, including Nine-Patch, Pinwheel, Sawtooth Star, Irish Chain, and Flying Geese. Quilters combined and varied these patterns to create hundreds more. Quiltmakers created patterns based on the lives they lived, the prairie paths they took, and the scenery from

FLYING GEESE c. 1838

Quiltmaker Sarah K. Headley created this quilt in Bucks County, Pennsylvania. Courtesy: University of Nebraska-Lincoln, No. 1997.007.0749

their surroundings—stars in the sky, furrows in the field, and even broken dishes.

Patterns traveled all over the country acquiring new names and variations.

Block names commemorated important people or significant events. Robbing Peter to Pay Paul was known as Dolley Madison's Workbox in another location. Beauregard's Surroundings was also known as Road to California, Wheel of Fortune, Coverlet Quilt, and Burgoyne Surrounded.

Between 1840 and 1860, the trend toward elaborate floral appliqués became popular, particularly in Pennsylvania and Maryland. Generally quilters used a variety of block designs in the appliquéd album quilts. Patchwork album quilts usually featured the same block but in different fabrics. Elegantly appliquéd quilts were particularly popular around Baltimore between 1846 and 1860. Even today these highly detailed and stunningly embellished projects are known as Baltimore album quilts.

Quilting Popularity

For everyday quilts the number of pieced patterns continued to grow, especially as roller-printed cotton fabrics in small prints became more available. As pioneers moved, so did the popularity of quilting. Pioneer women used quilting for practical and aesthetic purposes in their prairie homes, making bedding for their families and making shrouds to bury their dead. Lonely women often gathered to exchange news, quilt patterns, and fabric scraps. Young girls were taught to sew and quilt out of necessity.

Appliquéd quilts reached unparalleled heights of beauty and workmanship during the 10 years before the Civil War. To own such a quilt was a statement of affluence and

continued on page 12

Fabric of the Time

Although brown was a dependable color and often used in printed fabrics, quilts made in the mid-1800s were not drab. Green and turkey red were predominant colors. Unfortunately, some green dyes did not withstand the test of time. Fabrics treated with natural dyes retained green color; however, synthetic dyes developed in the late 1850s eventually became dull brown.

Turkey red and indigo blue were favorites due to their fade resistance.

Rich Prussian blue was another favorite. Pinks were dark or soft and featured florals or paisleys. Double pinks appear in quilts dating from the 1840s and 1850s. Yellow print was used as a background. Purples from this period are rare, since they often faded to brown. Permanent purple dye was not developed until 1862.

Linens and cottons were chosen instead of wool for their look and feel. Occasionally silk was used for coverlets.

Ombré print— fabric dyed light to dark to create an illusion of depth in appliquéd quilts—was used from 1830 to 1850.

Simple plaids and light-color backgrounds with large rows of prints also were popular.

status. Conventional appliqués, rich with flowers, birds, baskets, feathers, and other motifs, were dazzling.

In the South, where many slaves picked and cleaned the cotton that fueled the U.S. textile industry, some female slaves were lent from one plantation to another to do sewing. These women may have stitched many of the quilts we cherish today.

Piecing Gets Fancy

Plain piecing took a fancy turn too. Stars sprouted feathered edges, and triangles acquired curved corners. Overall patterns of diamonds formed cubes or blocks, and hexagons made complex honeycombs.

During this period the preference for white or light backgrounds for patchwork and appliqués developed. Colorwise, green and turkey red on white were popular. Appliquéd album blocks as well as other designs were executed in red and green calicos, the small prints that became popular during the 1840s and 1850s.

THREE-PATTERN APPLIQUÉ c. 1830

Look closely and you'll discover why this appliquéd sampler is called Three-Pattern Appliqué. The creative quilter used half blocks to reach the outer edge. This summer spread was created in Montgomery County, Pennsylvania.

Courtesy: University of Nebraska-Lincoln, No. 1997.007.0231

ERA TIMELINE

1830 *Godey's Lady's Book* begins publication. 1832 The Oregon Trail becomes a main route for settlers heading west. 1833 Oberlin College in Ohio, the first coeducational college and the first to admit blacks, opens. 1834 Cyrus McCormick gets a patent for the horse-drawn grain reaper. 1835 Samuel L. Clemens (Mark Twain) is born in Missouri. 1836 The Battle of the Alamo takes place in Texas. 1837 The U.S. consists of 13 free states and 13 slave states. 1838 Removal of nearly 17,000 Cherokee Indians from Georgia on the "Trail of Tears" results in 4,000 deaths; the Underground Railroad to help slaves move North is organized. 1841 William Henry Harrison becomes president on March 4 but dies of pneumonia on April 4. 1843 A large westward migration begins. 1845 A potato famine in Ireland brings great numbers of immigrants to the United States; Henry David Thoreau starts living at Walden

Quilting for Comfort

Many men heading west sought adventure, fortune, and open spaces. In contrast to the ladies of leisure in the cities, the pioneer women who accompanied these men knew they could carry along only a few essential possessions. Large furniture pieces and family treasures couldn't always make the trip.

Quilts, however, were justified being used to warm beds, cover cabin doors, shield crops from locusts, and shroud the dead. Just as importantly, they were cherished treasures of another way of life. Signature quilts were especially prized because they symbolized ties to distant family and friends.

Crossing the plains was a treacherous and desperately lonely life. Many women found that the social and aesthetic values of quiltmaking offered solace as they dealt with isolation.

Old patterns made the trip, and new ones were made and named for the journey, such as Road to California, Kansas Troubles, and Oregon Trail.

Young girls learned to sew so they could help produce and mend the family bedding and clothing. By the age of 10 or 11, girls were learning the methods of piecing and appliquéing and already had a few quilts to their credit.

Typically pioneer brides made five or six quilts to begin housekeeping. Completion of a wedding quilt, representing her finest stitched work, proved a girl's readiness for marriage. Made by brides alone or quilted with the help of friends or relatives, wedding quilts were the crowning glory of young women.

---

ond. 1846 U.S. annexes California and New Mexico; Iowa becomes a state. 1847 New congressman Abraham Lincoln delivers a speech opposing the Mexican War; Frederick Douglass founds *The North Star*, an abolitionist newspaper. 1848 Lucretia Mott and Elizabeth Cady Stanton organize the first American women's rights convention in Seneca Falls, New York. 1849 First gold seekers arrive in San Francisco; Amelia Bloomer publishes *The Lily*, a journal supporting women's rights and temperance. 1850 Nathaniel Hawthorne publishes *The Scarlet Letter*, which becomes a best seller. 1851 Horace Greeley may or may not have said it, but the word was to "Go west, young man, go west." 1852 Harriet Beecher Stowe's *Uncle Tom's Cabin* sells 1 million copies. 1854 Thoreau publishes *Walden*. 1856 Pro- and antislavery forces clash around the country. 1858 Lincoln is nominated to oppose Stephen Douglas for the Senate, and Lincoln and Douglas debate.

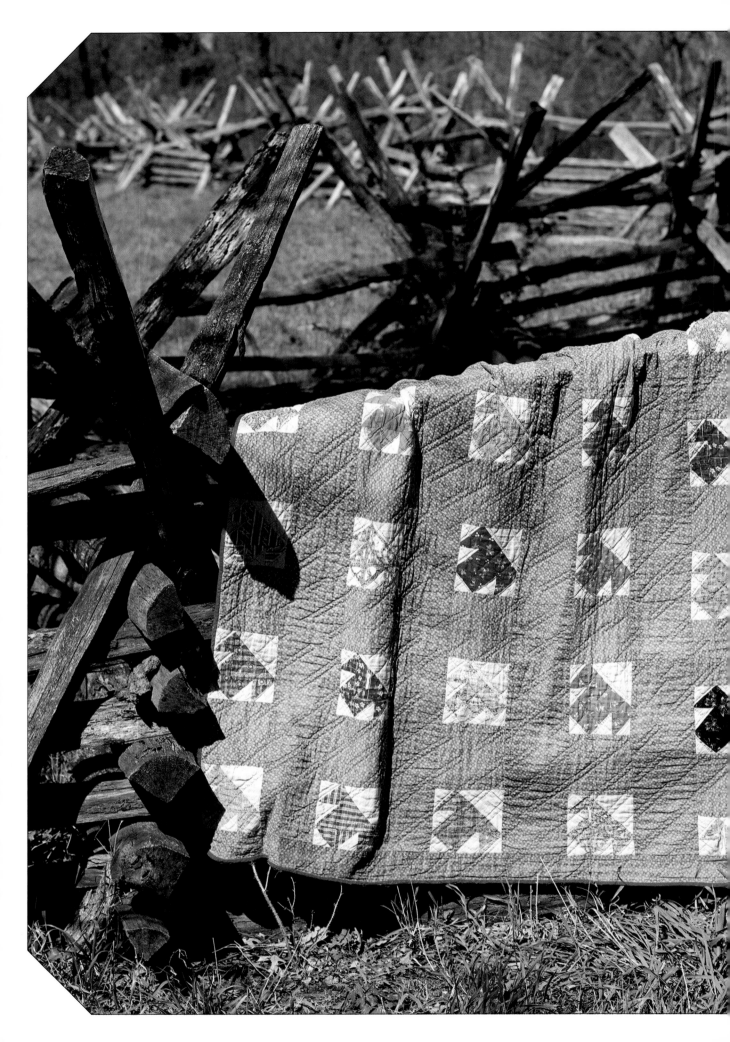

T-squares

1830–1860

This T-square quilt may have been made to symbolize the maker's last name or that she lived in Tennessee. A turkey red border completes the quilt.

Materials

1⅓ yards of assorted light and dark prints for blocks

1⅓ yards of light blue check for block backgrounds

3½ yards of green print for setting squares and sashing strips

⅝ yard of red print for binding

4⅞ yards of backing fabric

75×87 inches of quilt batting

Finished quilt: 68¼×80¾ inches
Finished block: 5¼ inches square

Quantities specified are for 44/45-inch-wide, 100-percent-cotton fabrics. All measurements include a ¼-inch seam allowance. Sew with right sides together unless otherwise stated.

Cut the Fabrics

To make the best use of fabrics, cut the pieces in the order that follows. Cut the sashing and border strips the length of the fabric (parallel to the selvage).

instructions continued on page 16

15

T-squares

1830–1860

From assorted light and dark prints, cut:

- 140—2⅝-inch squares, cutting each diagonally to make 280 triangles, or 280 of Pattern A
- 28—4⅜-inch squares, cutting each diagonally to make 56 triangles, or 56 of Pattern B

From light blue check, cut:

- 140—2⅝-inch squares, cutting each diagonally to make 280 triangles, or 280 of Pattern A
- 28—4⅜-inch squares, cutting each diagonally to make 56 triangles, or 56 of Pattern B

From green print, cut:

- 6—5¾×79¼-inch sashing strips
- 1—2½×68¾-inch border strip
- 49—5¾-inch setting squares

From red print, cut:

- 8—2½×42-inch binding strips

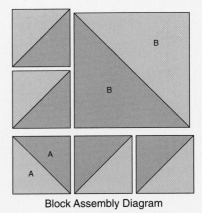

Block Assembly Diagram

Make the Blocks

1 Join an assorted light or dark print A triangle to an light blue check A triangle to make a small triangle-square. Press the seam allowance toward the print. Repeat to make five small triangle-squares.

2 Sew together an assorted light or dark print B triangle to a light blue check B triangle to make a large triangle-square. Press the seam allowance toward the dark print.

3 Referring to the Block Assembly Diagram, *above right*, join the five small triangle-squares and 1 large triangle-square to make one T-square block. Press the seam allowances toward the dark print. The block should measure 5¾ inches, including seam allowances.

4 Repeat steps 1–3 to make 56 T-square blocks.

Assemble the Quilt Top

1 Referring to the Quilt Assembly Diagram, *opposite,* for placement, lay out the 56 T-square blocks and 49 green print setting squares in seven rows. Join the rows. Press seam allowances toward the setting squares.

2 Referring to the diagram, lay out the seven pieced rows and six green print sashing strips in alternating rows. Join the rows. Press the seam allowances toward the green sashing strips.

3 Sew together the 2½×68¾-inch border strip to one 68¾-inch edge of the quilt top.

Complete the Quilt

1 Layer the quilt top, batting, and backing. Baste the layers (see tips for assembling the quilt in Quilter's Workshop beginning on *page 280*). Quilt as desired.

2 Use the red print 2½×42-inch strips to bind the quilt (see binding tips in Quilter's Workshop).

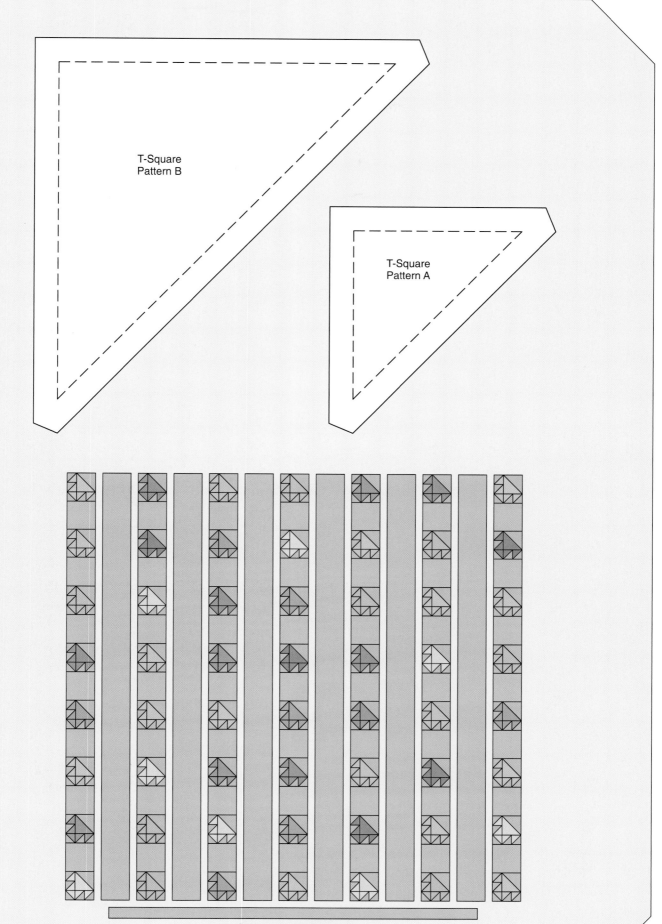

T-Square
Pattern B

T-Square
Pattern A

Quilt Assembly Diagram

criss—cross
1830–1860

Red and white was a favorite color combination used in quilts during the mid-1800s. The background fabric of this quilt is a tiny black-on-white print. The quilt was probably made in Iowa during the 1850s.

Materials

$3^1/_2$ yards of black-on-white print

2 yards of red print

$3^3/_4$ yards of backing

67×74 inches of quilt batting

Finished quilt: $60^1/_2$×$67^1/_2$ inches

Finished block: 10 inches square

Quantities specified are for 44/45-inch-wide, 100-percent-cotton fabrics. All measurements include a $^1/_4$-inch seam allowance. Sew with right sides together unless otherwise stated.

Cut the Fabrics

To make the best use of fabrics, cut the pieces in the order that follows. Cut the sashing and border strips the length of the fabric (parallel to the selvage). The measurements are mathematically correct. You may wish to cut your sashing and border strips longer than specified to allow for possible sewing differences. Trim the strips to the lengths needed before joining them to the quilt top.

From black-on-white print, cut:

- 2—$2^1/_2$×68-inch border strips (#3)
- 5—6×57-inch sashing strips (#2)
- 12—6×$10^1/_2$-inch sashing strips (#1)
- 48—$3^3/_4$-inch squares, cutting diagonally in an X to make 192 large triangles, or 192 of Pattern C

- 32—$2^1/_8$-inch squares, cutting once diagonally to make 64 small triangles, or 64 of Pattern D
- 64—$2^1/_4$-inch squares, or 64 of Pattern A

From red print, cut:

- 80—$2^1/_4$×$5^3/_4$-inch rectangles, or 80 of Pattern B
- 96—$2^1/_4$-inch squares, or 96 of Pattern A
- 7—$2^1/_2$×42-inch binding strips

Make the Blocks

1 For one Criss-Cross block, you will need: four black-on-white print Pattern A, 12 black-on-white print Pattern C, four black-on-white print Pattern D, six red print Pattern A, and five red print Pattern B (see *page 21*).

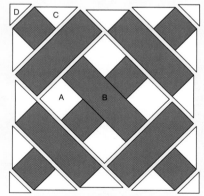

Block Assembly Diagram

2 Referring to the Block Assembly Diagram, join two black-on-white A squares to

instructions continued on page 20

opposite sides of a red print A square to make a pieced unit. Press the seam allowances toward the black-on-white squares. Repeat to make a second pieced unit. Sew a pieced unit to each long side of a B rectangle to make a pieced center unit. Press the seam allowances toward the red print.

3 Sew two black-on-white C triangles to opposite sides of a red print A square. Press the seam allowances toward the A square. Sew a B rectangle to one side to make a pieced corner unit. Press the seam allowance toward the B rectangle. Repeat to make four pieced corner units.

4 Join a pieced corner unit to opposite sides of the pieced center unit. Press the seam allowances toward the B rectangle.

5 Add a C triangle to opposite ends of the B rectangle of the remaining pieced corner units. Press the seam allowances toward the B rectangle. Sew to remaining sides of the pieced center unit.

6 Sew a D triangle to each corner of the pieced block.

7 Repeat steps 1–6 to make a total of 16 Criss-Cross blocks.

Assemble the Quilt Top

1 Sew a black-on-white print 6×10½-inch sashing strip (#1) to one side of 12 Criss-Cross blocks. Press the seams toward the sashing strips.

2 Referring to the Quilt Assembly Diagram, *left*, lay out 16 Criss-Cross blocks in four horizontal rows, beginning with a block with sashing and ending with a Criss-Cross block. Join the blocks and sashing in each row. Press the seam allowances toward the #1 sashing strips.

3 Lay out the rows and five 6×57-inch black-on-white print sashing strips (#2). Join the horizontal rows.

4 Sew a 2½×68-inch black-on-white print border (#3) to each long side of quilt top.

Complete the Quilt

1 Layer the quilt top, batting, and backing. Baste the layers. Quilt as desired.

2 Use the red print 2½×42-inch strips to bind the quilt (see binding tips in Quilter's Workshop beginning on *page 280*).

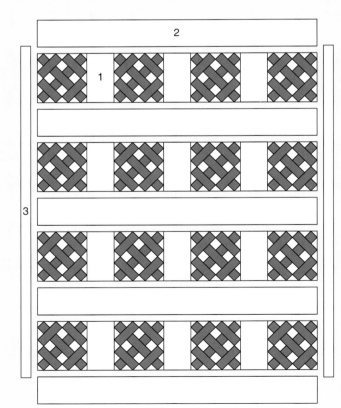

Quilt Assembly Diagram

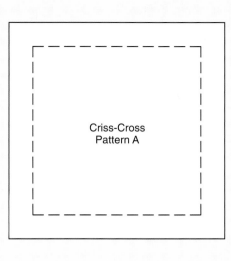

Criss-Cross
Pattern A

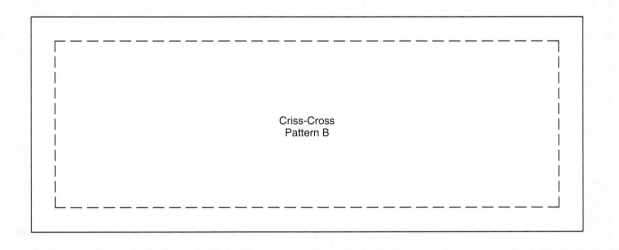

Criss-Cross
Pattern B

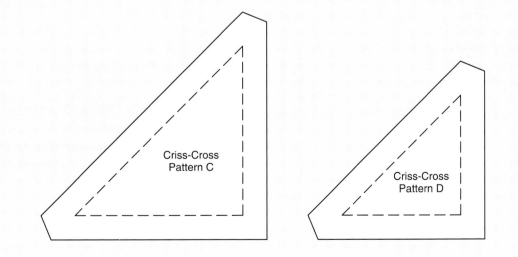

Criss-Cross
Pattern C

Criss-Cross
Pattern D

flying geese

1830–1860

This Flying Geese Variation uses red and white blocks set with white sashing. The turkey red prints are over-dyed with black and yellow.

Materials

3¼ yards *total* of assorted red prints
4¼ yards of solid white
4⅓ yards of backing
77×84 inches of quilt batting

Finished quilt: 71×77½ inches
Finished block: 10 inches square

Quantities specified are for 44/45-inch-wide, 100-percent-cotton fabrics. All measurements include a ¼-inch seam allowance. Sew with right sides together unless otherwise stated.

Cut the Fabrics

To make the best use of fabrics, cut the pieces in the order that follows. Cut the sashing and border strips the length of the fabric (parallel to the selvage). The measurements are mathematically correct. You may wish to cut your sashing and border strips longer than specified to allow for possible sewing differences. Trim the strips to the lengths needed before joining them to quilt top.

From assorted red prints, cut:
- 120—2⅞-inch squares, cutting once diagonally to make 240 B triangles, or 240 of Pattern B
- 120—2½-inch squares, or 120 of Pattern C

- 30—7¼-inch squares, cutting diagonally in an X to make 120 D triangles, or 120 of Pattern D
- 30—Pattern E

From solid white, cut:
- 6—4×78-inch sashing and border strips (#2)
- 25—4×10½-inch sashing strips (#1)
- 8—2½×42-inch binding strips
- 720—Pattern A

Make the Blocks

1 For one Flying Geese Variation block, you will need 24 white Pattern A, 8 red print Pattern B, 4 red print Pattern C, 4 red print Pattern D, and 1 red print Pattern E (see *page 25*).

2 Referring to the Block Assembly Diagram, sew an A triangle to each short side of a B triangle to make a Flying Geese unit. Press the seam allowances toward the B triangle. Repeat to make eight Flying Geese units.

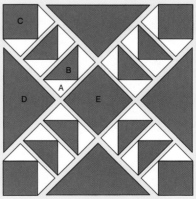

Block Assembly Diagram

instructions continued on page 24

3 Join two A triangles to adjacent sides of a C square to make a corner unit. Press the seam allowances toward the C square. Repeat to make a total of four corner units.

4 Sew together two Flying Geese units and a corner unit to make an ABC unit. Press the seam allowances in one direction. Repeat to make four ABC units.

5 Sew an ABC unit to opposite sides of the E square to make an ABCE unit. Press the seam allowances in one direction.

6 Sew a D triangle to each long side of two ABC units to make two ABCD units. Press the seam allowances in one direction.

7 Lay out the ABCE unit and two ABCD units in three rows. Join the rows to make a Flying Geese Variation block. Press the seam allowances in one direction.

8 Repeat steps 1–7 to make 30 Flying Geese Variation blocks.

Assemble the Quilt Top

1 Sew a solid white 4×10½-inch sashing strip to the bottom of 25 Flying Geese Variation blocks (#1), referring to the Quilt Assembly Diagram, *below left*. Press the seams toward the sashing strips.

2 Lay out 30 Flying Geese Variation blocks in five vertical rows, beginning the row with a block with sashing and ending with a block without sashing. Join the blocks and sashing in each row. Press the seam allowances toward the sashing strips.

3 Lay out five rows and the 4×78-inch solid white sashing and border strips (#2), beginning and ending with a border strip. Join the rows and sashing strips to complete the quilt top.

Complete the Quilt

1 Layer the quilt top, batting, and backing. Baste the layers (see tips for assembling the quilt in Quilter's Workshop beginning on *page 280*).

2 Quilt as desired. The original maker of the antique quilt quilted each block with vertical and horizontal lines and quilted a cable pattern in the sashing and borders.

3 Use the solid white 2½×42-inch strips to bind the quilt (see binding tips in Quilter's Workshop).

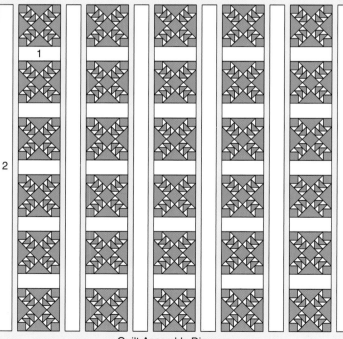

Quilt Assembly Diagram

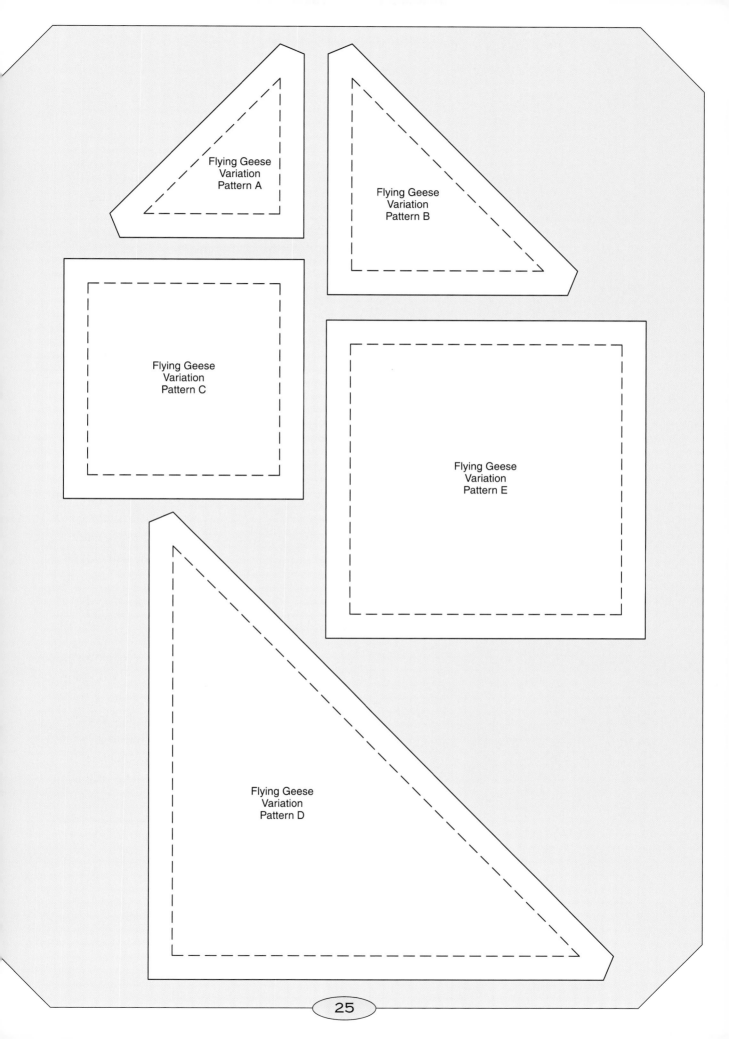

Flying Geese
Variation
Pattern A

Flying Geese
Variation
Pattern B

Flying Geese
Variation
Pattern C

Flying Geese
Variation
Pattern E

Flying Geese
Variation
Pattern D

nine-patch

1830–1860

Alternate and join contrasting white
and blue fabric squares as the foundation for this
checkerboard-style quilt.

Materials

7¼ yards of solid white or muslin fabric
2¾ yards of blue print
6⅛ yards of backing fabric
90×108 inches of quilt batting

Finished quilt: 82½×103½ inches
Finished Nine-Patch block: 10½ inches square

Quantities specified are for 44/45-inch-wide, 100-percent-cotton fabrics. All measurements include a ¼-inch seam allowance. Sew with right sides together unless otherwise stated.

Quilt Notes

This quilt is a 7×9-block alternate straight set. Each block is composed of four basic Nine-Patch units, joined by a center crossbar.

To piece the blocks, follow either the strip-piecing instructions or the traditional piecing instructions on *page 28*. Strip piecing also makes the assembly of the 1½-inch-square pieces (finished size) more accurate.

For more information on strip piecing, see tips in Quilter's Workshop beginning on *page 280*.

Cut the Fabrics

To make the best use of fabrics, cut the pieces in the order that follows. To minimize cutting and piecing, the fabric is cut into strips. These strips can be sewn together, then cut into pieced segments for the block assembly, or individual pieces can be cut from the strips for traditional piecing.

From blue print, cut:

◆ 43—2×42-inch strips. Set aside 10 strips for the middle border; use 33 strips for the Nine-Patch units.
◆ 2—2×33-inch strips for Strip Set 3

From solid white, cut:

◆ 35—2×42-inch strips. Set aside eight strips for borders; use the remaining strips for the Nine-Patch units.
◆ 31—11-inch squares
◆ 8—2×42-inch strips, cutting sixty-four 2×5-inch rectangles for the center crossbars
◆ 12—2×36-inch border strips
◆ 4—5×33-inch strips for Strip Set 3
◆ 9—2½×42-inch binding strips

Prepare the Strip Sets

Note: For traditional piecing, see "Make the Nine-Patch Blocks, Traditional Piecing," *page 28*.

1 For Strip Set 1, sew a 2-inch-wide blue print strip to each long edge of a 2-inch-wide solid

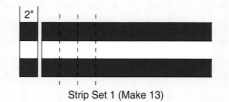

2"

Strip Set 1 (Make 13)

instructions continued on page 28

white print strip. Press the seam allowances toward the blue print. Make a total of 13 of Strip Set 1.

2 For Strip Set 2, sew a 2-inch-wide solid white strip to each long edge of one 2-inch-wide blue print strip. Press the seam allowances toward the blue print. Make a total of seven of Strip Set 2.

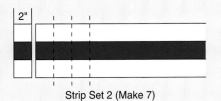

Strip Set 2 (Make 7)

3 For Strip Set 3, sew a 5×33-inch solid white strip to both sides of one 2×33-inch blue print strip. Press seam allowances toward the solid white. Make a total of two of Strip Set 3.

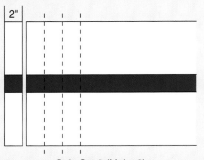

Strip Set 3 (Make 2)

Make the Nine–Patch Blocks

STRIP PIECING:

1 From *each* of Strip Sets 1 and 2, you can cut twenty 2-inch-wide segments. Cut a total of 256 segments of Strip Set 1 and 128 segments of Strip Set 2.

2 Make a total of 128 Nine-Patch blocks as shown in Diagram 1.

TRADITIONAL PIECING:

1 From 31 of the 2-inch-wide blue strips, cut a total of 640 print 2-inch squares. From 25 of the 2×42-inch solid white strips, cut a total of 512 white 2-inch squares to make the Nine-Patch blocks.

2 Make a total of 128 Nine-Patch blocks as shown in Diagram 1. Press the seam allowances toward the blue print.

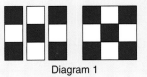

Diagram 1

Assemble the Units

1 Sew together two Nine-Patch blocks and a solid white 2×5-inch rectangle as shown in Diagram 2, to make a Nine-Patch unit. Press the seam allowances toward the solid white. Make a total of 64 Nine-Patch units.

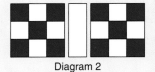

Diagram 2

2 Cut thirty-two 2-inch-wide pieces from Strip Set 3 to make a center crossbar. If piecing traditionally, use the remaining strips to cut blue print 2-inch squares and solid white 2×5-inch rectangles to make a total of 32 center crossbars.

3 Sew a Nine-Patch unit to each long edge of a 2-inch-wide crossbar to complete 1 four-block unit as shown in Diagram 3 (see *page 29*). Press the seam allowances toward the center crossbar. Make a total of 32 four-block units.

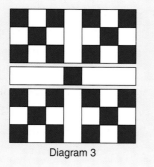

Diagram 3

Assemble the Quilt Top

1 Referring to the photograph on *page 26*, lay out the four-block units and solid white 11-inch squares in seven horizontal rows. Alternating pieced blocks with solid white squares, lay out five rows that begin and end with a four-block unit and four rows that begin and end with a solid white 11-inch square.

2 Join the blocks in each row. Press the seam allowances toward the solid white squares.

3 Join the horizontal rows. Press the seam allowances in one direction. The quilt top should measure 73½×94½ inches.

Add the Borders

1 Stitch together three solid white 2×36-inch strips end to end to make an inner border strip long enough for each side. Sew inner border strips to opposite sides of the quilt top; trim excess border fabric.

2 Sew together two white 2×42-inch strips to make the top and bottom inner border strips. Stitch an inner border onto each end of the quilt top; trim excess border fabric. Press seam allowances toward the inner border.

3 Make the middle border in the same manner as the inner border, piecing three blue print 42-inch-long strips for the side borders and two blue print strips for the top and bottom borders.

4 Sew the side middle borders onto the quilt top first; then join the top and bottom borders. Press the seam allowances toward the middle border.

5 Use the remaining solid white 2×42-inch strips to piece the outer borders. Join three 42-inch-long strips for each side outer border and two 42-inch-long strips for top and bottom outer border. Add the borders onto the quilt top, sewing the side borders first and then the top and bottom borders. Press the seam allowances toward the blue print middle border.

Complete the Quilt

1 Layer the quilt top, batting, and backing. Baste the layers (see tips for assembling the quilt in Quilter's Workshop beginning on *page 280*).

2 Quilt as desired. This Nine-Patch has straight lines of quilting that cross through each square of the patchwork and across the borders. A maple leaf design is quilted in the plain squares; the pattern for the leaf design is on the Pattern Sheet.

3 Use the solid white 2½×42-inch strips to bind the quilt (see binding tips in Quilter's Workshop).

sawtooth star

1830–1860

Dainty prints dance on this starry quilt set with solid brown squares. Each of the stars is constructed with a light-color center square encircled by dark points.

Materials

4$\frac{1}{4}$ yards of brown fabric

2$\frac{3}{4}$ yards of muslin

41—5$\frac{1}{2}$-inch squares of assorted light prints for the star centers

41—9-inch squares of assorted dark prints for the star points

$\frac{3}{4}$ yard of green print for binding

2$\frac{7}{8}$ yards of 90-inch-wide backing fabric

90×109 inches of quilt batting

Finished quilt: 85$\frac{1}{2}$×94$\frac{1}{2}$ inches.
Finished Sawtooth Star block: 4$\frac{1}{2}$ inches square

Quantities specified are for 44/45-inch-wide, 100-percent-cotton fabrics. All measurements include a $\frac{1}{4}$-inch seam allowance. Sew with right sides together unless otherwise stated.

Quilt Notes

This quilt is a 17×19-block alternate straight set, with 161 star blocks and 162 setting squares. Each star has a light center and dark points against a muslin background.

Use a variety of colors and prints for a genuine scrap quilt. Plaids, shirtings, calicos, pindots, solids, and stripes were used in the original quilt.

Cut the Fabrics

To make the best use of fabrics, cut the pieces in the order that follows.

From brown fabric, cut:

◆ 4—5×90-inch border strips

◆ 162—5-inch squares for setting squares

From muslin, cut:

◆ 26—1$\frac{5}{8}$×42-inch strips, cutting twenty-five $\frac{5}{8}$-inch squares from each strip for patch A. Cut a total of 644 A squares.

◆ 14—3$\frac{1}{2}$×42-inch strips, cutting twelve 3$\frac{1}{2}$-inch squares from each strip. Cut each square diagonally in an X, creating four C triangles. Cut a total of 644 C triangles.

From each assorted light print, cut:

◆ 4—2$\frac{3}{4}$-inch squares for star centers. Cut a total of 161 center squares.

From each assorted dark print, cut:

◆ 16—2-inch squares, cutting each square in half diagonally to make 32 B triangles. Cut eight triangles for each star, or a total of 1,288 triangles.

From green print, cut:

◆ 8—2$\frac{1}{2}$×42-inch strips

Make the Blocks

1 Each block requires one center square, four *each* of square A and triangle C, and eight B triangles.

Note: Although seam allowances are usually pressed toward darker fabrics, it is important to avoid building up bulk where seam allowances meet. This requires pressing toward the lighter fabrics in this patchwork.

Assemble the Quilt Top

1 Referring to the photograph, *left*, lay out the Sawtooth Star blocks and brown setting squares in 19 horizontal rows.

2 Join the Sawtooth Star blocks and setting squares in each row. Press the seam allowances toward the setting squares.

3 Join the rows. Press the seam allowances in one direction.

Add the Borders

1 Stitch a brown 5×90-inch strip onto each long side of the quilt top. Press seam allowances toward the border strip. Trim excess border fabric.

2 Join a brown 5×90-inch strip to the top and bottom of the quilt top as in *Step 1*.

Complete the Quilt

1 Layer the quilt top, batting, and backing. Baste the layers (see tips for assembling the quilt in Quilter's Workshop beginning on *page 280*).

2 Quilt as desired. This quilt has quilting that outlines the seams of the star points. Diagonal lines, 1/4 inch apart, are quilted in the star centers, the setting squares, and the borders.

3 Use the green print 2½×42-inch strips to bind the quilt (see binding tips in Quilter's Workshop).

2 Referring to the Block Assembly Diagram, sew together a dark print B triangle to each short side of a muslin C triangle to make a Flying Geese unit. Press the seam allowances toward the C triangle. Make four Flying Geese units.

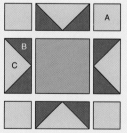

Block Assembly Diagram

3 Sew a Flying Geese unit to opposite sides of a light print 2³/₄-inch square. Press the seam allowances toward the center.

4 Join muslin A square to each end of the remaining Flying Geese units. Press the seam allowances toward the A squares.

5 Lay out the pieces in three rows. Join the rows to make a Sawtooth Star block. Press the seam allowances toward the center square. Make a total of 161 Sawtooth Star blocks.

irish chain

1830–1860

Tiny squares of white, tan, and red fabrics
arranged on a white background create a covering
of large graphic diamonds.

Materials

4 yards of muslin
3 yards of tan print
2$\frac{1}{2}$ yards of red print
6 yards of backing fabric
90×108 inches of quilt batting

Finished quilt: 73$\frac{1}{4}$×97$\frac{1}{4}$ inches
Finished block: 12$\frac{1}{4}$ inches square

Quantities specified are for 44/45-inch-wide,
100-percent-cotton fabrics. All measurements
include a $\frac{1}{4}$-inch seam allowance. Sew with right
sides together unless otherwise stated.

Quilt Notes

This quilt is a 5×7-block alternate straight set.
However, instead of being a plain square, the
alternating block is pieced to connect to
the main block, creating the illusion of a
continuous chain.

Although the pieces for this quilt can be cut
and sewn traditionally, instructions are included
for strip piecing, which reduces cutting and
sewing time and improves the accuracy of
sewing the small squares.

Cut the Fabrics

To make the best use of fabrics, cut the pieces in
the order that follows. Cut all fabrics in strips, as
indicated. For traditional patchwork, individual

pieces are cut from these strips. For strip piecing,
the strips are sewn together, then cut into segments.

From tan print, cut
- 1—23×42-inch rectangle to equal 350 inches
  total of 2$\frac{1}{2}$-wide binding (see tips for making
  binding in Quilter's Workshop beginning on
  page 280)
- 10—2$\frac{1}{4}$×42-inch strips for the outer border
- 20—2$\frac{1}{4}$×42-inch strips. Set aside 12 strips for
  Block A and eight strips for Block B.

From red print, cut:
- 10—2$\frac{1}{4}$×42-inch strips for the inner border.
- 24—2$\frac{1}{4}$×42-inch strips. Set aside 20 strips for
  Block A and four strips for Block B.

From muslin, cut:
- 10—2$\frac{1}{4}$×42-inch strips for the middle border
- 17—2$\frac{1}{4}$×42-inch strips for Block A
- 4—5$\frac{3}{4}$×42-inch strips for Block B
- 18—9$\frac{1}{4}$-inch squares

Prepare the Strip Sets

Note: For traditional piecing, see *page 34*.

The six strip sets are illustrated on *page 34*.
Strip Sets 1–4 are for Block A; each is made by
sewing together seven 2$\frac{1}{4}$×42-inch strips. Strip
Sets 5 and 6 are for the pieced edge of Block B.

1 Using the colors indicated in the illustration
of each strip set, sew together seven strips to
make Strip Sets 1, 2, 3, and 4 as shown.

instructions continued on page 34

2 Make Strip Sets 5 and 6 in the same manner, positioning a muslin 5³/₄-inch-wide strip in the center of each set as illustrated.

3 Make one of Strip Set 4. Make two of all the other sets. Press all the seam allowances in one direction.

Assemble the A Blocks

Block A is assembled in seven rows. Refer to the Assembly Diagram, Block A, for placement of each square or strip segment. Position each unit carefully for correct color placement.

TRADITIONAL PIECING:

1 Cut the 2¹/₄-inch-wide strips designated for Block A into 2¹/₄-inch squares. Cut a total of 340 red print squares, 204 tan print squares, and 289 muslin squares.

2 Assemble the squares in horizontal rows as shown in the Assembly Diagram. Press the seam allowances toward the dark fabric. Join the rows as shown. Make a total of 17 of Block A.

STRIP PIECING: Each strip segment represents one horizontal row of the block.

1 From *each* of Strip Sets 1, 2, and 3, cut thirty-four 2¹/₄-inch-wide units. Cut 17 units 2¹/₄ inches wide from Strip Set 4.

2 Each block requires two units from Strip Sets 1, 2, and 3, and one unit from Strip Set 4.

3 Join the seven segments into a block in a 1-2-3-4-3-2-1 sequence (see Assembly Diagram, Block A). Make a total of 17 of Block A.

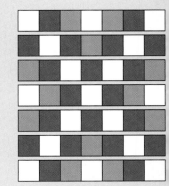

Assembly Diagram
Block A

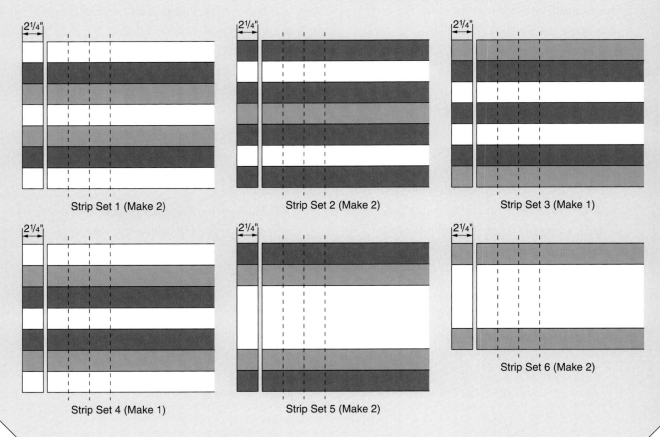

Strip Set 1 (Make 2)

Strip Set 2 (Make 2)

Strip Set 3 (Make 1)

Strip Set 4 (Make 1)

Strip Set 5 (Make 2)

Strip Set 6 (Make 2)

Assemble the B Blocks

Block B is assembled by sewing pieced rows around a muslin square. Refer to the Assembly Diagram, Block B, for placement of each unit.

TRADITIONAL PIECING:

1 Cut the 2¼-inch-wide strips designated for Block B into 2¼-inch squares. Cut 72 red print squares and 144 tan print squares.

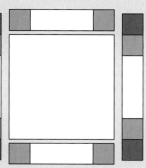

Assembly Diagram Block B

From each 5¾-inch-wide muslin strip, cut eighteen 2¼×5¾-inch units. Cut a total of 72 units.

2 Assemble Block B as shown. For each block, make two units consisting of a muslin strip with a tan print square sewn to each end. Make two more units in the same manner, adding red print squares at each end.

3 Sew the short units to opposite sides of a 9¼-inch muslin square. Sew the long units to the remaining sides. Press the seam allowances toward the muslin square. Make a total of 18 of Block B.

STRIP PIECING: Block B is made by sewing units of Strip Sets 5 and 6 to a center muslin square.

1 Cut *each* of Strip Sets 5 and 6 into eighteen 2¼-inch-wide units. Each block requires two units from each of these strip sets.

2 Sew units from Strip Set 6 onto opposite sides of one 9¼-inch muslin square. Sew units from Strip Set 5 onto the remaining sides of the square. Press seam allowances toward the muslin square. Make a total of 18 of Block B.

Assemble the Quilt Top

1 Referring to the photograph on *page 32*, lay out blocks A and B in seven horizontal rows with five blocks to a row, alternating A and B blocks. Make four rows that begin and end with a B block and three rows that begin and end with an A block.

2 Join the blocks in each row. Press the seam allowances toward Block B.

3 Sew together the rows. Press the seam allowances in one direction. The quilt top should measure 61¼×85¾ inches.

Add the Borders

1 Join three 2¼×42-inch red print strips end to end to make an inner border strip long enough for each side. Sew border strips to sides of the quilt top; trim excess border fabric.

2 Sew together two red print strips for the top and bottom inner border strips. Stitch a strip onto each end of the quilt top; trim excess border fabric.

3 Sew together the middle and outer border strips in the same manner. Join the middle border, then the outer border to the quilt top. With each border, sew the side border strips first and then the top and bottom border strips.

Complete the Quilt

1 Layer backing, batting, and quilt top. Baste the three layers together (see tips for assembling the quilt in Quilter's Workshop beginning on *page 280*).

2 Quilt as desired. The quilt shown on *page 32* features straight lines of quilting that form a crosshatch pattern through each square of the patchwork and across the borders.

3 Use the tan print 2½×42-inch strips to bind the quilt (see binding tips in Quilter's Workshop).

robbing peter

1830–1860

*A lovely example from the
two-color quilt era, this antique appliquéd
red and white quilt is bordered
with a trio of stripes.*

Although this block appears to be pieced, the
curves are achieved by appliquéing four
melon-shape pieces (Pattern A) onto a solid
fabric square.

Materials

6 yards *each* of white and red fabrics
$5^3/_4$ yards of backing fabric
90×108 inches of quilt batting

Finished quilt: 68×96 inches
Finished block: 7 inches square

Quantities specified are for 44/45-inch-wide,
100-percent-cotton fabrics. All measurements
include a $^1/_4$-inch seam allowance. Sew with right
sides together unless otherwise stated.

Quilt Notes

Trace and make a template for Pattern A on
page 39 (see tips for making templates in Quilter's
Workshop beginning on *page 280*).

instructions continued on page 38

Cut the Fabrics

To make the best use of fabrics, cut the pieces in the order that follows.

From white fabric, cut:

- 1—20×108-inch rectangle. From this piece, cut four 2½×108-inch border strips and four 2½×80-inch border strips.
- 48—7½-inch squares
- 192—Pattern A

From red fabric, cut:

- 1—10×108-inch rectangle. From this piece, cut two 2½×80-inch border strips and two 2½×108-inch border strips.
- 8—2½×42-inch binding strips
- 48—7½-inch squares
- 192—Pattern A

Make the Blocks

1 On each A piece, turn under the seam allowance on the curved edges only. Clip the seam allowance, if necessary, to achieve a smooth curve. Press or baste the seam allowance in place if desired. Leave the straight edge flat; this is sewn into the seam when blocks are joined.

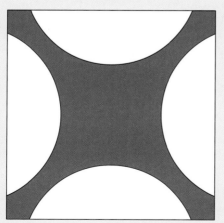

Quilt Block

2 Align the straight edge of one white A piece with one edge of a red 7½-inch square. There should be approximately ¾ inch of red showing above and below the white melon shape on the straight edge. Appliqué the curved edge onto the red fabric.

3 Appliqué a white A piece onto each of the three remaining sides of the red square in the same manner.

4 Repeat, sewing four white A pieces onto each red square and four red A pieces onto each white square. Make a total of 48 blocks of each color combination.

Assemble the Quilt Top

1 Referring to the Quilt Assembly Diagram, *opposite*, lay out the blocks in 12 horizontal rows of eight blocks each, alternating red and white centers. Position blocks so six rows begin with a red print square and six rows begin with a white print square.

2 Sew together the blocks in each row. Press the seam allowances in one direction, alternating the direction with each row.

3 Join the rows, matching seam lines carefully. Press the seam allowances in one direction. The quilt top should measure 56×84 inches.

Add the Borders

1 Match two white border strips with one red border strip of the same length. Sew together the strips lengthwise, with the red strip in the center. Repeat to make a total of four white-red-white border sections. Press the seam allowances in one direction.

Robbing Peter to Pay Paul
Pattern A

2 Sew the long border sections to the sides of the quilt top, starting and stopping ¹/₄ inch from each end. Repeat with the short border sections, adding them to the top and bottom edges. Miter the border corners (see tips for mitering border corners in Quilter's Workshop beginning on *page 280*).

Complete the Quilt

1 Layer backing, batting, and quilt top. Baste the three layers together (see tips for assembling the quilt in Quilter's Workshop).

2 Quilt as desired. This quilt has outline quilting around each A piece and the border seams.

3 Use the red 2¹/₂×42-inch strips to bind the quilt (see binding tips in Quilter's Workshop).

Quilt Assembly Diagram

peony

1830–1860

*Beautifully pieced floral blocks are
accented with appliquéd stems, leaves, and buds, with outer blocks
turned to face the center of the quilt top.*

Materials

10 yards of muslin
2 yards of red-orange print
1½ yards of green print
9 yards of backing fabric
107-inch square of quilt batting

Finished quilt: 101 inches square
Finished block: 15 inches square

Quantities specified are for 44/45-inch-wide,
100-percent-cotton fabrics. All measurements
include a ¼-inch seam allowance. Sew with right
sides together unless otherwise stated.

Quilt Notes

Trace and make templates for Patterns A, B, C, D,
F, G, and H on Pattern Sheet (see tips for making
templates in Quilter's Workshop beginning on
page 280). *Note:* Add ¼-inch-wide seam allowances
to pattern pieces before cutting them from
fabric. For the E piece, cut a 7½-inch-square
template. For the setting squares and triangles,
cut a 15-inch square template.

Cut the Fabrics

To make the best use of fabrics, cut the pieces
in the order that follows.

Adding ¼-inch seam allowances, use the
15-inch-square template to mark and cut nine
setting squares—the cut square will measure
15½ inches. Set the squares aside.

For the setting triangles, draw a diagonal line
between opposite corners of the 15-inch-square
template. Draw a second diagonal line in the
opposite direction, through the lower section of
the template (see Diagram 1).

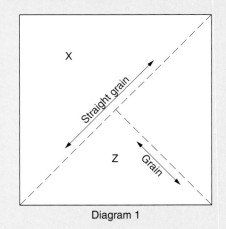

Diagram 1

Cut on the drawn lines to form templates
X and Z.

Using template X, mark 12 setting triangles on
muslin, the long side of the triangle on the
straight grain. Adding ¼-inch seam allowances,
cut out the triangles.

Using template Z, mark four corner-setting
triangles on the muslin, with the legs of the
triangle template on the straight grain. Adding
¼-inch seam allowances, cut out the triangles
and set aside.

Measurements for the borders are 3 to
4 inches longer than necessary; trim excess
after sewing borders in place.

instructions continued on page 42

Note: The number of pieces to cut for the entire quilt is listed first; the number to cut for one block follows in parentheses.

From muslin, cut:

- 4—8$\frac{1}{2}$×104-inch border strips
- 10—2$\frac{1}{2}$x42-inch binding strips
- 144—Pattern B (9)
- 144—Pattern C (9)
- 48—Pattern D (3)
- 16—Pattern E (1)

From red-orange print, cut:

- 288—Pattern A (18)
- 32—Pattern F (buds, 2). When cutting buds, trace template onto right side of fabric, add seam allowance, and cut out.

From green print, cut:

- 32—Pattern G (large leaves, 2)
- 32—Pattern F (small leaves, 2)
- 32—Pattern H (bud stems, 2)
- 480 inches of 1-inch-wide bias strips for stems. Each block requires approximately 30 inches of bias—about 16 inches for the center flower and 7 inches for each side flower.

Make the Blocks

The flowers that make up most of the Peony block are pieced. Because the muslin squares and triangles in these areas must be set in, hand piecing is recommended. (Stitch from seam line to seam line, rather than to raw edges.)

1 Referring to Diagram 2, sew diamonds in pairs; make a total of three pairs.

2 Join the pairs to make a six-diamond flower. Make three six-diamond flowers for each block.

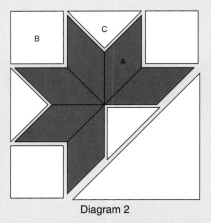

Diagram 2

3 Set three B squares and three C triangles into each section (see Diagram 2). When joining the C pieces that fit into the base of the flower, leave the seams open at the corner so the stem can be tucked in later (see tips for sewing set-in seams in Quilter's Workshop beginning on *page 280*).

Diagram 3

Diagram 4

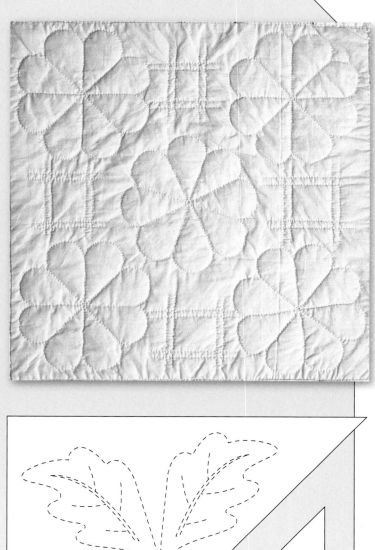

Diagram 5   Diagram 6

4 Sew D pieces to each flower section. Join flower sections and E piece to complete the piecing of each block (see Diagram 3).

5 Prepare bias strips for stems(see tips for cutting and folding bias strips in Quilter's Workshop). Finished width of the stems is about $3/8$ inch.

6 For appliquéd leaves, turn under seam allowances; baste along fold lines. At ends of bud stems, trim seam allowances to $1/8$ inch.

7 Referring to Diagram 3 for placement, arrange stems, buds, and leaves. Using matching thread, appliqué center flower stem first, leaving openings for leaves and side stems. After tucking stems under flower diamonds, sew openings closed. For bud ends, first appliqué bud. Use the end of the needle to turn back seams of the bud covering as you appliqué it over each bud.

8 Repeat steps 1–7 to make a total of 16 Peony blocks.

instructions continued on page 44

43

Assemble the Quilt Top

1 Use quilting designs on *page 43* and a water-erasable pen to mark designs on muslin squares and triangles (see Diagrams 4, 5, and 6). Fold and lightly press the muslin pieces in half or in quarters; the creases form the placement guidelines.

Diagram 7

2 Stitch the pieced and plain blocks together in diagonal rows, turning the pieced blocks along the sides of the quilt toward the center (see Diagram 7). The quilt top should measure 85½ inches square, including the seam allowances.

Add the Border

1 Cut border strips to exact size and stitch them to the quilt top, mitering corners (see tips for mitering border corners in Quilter's Workshop).

2 Using the quilting patterns on the Pattern Sheet and referring to Diagram 8, mark the border designs with a water-erasable pen, chalk, or marker. For placement of motifs in the border, see Diagram 8.

Complete the Quilt

1 Layer backing, batting, and quilt top. Baste the three layers together (see tips for assembling the quilt in Quilter's Workshop).

2 Quilt all motifs along marked lines. Also quilt in-the-ditch (along seams) around each flower diamond, along the stems, around the leaves, along seams between quarter-block sections, and between whole blocks. In addition, quilt segments of the large leaves as shown on the pattern piece.

3 Use the muslin 2½×42-inch strips to bind the quilt (see binding tips in Quilter's Workshop).

Diagram 8

1860-1890

In the late 1800s, quilts were as varied as the reasons for making them. War and necessity inspired many works of the time.

Log Cabin blocks date from the 1860 presidential campaign of Abraham Lincoln, whose origins were represented by the humble cabin of his birth. The block is symbolic of the American frontier, with strips of fabric representing the interlocking logs of a cabin stacked row upon row. The red center square often used represents the hearth as the center of the cabin. Yellow centers signify candles in the cabin window.

Log Cabin blocks in a Barn Raising setting depict the beams of a new barn. The Straight Furrows setting reflects patterns in a plowed field, and Zigzag sets imitate the jagged split-rail fences of rural fields and gardens. Other variations include Courthouse Steps and Pineapple.

During the time of the Civil War (1861–1865), quilts were part of a divided nation's social consciousness. Women in both the North and the South supplemented supplies by making quilts for their husbands, brothers, and sons at war. They made elegant quilts to raffle to raise funds for the cause, and simpler ones to supply bedding for hospitals.

Strong feelings on both sides of the war effort inspired patriotic quilt designs. Red, white, and blue quilts were encouraged in such publications as *Peterson's Magazine*, and 34 stars for the number of states often were incorporated. Eagles, arrows, laurel leaves, and other emblems of war and peace were added. More quilts survived in the North, which suffered less physical destruction than the South.

HEXAGON MOSAIC c. 1860

Created in Pennsylvania in the mid-1800s, this geometric quilt is created from thousands of hexagon pieces.

Courtesy: University of Nebraska-Lincoln, No. 1997.007.0145

Making Do

Immediately after the war, life changed dramatically as people experienced shortages of supplies for their homes. With no money for new fabric, quilters often cut up worn clothing, including fancy ball gowns. Quilts also reflected the somber times, as many women grieved over lost family members, and many quilts were made using gray, black, white, and deep purple.

Fabric of the Time

In the later decades of prosperity in the 1800s, Northern textile mills moved to full production. Technology increased the variety of cotton print designs, and included celebratory, commemorative, and playful designs. Paisleys were everywhere—from tiny prints on fabrics to large motifs on woolen shawls.

Aniline chemical dyes, discovered in 1856, were responsible for a broad range of bright, sharp colors. One design could be printed in several different color schemes.

Expositions increased the popularity of fabrics. Japanese influence was seen in formal and asymmetrical designs, while Europeans promoted symmetrical patterns.

Muddy brown, dark chocolate, and cocoa brown were common during this time. Often a geometric or floral element was used as the main design. Double and cinnamon pinks were popular.

Elegant silks and rich velvets were used in crazy quilts. Any elegant fabric—even silk from patriotic ribbons—was stitched into quilts for richness.

For new opportunities, many people traveled by train to the West. Towns sprang up around railroad depots across the plains. With distribution available, general stores carried calico fabrics. When combined with geometric pieces cut from cast-off clothing, calico added color to quilters' handwork. By 1870 the sewing machine, patented by Elias Howe in 1846, was commonplace. A decade later 600,000 machines were in use, freeing women from hand piecing.

Quilting bees and county fairs were social highlights during the late 1800s when there were great distances between homesteads and towns. Showing livestock and quilts at the fair were anticipated as special times.

Mail-order supplies changed quilting forever. In 1872 Montgomery Ward was the first to make quilting products—fabrics, sheeting, batting, and some patterns—available by catalog. Sears, Roebuck & Co., followed in 1887. Ladies Art Company of

continued on page 50

Stores and mail-order suppliers increasingly carried more quilting supplies—including fabric for as little as 10 cents a yard.

49

St. Louis was the first to specialize in quilt templates and directions by mail. Catalogs popularized quilt patterns that had been previously known only to a few. For example, Clamshell and Postage Stamp, popular in the East, became favorites across the country.

Millinery goods were easy to find—even being offered in early magazines.

Crazy Quilt Craze

Philadelphia's Exposition in 1876 is credited with spawning the silk crazy quilt, made from random-shape pieces of rich satin, silk, and velvet, and embellished with fancy decorative embroidery stitches. The quilt's name came from the look of crazed porcelain and likely was tied to the country's fascination with Japanese designs.

NORTH CAROLINA LILY c. 1880–1900
Pieced lilies are the focus in this graphic quilt from Indiana County, Pennsylvania. Courtesy: University of Nebraska-Lincoln, No. 1997.007.0042

ERA TIMELINE

1860 Abraham Lincoln is elected president. 1861 The attack on Fort Sumter near Charleston, South Carolina, signals the beginning of the Civil War. 1862 The Homestead Act allows citizens to acquire up to 160 acres after farming it for five years. 1863 The President's Emancipation Proclamation is signed; first Conscription Act requires males from ages 20–45 to register for service in the Army; Lincoln gives the "Gettysburg Address." 1865 The Civil War ends when General Robert E. Lee surrenders to General U. S. Grant at Appomattox Courthouse; Lincoln is shot by John Wilkes Booth while watching a play at Ford's Theater in Washington, D.C.; 13th Amendment abolishes slavery. 1866 First 5-cent coins, called nickels, are introduced. 1867 All males over 21 can vote; Alaska is purchased from Russia for $7. million. 1869 Union Pacific Central Pacific transcontinenta railroad is completed as the two lines meet at Promontor Point, Utah. 1870 John D. Rockefeller develops Standar Oil Co. 1871 The "Great

This striking quilt from Providence, Rhode Island, highlights 16 Basket blocks set on point against a print background.

Courtesy: University of Nebraska-Lincoln, No. 1997.007.0694

The new social consciousness of women of the 1880s reflected their desire for elegance, culture, and harmony. Women followed European designs in the press and eagerly imitated Britain's Queen Victoria, whose name became synonymous with the era. In keeping with her style, American women embellished their homes with lace, ribbons, ruffles, and fringe. Crazy quilting was a natural outgrowth of this decorative style. With satin stitches, French knots, stem stitches, and featherstitches, quilts became more decorative.

Design Days

As people adjusted to time of prosperity, Northern textile mills began producing a grand variety of fabrics, colors, and prints, allowing quilters extraordinary options. There were paisleys, calicos, bold graphics, and formal and asymmetrical Japanese patterns.

Colorwise, muddy brown, dark chocolate, and cocoa brown were common. Double or cinnamon pinks were also popular.

Elegant fabrics, such as colorful silks from ribbons and scarves, were stitched into quilts for richness and interest.

While fashionable city women fussed over fancy crazy quilts, rural quilters continued to piece scrap quilts as part of the daily routine.

Chicago Fire" almost destroys the Midwestern city. 1874 barbed wire becomes available, making grazing possible; the Chautauqua Movement of educational and religious lectures begins in New York State. 1876 Alexander Graham Bell invents the telephone; General Custer and 250 men attack Sitting Bull and Crazy Horse at Little Big Horn. 1877 Thomas Edison patents the phonograph. 1878 The first central switchboard opens for telephone service in New York City. 1879 Edison invents a working lightbulb. 1880 George Eastman patents a flexible roll of camera film. 1881 Clara Barton organizes the Red Cross; President Garfield is assassinated. 1883 The Brooklyn Bridge opens to the public. 1884 Chicago has the first skyscraper, a 10-story building; the first long-distance telephone service is established between New York and Boston. 1885 Washington Monument is dedicated after 36 years of construction. 1886 Statue of Liberty is dedicated in New York Harbor. 1888 The U.S. introduces the secret-ballot system for voting. 1889 Jane Addams opens Hull House; 50,000 settlers lay claims in first Oklahoma land rush.

feathered star
1860–1890

This star quilt is an example of pieced work. Created with indigo blue calicoes set on white, it is a striking quilt from this era.

Materials

5 yards of navy blue print
2^3/$_4$ yards of solid white
4^1/$_8$ yards of backing fabric
74×86 inches of quilt batting

Finished quilt: 68×77^3/$_4$ inches
Finished block: 13^1/$_2$ inches square
Finished half block: 6^3/$_4$×13^1/$_2$ inches

Quantities specified are for 44/45-inch-wide, 100-percent-cotton fabrics. All measurements include a ^{1}/$_4$-inch seam allowance. Sew with right sides together unless otherwise stated.

Cut the Fabrics

To make the best use of your fabrics, cut the pieces in the order that follows. Cut the sashing and border strips the length of the fabric (parallel to the selvage). The measurements are mathematically correct. You may wish to cut your border strips longer than specified to allow for possible sewing differences. Trim the strips to the lengths needed before joining them to the quilt top. The patterns are on the Pattern Sheet.

From navy blue print, cut:
- 2—3×78^1/$_4$-inch border strips (#1)
- 2—3×63^1/$_2$-inch border strips (#2)
- 3—3^1/$_2$×73^1/$_4$-inch sashing strips (#3)

- 16—3^1/$_2$×14-inch sashing strips (#4)
- 20—6^1/$_2$-inch squares, or 20 of Pattern E
- 72—3^1/$_8$-inch squares, cutting each once diagonally for 144 medium triangles, or 144 of Pattern B
- 144—2^3/$_4$-inch squares, cutting each diagonally twice in an X for 576 small triangles, or 576 of Pattern A
- 8—2^1/$_2$×42-inch binding strips

From solid white, cut:
- 19—7^1/$_4$-inch squares, cutting each diagonally twice in an X for 76 large triangles, or 76 of Pattern C
- 72—4^1/$_4$-inch squares, or 72 of Pattern D
- 127—2^3/$_4$-inch squares, cutting each diagonally twice in an X for 508 small triangles, or 508 of Pattern A

Make the Blocks

1 For one Feathered Star block, you will need 32 navy blue print Pattern A, 28 solid white Pattern A, 8 navy blue print Pattern B, 4 solid white pattern C, 4 solid white Pattern D, and 1 navy blue print Pattern E.

2 Sew a solid white A triangle to a navy blue print A triangle to make a triangle-square. Press the seam allowances toward the navy blue print. Repeat to make 24 triangle-squares.

instructions continued on page 54

3 Referring to the Block Assembly Diagram, join three triangle-squares in a row to make a triangle-square unit. Repeat eight times. Lay out four left and four right triangle-square units in diagonal rows, placing the light side of the triangle-squares in the correct position.

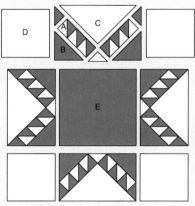

Block Assembly Diagram

Left Side Diagonal Row: Sew a navy blue print A triangle to the top of each triangle-square unit. Sew a navy blue print B triangle to the left side of each; join the short side of a solid white C triangle to the right side.

Right Side Diagonal Row: Sew a navy blue print A triangle to the top of each triangle-square unit. Sew a short side of a solid white triangle A to the bottom of each. Sew a navy blue print B triangle to the right side. Stitch the right side to the left side to make an ABC unit.

4 Sew a solid white D square to opposite sides of an ABC unit to make Row 1 and Row 3.

5 Sew an ABC unit to opposite sides of a navy blue print E square to make Row 2. Join Rows 1–3. Press the seam allowances in one direction. Repeat to make 16 Feathered Star blocks.

Make the Half Blocks

1 For one Feathered Star half-block, you will need 16 navy blue print Pattern A, 15 solid white Pattern A, 4 navy blue print Pattern B, 3 solid white Pattern C, 2 solid white Pattern D, and 1 navy blue print Pattern E.

2 Follow steps 1–5 to make the 13$\frac{1}{2}$-inch Feathered Star block, completing only Rows 1 and 2. Trim the half block to measure 7$\frac{1}{4}$×14 inches, including seam allowances (see Feathered Star Half Block Diagram). Repeat to make 4 half blocks.

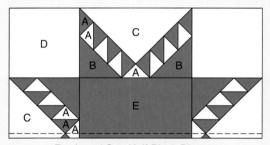

Feathered Star Half-Block Diagram

Assemble the Quilt Top

1 Sew a 3$\frac{1}{2}$×14-inch navy blue print sashing strip (#4) to one side of each of 12 whole blocks and the 4 half blocks.

2 Lay out the blocks in four vertical rows, beginning with a half block and ending with a full block without sashing.

3 Join the blocks in each row. Press the seam allowances toward the sashing strips.

4 Lay out the four block rows and three long navy blue print sashing strips. Join the rows to the sashing strips (#3). Press the seam allowances toward the long sashing strips.

Quilt Assembly Diagram

Add the Borders

Sew a short navy blue print border strip (#2) to the top and bottom of the quilt top. Join a long navy blue print border strip (#1) to each side edge of the quilt to complete the quilt top.

Complete the Quilt

1 Layer the quilt top, batting, and backing. Baste the layers (see tips for completing the quilt in Quilter's Workshop beginning on *page 280*).

2 Quilt as desired. The original maker of the quilt quilted a diamond grid on the Feathered Star blocks and parallel grid lines on the sashing and borders.

3 Use the navy blue print 2½×42-inch strips to bind the quilt (see binding tips in Quilter's Workshop).

colorado block

1860-1890

Colorado became a state on August 1, 1876. It's possible this quilt was made to commemorate Colorado's statehood because the fabrics used date from the same era.

Materials

3 yards *total* of assorted dark prints

$2\frac{1}{2}$ yards of cream print for the block background

3 yards of tan print for setting blocks and binding

4 yards of backing fabric

72×84 inches of quilt batting

Finished quilt: 66×78 inches

Finished block: 6 inches square

Quantities specified are for 44/45-inch-wide, 100-percent-cotton fabrics. All measurements include a $\frac{1}{4}$-inch seam allowance. Sew with right sides together unless otherwise stated.

Cut the Fabrics

To make the best use of your fabrics, cut the pieces in the order that follows.

From assorted dark prints (you will need 8 squares or 16 triangles from one print to complete a single block), cut:

◆ 576—$2\frac{3}{8}$-inch squares, cutting each diagonally once to make 1,152 triangles, or 1,152 of Pattern A

instructions continued on page 58

colorado block

1860-1890

From cream print, cut:

- 72—4¼-inch squares, cutting each diagonally twice in an X for a total of 288 quarter-square triangles, or 288 of Pattern B
- 288—2⅜-inch squares, cutting each diagonally once to make 576 triangles, or 576 of Pattern A

From tan print, cut:

- 71—6½-inch setting squares
- 8—2½×42-inch binding strips

Make the Blocks

1 For one block you will need 16 matching dark print A triangles, 8 cream print A triangles, and 4 cream print B triangles.

2 Referring to Diagram 1, sew a cream print A triangle to a matching dark print A triangle to make a triangle-square. Repeat to make eight triangle-squares. Sew a matching dark print A triangle to each short side of a cream print B triangle to make a Flying Geese unit (see Diagram 2). Repeat to make four Flying Geese units.

3 For center block unit: Sew together two triangle-squares (see Block Assembly Diagram). Repeat. Join the pairs to make the center block.

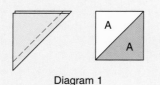

Diagram 1

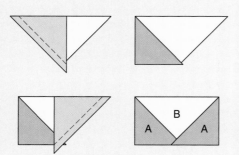

Diagram 2

4 Join a triangle-square to opposite ends of two Flying Geese units to make Row 1 and Row 3. Sew a Flying Geese unit to opposite sides of the center unit to make Row 2. Join the rows to make one Colorado block. Press the seam allowances in one direction. Repeat to make 72 Colorado blocks.

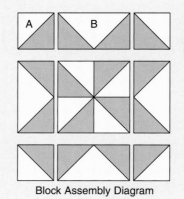

Block Assembly Diagram

Assemble the Quilt Top

1 Referring to the Quilt Assembly Diagram for placement, lay out 72 Colorado blocks and 71 setting blocks in 13 horizontal rows with 11 blocks in each row. Sew the blocks together in each row. Press the seam allowances in one direction, alternating the direction with each row.

2 Join the rows. Press the seam allowances in one direction. The pieced quilt top should measure 66½×78½ inches, including the seam allowances.

Complete the Quilt

1 Layer the quilt top, batting, and backing. Baste the layers (see tips for completing the quilt in Quilter's Workshop beginning on *page 280*). Quilt as desired.

2 Use the tan print 2½×42-inch strips to bind the quilt (see binding tips in Quilter's Workshop).

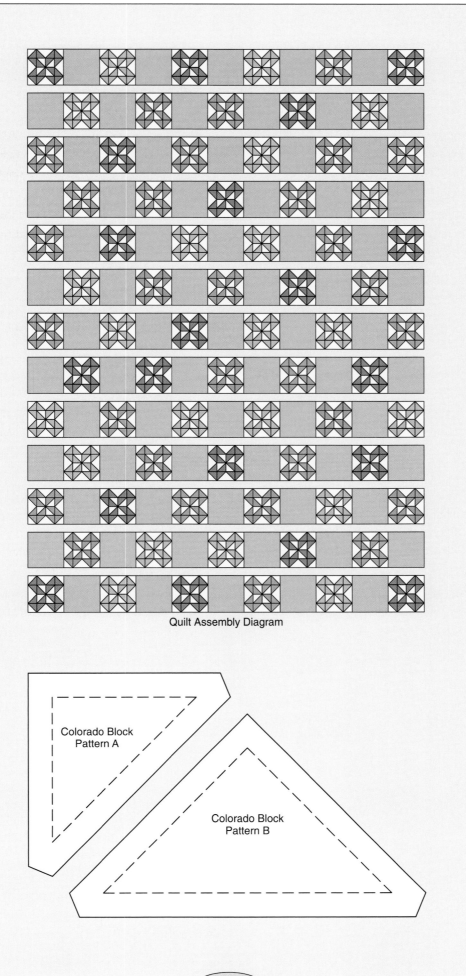

Quilt Assembly Diagram

Colorado Block
Pattern A

Colorado Block
Pattern B

sweet stripes

1860-1890

A lively rendition of the traditional Courthouse Steps block, this quilt incorporates a variety of red and cream prints and stripes to capture a playful look.

Materials

1³/₈ yards of red print for block centers, inner border, and binding

1¹/₂ yards *total* of assorted cream shirting prints for blocks and outer border

1¹/₂ yards *total* of assorted red-and-white stripes for blocks

2²/₃ yards of backing fabric

48×55 inches of quilt batting

Finished quilt top: 41¹/₂×49 inches

Finished block: 7¹/₂ inches square

Quantities specified are for 44/45-inch-wide, 100-percent-cotton fabrics. All measurements include a ¹/₄-inch seam allowance. Sew with right sides together unless otherwise stated.

Cut the Fabrics

To make the best use of your fabrics, cut the pieces in the order that follows. Cut the border strips the length of the fabric (parallel to the selvage). The red-and-white stripes are cut with the stripes running parallel to the long edges.

From red print, cut:

- 5—2¹/₂×42-inch binding strips
- 2—1¹/₂×47-inch inner border strips
- 2—1¹/₄×38-inch inner border strips
- 30—2-inch squares

From assorted cream shirting prints, cut:

- 2—1³/₄×49¹/₂-inch outer border strips
- 2—1³/₄×39¹/₂-inch outer border strips
- 60—1¹/₂×6-inch rectangles
- 60—1¹/₂×4-inch rectangles
- 60—1¹/₂×2-inch rectangles

From assorted red-and-white stripes, cut:

- 60—¹/₂×8-inch rectangles
- 60—1¹/₂×6-inch rectangles
- 60—1¹/₂×4-inch rectangles

Make the Blocks

For one Courthouse Steps block, you'll need one red print 2-inch square, two each cream print 1¹/₂×2-, 1¹/₂×4- and 1¹/₂×6-inch rectangles from the same print, and two red-and-white stripe 1¹/₂×4-, 1¹/₂×6-, and 1¹/₂×8-inch rectangles from the same print.

1 Sew matching cream print 1¹/₂×2-inch rectangles to opposite sides of a red print 2-inch square (see Diagram 1). Press the seam allowances toward the cream print rectangles.

Diagram 1

instructions continued on page 62

2 Sew matching red-and-white stripe 1¹/₂×4-inch rectangles to opposite sides of the pieced step 1 unit (see Diagram 2). Press the seam allowances toward the red-and-white stripe rectangles.

Diagram 2

3 Referring to Diagram 3 for placement, continue sewing matching pairs of rectangles to the pieced unit until you have three rectangles on each side of the red print square, completing a Courthouse Steps block. Always press the seam allowances toward the outside. The pieced block should measure 8 inches square, including the seam allowances.

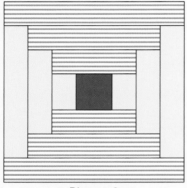

Diagram 3

4 Repeat steps 1–3 to make a total of 30 Courthouse Steps blocks.

Assemble the Quilt Center

1 Referring to the photograph on *page 63* for placement, lay out the 30 Courthouse Steps blocks in six horizontal rows, keeping each block's red-and-white stripes at the top and bottom.

2 Sew together the blocks in each row. Press the seam allowances in one direction, alternating the direction with each row. Then join the rows to complete the quilt center. Press the seam allowances in one direction. The pieced quilt center should measure 38×45¹/₂ inches, including the seam allowances.

Add the Borders

1 Sew the red print 1¹/₄×38-inch inner border strips to the top and bottom edges of the pieced quilt center. Then add the 1¹/₂×47-inch inner border strips to the side edges of the pieced quilt center. Press the seam allowances toward the red print inner border.

2 Sew the cream print 1³/₄×39¹/₂-inch outer border strips to the top and bottom edges of the pieced quilt center. Then add the cream print 1³/₄×49¹/₂-inch outer border strips to the side edges of the pieced quilt center to complete the quilt top. Press the seam allowances toward the cream print outer border.

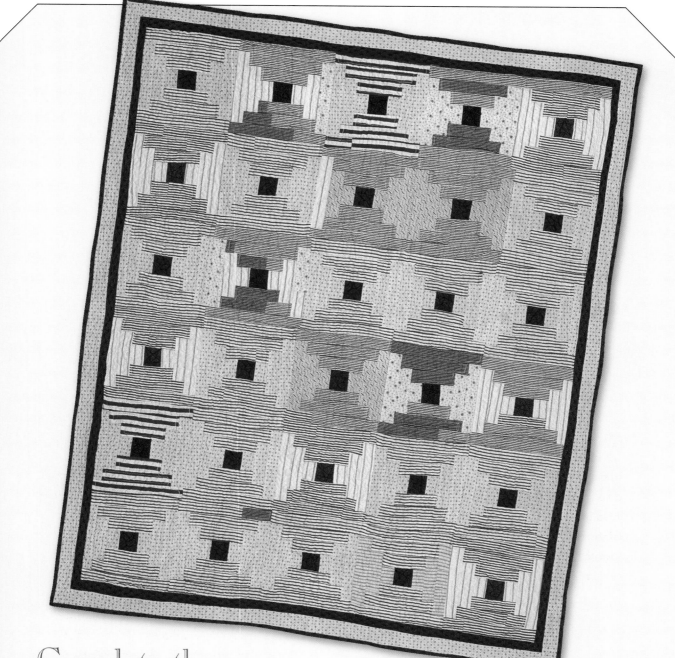

Complete the Quilt

1 Layer the quilt top, batting, and backing. Baste the layers (see tips for completing the quilt in Quilter's Workshop beginning on *page 280*).

2 Quilt as desired. The original quiltmaker quilted a star in the center of each block, then stipple-quilted the cream print areas. She stitched $1/4$ inch inside each red-and-white stripe rectangle and stitched a swirl and stipple design in the borders.

3 Use the red print $2^{1}/_{2} \times 42$-inch strips to bind the quilt (see binding tips in Quilter's Workshop beginning on *page 280*).

burgoyne

1860–1890

A geometric muslin design is striking
against a dark blue background.
To create this quilt quickly, use the
strip piecing method.

Materials

7¼ yards of dark blue print
3½ yards of muslin
6 yards of backing fabric
90×108 inches of quilt batting

Finished quilt: 83×101 inches
Finished Burgoyne Surrounded block:
    15 inches square

Quantities specified are for 44/45-inch-wide,
100-percent-cotton fabrics. All measurements
include a ¼-inch seam allowance. Sew with right
sides together unless otherwise stated.

Quilt Notes

This quilt is a 4×5-block straight set with sashing.
The continuous design is achieved using pieced
Nine-Patch sashing squares that connect the
paths of squares in the surrounding blocks.

Although the blocks for this quilt can be cut
and sewn traditionally, instructions are also given
for quick strip piecing, which reduces cutting and
sewing time. These techniques also are likely to
improve the accuracy in combining the 1-inch
squares (finished size).

instructions continued on page 66

burgoyne

1860–1890

Cut the Fabrics

To make the best use of your fabrics, cut the pieces in the order that follows. First cut large pieces across the 42-inch width of the fabric as indicated. From each large piece, cut the strips and rectangles that are listed.

Use the 42-inch-long strips for strip piecing or, if you prefer, cut pieces from these strips for traditional piecing.

The borders are cut longer than necessary and are trimmed to fit after they are sewn to the quilt top.

From dark blue print, cut:

◆ 1—109×42-inch rectangle. Cut eleven $3^{1}/_{2}$×109-inch strips. Set aside four of the 11 strips for borders. From each remaining strip, cut seven $3^{1}/_{2}$×$15^{1}/_{2}$-inch strips for a total of 49 sashing strips.

◆ 1—40×42-inch rectangle. Cut seven $5^{1}/_{2}$×42-inch strips. From each strip, cut twelve $3^{1}/_{2}$×$5^{1}/_{2}$-inch pieces for piece A. Cut a total of 80 A pieces.

◆ 1—36×42-inch rectangle. Cut fourteen $2^{1}/_{2}$×42-inch strips. From each strip, cut twelve $2^{1}/_{2}$×$3^{1}/_{2}$-inch pieces for piece B. Cut a total of 160 B pieces.

◆ 1—42-inch square. Cut 28 strips, $1^{1}/_{2}$×42 inches each, for Strip Sets 1, 2, 3, and 5.

◆ 1—21×42-inch rectangle. Cut eight $2^{1}/_{2}$×42-inch strips for Strip Set 4.

From muslin, cut:

◆ 40—$1^{1}/_{2}$×42-inch strips. Set aside 10 strips for the inner border. Use the remaining 30 strips for Strip Sets 1, 2, 4, and 5.

◆ 20—$2^{1}/_{2}$×42-inch strips. Set aside 8 strips for binding. Use 12 strips for Strip Set 3.

Prepare the Strip Sets

Note: For traditional piecing, see "Make the Nine-Patch Units," *opposite.*

1 The five strip sets are illustrated *below.* Begin with Strip Set 5. Sew one $1^{1}/_{2}$-inch-wide muslin strip to a $1^{1}/_{2}$-inch-wide dark blue print strip as shown. Sew together six pairs of strips, making six of Strip Set 5.

2 Make Strip Sets 1 and 2 in the same manner, adding a third $1^{1}/_{2}$-inch strip to each set as shown. Make four of Strip Set 1 and eight of Strip Set 2.

3 Use one $1^{1}/_{2}$-inch-wide dark blue print strip and two $2^{1}/_{2}$-inch-wide muslin strips to make one of Strip Set 3. Strip Set 4 is made in the same

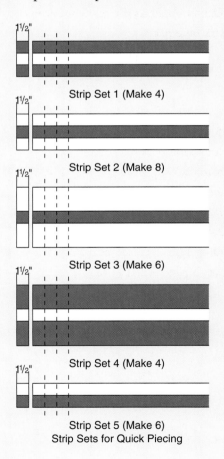

1½"

Strip Set 1 (Make 4)

1½"

Strip Set 2 (Make 8)

1½"

Strip Set 3 (Make 6)

1½"

Strip Set 4 (Make 4)

1½"

Strip Set 5 (Make 6)
Strip Sets for Quick Piecing

manner, with the colors reversed. Make six of Strip Set 3 and four of Strip Set 4.

4 Press all seam allowances toward the dark blue print.

Make the Nine-Patch Units

TRADITIONAL PIECING:

1 From the 1¹/₂-inch-wide dark blue print and muslin strips, cut 1¹/₂-inch squares. Cut 440 blue squares and 550 muslin squares.

2 Assemble 110 Nine-Patch units as shown in Diagram 1. Press the seam allowances toward the dark blue print.

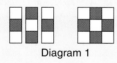
Diagram 1

STRIP PIECING:

1 Cut twenty-eight 1¹/₂-inch-wide segments from each of Strip Sets 1 and 2, cutting perpendicular to the strip edges as shown in Diagram 2.

2 Assemble 110 Nine-Patch units as shown in Diagram 1. Press the seam allowances toward the dark blue print.

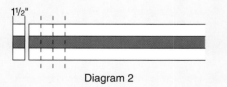

1¹/₂"

Diagram 2

Make the Four-Patch Units

TRADITIONAL PIECING:

1 Cut six 1¹/₂-inch-wide strips of each fabric into 1¹/₂-inch squares, cutting 160 squares of each color.

2 Referring to Diagram 3, assemble 80 Four-Patch units.

Diagram 3

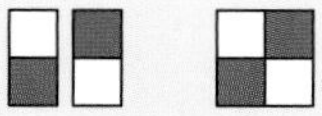

STRIP PIECING:

1 From each Strip Set 5, cut 1¹/₂-inch segments, cutting 160 total.

2 Assemble 80 Four-Patch units as shown in Diagram 3.

Make the Side Units

TRADITIONAL PIECING:

1 Cut 1¹/₂-inch-wide strips of each fabric into 1¹/₂-inch squares, cutting 80 squares of each color. From the 2¹/₂-inch-wide strips, cut 1¹/₂×2¹/₂-inch segments, cutting 160 pieces of each fabric.

2 Referring to Diagram 4, assemble 80 side units. Press all seam allowances toward the dark blue print.

Diagram 4

STRIP PIECING:

1 From Strip Sets 3 and 4, cut 1¹/₂-inch-wide segments, cutting 80 of each.

2 Assemble 80 side units as shown in Diagram 4.

instructions continued on page 68

Make the Center Units

TRADITIONAL PIECING:

1 Cut the remaining muslin strips into eighty $2^1/_2$-inch squares and twenty $1^1/_2$-inch squares. From the dark blue print strips, cut eighty $1^1/_2 \times 2^1/_2$-inch pieces.

2 Assemble 20 center units as shown in Diagram 5. Press all seam allowances toward the dark blue print.

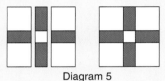

Diagram 5

STRIP PIECING:

1 From the remaining Strip Set 3, cut forty $2^1/_2$-inch-wide segments. From Strip Set 4, cut twenty $1^1/_2$-inch-wide segments.

2 Assemble 20 center units as shown in Diagram 5.

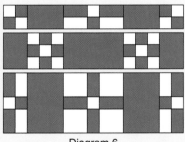

Diagram 6

Make the Block

To assemble one Burgoyne Surrounded block, refer to Diagram 6 and to the Burgoyne Surrounded Block illustration, *top right*, to assemble the five rows. Position each unit carefully for correct color placement.

Burgoyne Surrounded Block

1 For Row 1, sew a B piece to each short side of one side unit. Complete the row with one Four-Patch unit on each end. Press all seam allowances toward the B pieces. Repeat to make Row 5.

2 For Row 2, stitch a Nine-Patch unit to each short side of one A piece. Complete the row with a B piece on each end. Press the seam allowances toward the A and B pieces. Repeat to make Row 4.

3 To make Row 3, sew an A piece to opposite sides of one center unit. Complete the row with a side unit on each end. Press the seam allowances toward the A pieces.

4 Join the five rows to make one Burgoyne Surrounded block. Make a total of 20 Burgoyne Surrounded blocks.

Assemble the Block Rows

1 Join four blocks in a horizontal row, sewing a sashing strip between each block.

2 Finish the row by stitching a sashing strip onto each end.

3 Make five block rows. Press seam allowances toward the sashing.

Make the Sashing Rows

There are 30 Nine-Patch units left for the pieced sashing.

1 Sew a Nine-Patch unit onto one end of 24 sashing strips; press seam allowances toward the sashing.

2 Starting with a Nine-Patch unit, join four sets of pieced sashing into a horizontal row so that Nine-Patch units and sashing strips alternate.

3 End the row by sewing one of the six remaining Nine-Patch units onto the end of the last sashing strip.

4 Make six rows of sashing. Press seam allowances toward the sashing.

Assemble the Quilt Top

Referring to the photograph, join the rows, alternating sashing rows and block rows. The first and last rows are sashing. Press the seam allowances toward the sashing rows. The quilt top should measure $75\frac{1}{2} \times 93\frac{1}{2}$ inches.

Add the Borders

1 Stitch three $1\frac{1}{2} \times 42$-inch muslin strips together end to end for each side border strip. Sew the border strips to the sides of the quilt top; trim the excess border fabric.

2 Sew two muslin strips together end to end to make one border for the top edge; repeat for the bottom border. Sew a border to each end of the quilt top; trim the excess border fabric.

3 Assemble the outer dark blue print borders in the same manner. Stitch them onto the quilt top as for the muslin border, sewing side borders first, then the top and bottom borders. Press.

Complete the Quilt

1 Layer the quilt top, batting, and backing. Baste the three layers together (see tips for completing the quilt in Quilter's Workshop beginning on *page 280*).

2 Quilt as desired. The quilt shown has straight lines of quilting that form a crosshatch pattern through each square of the patchwork and across the borders.

3 Use the muslin $2\frac{1}{2} \times 42$-inch strips to bind the quilt (see binding tips in Quilter's Workshop).

fruit basket

1860-1890

*Wide borders, yellow sashing,
and red posts frame Fruit Basket blocks
set on point, making a bold
two-color quilt.*

Materials

5½ yards *each* of red and yellow print
3 yards of 90-inch-wide backing fabric
90×108 inches of quilt batting

Finished quilt: 81½×98½ inches
Finished Fruit Basket block: 8 inches square

Quantities specified are for 44/45-inch-wide,
100-percent-cotton fabrics. All measurements
include a ¼-inch seam allowance. Sew with right
sides together unless otherwise stated.

Quilt Notes

This quilt consists of 32 basket blocks set on
point with wide sashing strips and squares
between them. Half-block "basket tops" edge
the sides.

Cut the Fabrics

To make the best use of your fabrics, cut the
pieces in the order that follows. Refer to Quilter's
Workshop beginning on *page 280* for tips on
making templates for hand or machine

instructions continued on page 72

patchwork. Prepare templates for Patterns A, B, C, D, E, and F on Pattern Sheet.

Before cutting the fabrics, read the following assembly instructions to decide whether to use traditional or quick-piecing techniques to piece the triangle-squares.

From red print, cut:

- 1—27×42-inch rectangle for bias binding. (See tips for making and applying binding in Quilter's Workshop.)
- 1—18×94-inch rectangle. Cut two 4$\frac{1}{2}$×94-inch borders and two 4$\frac{1}{2}$×86-inch borders.
- 1—22×72-inch rectangle. For quick piecing cut four 18×22-inch rectangles; for traditional piecing cut 322 of Pattern A triangles.
- 1—12×24-inch rectangle. Cut 14 of Pattern D for the side triangles.
- 1—19×42-inch rectangle. For quick piecing cut two 19-inch squares; for traditional piecing cut 32 of Pattern D.
- 6—4$\frac{1}{2}$×42-inch strips. Cut 49 sashing posts, each 4$\frac{1}{2}$ inches square.
- 1—3×42-inch strip. Cut 28 of Pattern A for the side setting triangles.
- 1—4×42-inch strip. Cut four of Pattern F and 28 of Pattern E for the corner setting triangles.
- 64—Pattern B
- 32—Pattern C

From yellow print, cut:

- 1—14×88-inch rectangle. Cut two 3$\frac{1}{2}$×88-inch borders and two 3$\frac{1}{2}$×77-inch borders.
- 16—4$\frac{1}{2}$×42$\frac{1}{2}$-inch strips. Cut eighty 4$\frac{1}{2}$×8$\frac{1}{2}$-inch sashing strips.
- 1—22×72-inch rectangle. For quick piecing cut four 18×22-inch rectangles; for traditional piecing cut 322 of Pattern A triangles.

- 1—19×42-inch rectangle. For quick piecing cut two 19-inch squares; for traditional piecing cut 32 of Pattern D.
- 64—Pattern A
- 20—Pattern E

Make the Basket Triangle-Squares

TRADITIONAL PIECING:

Join yellow print and red print A triangles to assemble 322 small triangle-squares. Make 32 large triangle-squares with red print and yellow print D triangles.

QUICK PIECING:

For step-by-step instructions for quick-pieced triangle-squares, see Quilter's Workshop beginning on *page 280* for tips to stitch the grids described *below*.

1 For the D triangle-squares, mark the wrong side of each 19-inch yellow print square with a 3×3 grid of 5$\frac{3}{4}$-inch squares as shown in Diagram 1. Layer the yellow fabric, marked side up, atop a matching red fabric piece.

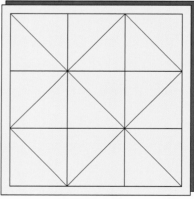

Diagram 1

2 Machine-stitch the grid as described in Step 3 of the tips on Quick Piecing Triangle-Squares in the Quilter's Workshop. Each grid makes 18 triangle-squares, so you'll have 36 total. Thirty-two triangle-squares are needed; discard any damaged or distorted ones.

3 To make the A triangle-squares, repeat the procedure with the 18×22-inch fabrics, marking each yellow print with a 6×7 grid of $2\frac{1}{2}$-inch squares (see Diagram 2). Each grid makes 84 triangle-squares. The total of 336 is 14 more than the 322 needed.

Diagram 2

4 Press all seam allowances toward the yellow print.

Assemble the Fruit Basket Block

1 Referring to the Block Assembly Diagram, join four of the small triangle-squares in a row. Make another row of three triangle-squares. Press the seam allowances toward the yellow print triangles.

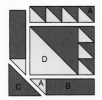

Block Assembly Diagram

2 Stitch the shorter row to one large triangle-square, joining the small yellow print triangles to the red print D triangle and positioning the units as shown in the Block Assembly Diagram. Press the seam allowance toward the large triangle; then sew the four-square row to the top of this unit.

3 Sew a yellow print A triangle to one end of a B rectangle as shown. Press the seam allowance toward the rectangle. Stitch this piece to the bottom edge of the center unit; press the seam allowance toward the outside of the block. Make another AB strip; add it to the left side of the unit.

4 Complete the Fruit Basket block by sewing a C triangle across the base of the basket as shown. Make a total of 32 Fruit Basket blocks.

Make the Setting Triangles

Combine small triangle-squares and red print D triangles to make the basket tops for the side triangles of the quilt.

1 Follow step 1 of "Assemble the Fruit Basket Block" to prepare two rows of triangle-squares.

instructions continued on page 74

fruit basket

1860-1890

2 Stitch the triangle-squares to a red D triangle in the same manner as in the block assembly. Add a red A triangle to each corner, creating a right triangle as shown in Diagram 3. Make a total of 14 basket top side triangles.

Diagram 3

3 Use E and F triangles to piece four corner triangles as shown in Diagram 4.

Diagram 4

Assemble the Quilt Top

1 Refer to the Quilt Assembly Diagram, *opposite*, to arrange the basket blocks, setting side and corner triangles, sashing, and posts in diagonal rows. *Note:* The sashing posts at the end of each diagonal row extend beyond the adjacent setting triangles.

2 Assemble the blocks and side setting triangles in diagonal rows, stitching a sashing strip between basket blocks and between posts and side setting triangles. Press the seam allowances toward the sashing.

3 Alternating rows of basket blocks and sashing, assemble the quilt top as shown. Match seam lines of sashing strips and squares carefully.

4 When the assembly is complete, trim excess fabric from the sashing posts even with edges of adjacent side setting triangles.

Add the Borders

1 Stitch the 88-inch yellow print borders to the quilt sides. Trim excess border fabric; press seam allowances toward the border fabric. Sew the remaining yellow borders to the top and bottom edges in the same manner.

2 Join the red borders to the quilt top in the same manner, first stitching the longer border strips to the sides, then the shorter border strips to the top and bottom.

Complete the Quilt

1 Layer the quilt top, batting, and backing. Baste the three layers together (see tips for completing the quilt in Quilter's Workshop beginning on *page 280*).

2 Quilt as desired. A grid of 1-inch squares is quilted over the surface of the quilt shown on *page 71*. The grid is straight over the basket blocks and sashing and diagonal in the borders.

3 Use the red print 27×42-inch rectangle to make about 360 inches of bias or straight-grain binding. Bind the quilt. (See tips for making and applying binding in Quilter's Workshop.)

Quilt Assembly Diagram

wertman family

1860–1890

Each name of the Wertman family
appears inside several different color
combinations of appliquéd work.
Eight colors are shown here against a
quilted muslin background.

Materials

7 yards of muslin

3½ yards of red print for appliqués, sashing,
and binding

¾ yard *each* of green, dark green, pink, and
brown prints for appliqués

1⅜ yards *each* of navy blue, gold, and yellow
prints for appliqués

3⅜ yards of 108-inch-wide backing fabric

120—inch square of quilt batting

Finished quilt: 93×108 inches

Finished appliquéd block: 13 inches square

Quantities specified are for 44/45-inch-wide,
100-percent-cotton fabrics. All measurements
include a ¼-inch seam allowance. Sew with right
sides together unless otherwise stated.

Quilt Notes

This quilt has 30 appliquéd blocks in a straight
set with sashing between the blocks. Each block
is the same pattern, a design reminiscent of
Pennsylvania Dutch designs.

Eight solid-color fabrics in 12 combinations of
light and dark fabrics give the quilt a colorful
appearance. Use additional fabrics if you want to
achieve a more scrappy look.

instructions continued on page 78

wertman family
1860~1890

If desired, use a fine-point permanent ink fabric marker to inscribe signatures in the center of each block.

Cut the Fabrics

To make the best use of your fabrics, cut the pieces in the order that follows. Refer to Quilter's Workshop beginning on *page 280* for tips on making templates for appliqués. Prepare templates for patterns A through H on Pattern Sheet. When cutting the appliqués from fabric, add a ³/₁₆-inch seam allowance around each piece.

From muslin, cut:

- 2—8¹/₂×110-inch border strips
- 2—8¹/₂×80-inch border strips
- 30—13¹/₂-inch squares

From red print, cut:

- 6—2¹/₂×95-inch sashing strips
- 4—2¹/₄×104-inch strips for straight-grain binding
- 1—26×33-inch piece for appliqués
- 35—2¹/₂×13¹/₂-inch strips for horizontal sashing

From red, green, dark green, brown, and navy blue prints, cut:

- 30 sets of dark print appliqués, each set consisting of one of Pattern A, two each of Patterns B and G, four of Pattern F, and eight of Pattern E. The quilt shown has 10 blocks made with navy blue fabric, six blocks each with the dark green and red fabrics, and four blocks each with the green and brown fabrics.

From pink, yellow, and gold prints, cut:

- 30 sets of light print appliqués, each set consisting of two of Patterns C and H, four of Pattern D, and four 1×3¹/₄-inch stem pieces. This quilt has six blocks with pink fabric and 12 blocks each with the yellow and gold fabrics.

Prepare the Appliqués

Arrange the light and dark prints in pairs for 30 blocks.

1 On the quilt shown, the G and H pieces are seamed together at the straight edge rather than appliquéd. You may join these pieces with a ³/₁₆-inch seam or appliqué one piece on the other.

2 Turn under the seam allowances on all appliqué pieces except the C circles. (These get slipped under the B posies.) On the other pieces, do not baste under edges that will be covered by another piece, such as the straight edges of the F pieces.

3 For the A, B, D, and H pieces, clip the seam allowances as needed to achieve nicely curved edges.

4 Cut out the center of the B posy, trimming the seam allowance to ¹/₈ inch. Do not turn this edge under yet.

5 Baste or press under ¹/₄ inch on each long side of the stem strips.

Appliqué the Blocks

1 Fold each muslin square vertically, horizontally, and diagonally; press each fold to mark placement lines.

2 Referring to the Block Appliqué Diagram, *opposite*, position and pin appliqués in place.

Block Appliqué Diagram

Align the center curves of the A piece on the horizontal and vertical placement lines on the muslin block.

Tuck stems under the A piece on the diagonal placement lines; position a B or GH flower at the top of each stem as shown. Place a C circle under the opening in the B flower.

Tuck a D piece under the A fabric on the horizontal placement line as shown. Position two E leaves in the center of each D stem, and an F piece at the top.

3 When all the pieces are correctly positioned, appliqué them in place. For the center of the B posy, use your needle to turn back and appliqué the edge of the flower fabric, revealing the C circle underneath.

Make a total of 30 appliquéd blocks.

Assemble the Quilt Top

1 Arrange the completed blocks in five vertical rows of six blocks each. In the quilt pictured on *pages 76–77*, all the blocks in a vertical row use the same light print—blocks in Rows 1 and 5 have gold fabric, Rows 2 and 4 have yellow fabric, and the middle row is made with pink fabric.

Join the vertical rows by sewing the blocks together with a short sashing strip between blocks. Finish each row with a sashing strip at the top and bottom edges. Press the seam allowances toward the sashing.

2 Assemble the rows, sewing a 95-inch-long sashing strip between the rows. Complete the quilt top by sewing a sashing strip to both sides of the assembled rows. Trim the excess sashing fabric even with the bottom of the quilt top.

3 Sew the 80-inch muslin border strips to the top and bottom edges of the quilt. Press seam allowances toward the borders; trim excess border fabric. Repeat to add side borders.

Complete the Quilt

1 Layer the quilt top, batting, and backing. Baste the three layers together (see tips for completing the quilt in Quilter's Workshop).

2 Quilt as desired. The quilt shown has outline quilting around the appliqués, diagonal lines in the sashing, and a cable quilted in the wide borders.

3 Use the four red print 2¼×104-inch strips to make 416 inches of straight-grain binding. (See tips for making and applying binding in Quilter's Workshop.)

checkers & rails

1860–1890

Handsome and streamlined, this traditional
Checkers & Rails pattern is brilliant in blue and cream.

Materials

$6^1/2$ yards *each* of muslin and blue print for blocks,
   borders, and binding
$3^3/8$ yards of 90-inch-wide backing fabric
120-inch square of quilt batting

Finished quilt: $83 \times 110^1/4$ inches

With the exception of the backing, quantities
specified are for 44/45-inch-wide,
100-percent-cotton fabrics. All measurements
include a $^1/4$-inch seam allowance. Sew with right
sides together unless otherwise stated.

Quilt Notes

This quilt is unusual because the design is
formed by pieced sashing rather than blocks. The
quilt is assembled as a diagonal set.

Cut the Fabrics

To make the best use of your fabrics, cut the
pieces in the order that follows. Cut large cross-
grain pieces as stated below; then cut these into
the strips and squares listed below the large
pieces. Rotary cutting is recommended.

From muslin, cut:

◆ 10—$2 \times 42^1/2$-inch strips for inner border
◆ 10—$3 \times 42^1/2$-inch strips for outer border
◆ 10—$6^1/2 \times 42$-inch strips. Cut fifty-nine
   $6^1/2$-inch squares.
◆ 60—$1^1/4 \times 42$-inch strips for checkerboards and
   rails patchwork

◆ 2—$9^3/4 \times 42$-inch strips. Cut five $9^3/4$-inch
   squares; cut each square in quarters diagonally
   to obtain 20 side setting triangles.
◆ 2—$5^1/8$-inch squares. Cut each square in half
   diagonally to obtain four corner triangles.

From blue print, cut:

◆ 1—$^3/4$-yard piece for binding
◆ 20—$2 \times 42^1/2$-inch border strips
◆ 7—$4^1/4 \times 42$-inch strips. Cut fifty-eight
   $4^1/4$-inch sashing squares.
◆ 84—$1^1/4 \times 42$-inch strips for the patchwork
◆ 6—$6^1/2$-inch squares. Cut each square in
   quarters diagonally for 24 side setting triangles.

Piecing and Sashing

Note: For this assembly press all seam allowances
toward the blue print.

TRADITIONAL PIECING:

1 Use 24 muslin strips and 48 blue strips, each
$1^1/4$ inches wide, for the rail units. Cut six
$6^1/2$-inch-long pieces from each strip.

2 Sew one $1^1/4 \times 6^1/2$-inch muslin strip between
two matching blue pieces to make one rail
unit (see Diagram 1 on *page 82*). Make a total of
140 rails.

3 Cut the remaining $1^1/4$-inch-wide blue print
and muslin strips into $1^1/4$-inch squares for
the checkerboards. Cut a total of 1,120 squares of
each fabric.

instructions continued on page 82

checkers & rails
1860–1890

4 Use four squares of each color to assemble an eight-square row, alternating colors. Make a total of 280 rows.

5 Join rows in pairs to complete the checkerboard units, turning one row upside down so the fabric colors alternate. Make a total of 140 checkerboard units.

STRIP PIECING:

1 Stitch one 1¼-inch-wide muslin strip between two blue print 1¼-inch-wide strips. Make a total of 24 sets of pieced strips in this manner.

2 Cut six 6½-inch-long units from each pieced strip as shown in Diagram 1. Cut a total of 140 rail units.

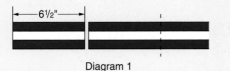

Diagram 1

3 For the checkerboard units, stitch together four 1¼-inch-wide strips of each fabric, alternating the colors as shown in Diagram 2. Make a total of nine strip sets in this manner.

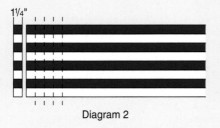

Diagram 2

4 Cut thirty-three 1¼-inch-wide segments from each strip set as shown in Diagram 2.

5 Join the checkerboard segments in pairs, turning one upside down so fabric colors alternate. Make a total of 14 checkerboard units.

JOINING SASHING UNITS: Sew one rail unit to each checkerboard unit, positioning the fabrics as shown in Diagram 3. Press the seam allowances toward the rails.

Diagram 3

Assemble the Quilt Top

1 Referring to the Quilt Assembly Diagram, *opposite*, lay out and join diagonal rows of muslin squares and sashing units. Note the positions of the checkerboards and rails in each sashing strip. Each diagonal row ends with a muslin side setting triangle. Press the seam allowances toward the muslin squares.

2 Assemble diagonal rows of the sashing units and blue print sashing squares. Refer to the Quilt Assembly Diagram to position the checkerboards and rails in each row. Each of these rows ends with a blue print side setting triangle. Press the seam allowances toward the blue print sashing squares.

3 Starting at the bottom left corner of the Quilt Assembly Diagram, stitch the rows together, matching the seam lines carefully.

Add the Borders

1 Piece matching border strips end to end to make borders long enough for each side. With the blue print strips, make four 2×126-inch borders and four 2×84-inch borders. In the same manner, use the muslin strips to assemble two 2×84-inch borders, two 2×126-inch borders, two 3×84-inch borders, and two 3×126-inch borders.

2 Referring to the photograph on *page 80* for color placement for each side of the quilt, sew four border strips together lengthwise to make a single unit four strips wide, with the widest (muslin) strip on the outside.

3 Pin the border units on the quilt top. Sew the borders to the quilt, mitering border corners (see tips for mitering borders in Quilter's Workshop beginning on *page 280*).

Complete the Quilt

1 Layer the quilt top, batting, and backing. Baste the three layers together (see tips for completing the quilt in Quilter's Workshop).

2 Quilt as desired. The quilt features diagonal quilting with a grid of $3/4$-inch squares. Diagonal lines are quilted in the borders.

3 Use the remaining blue print to make approximately 400 inches of binding (see tips for making and applying binding in Quilter's Workshop).

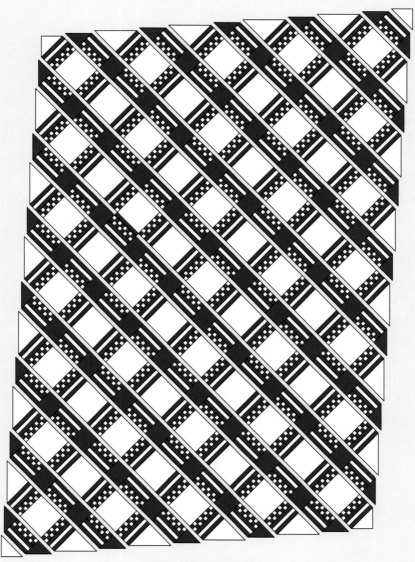

Quilt Assembly Diagram

sickle

1860–1890

*Smart-looking four-patch squares
and quick-to-stitch triangle-squares
make piecing this quilt a breeze
for beginners.*

Materials

3 yards of black print

2⅝ yards of white print

1⅛ yards of burgundy stripe

⅛ yard *each* of nine light and nine dark
   assorted scrap prints

¾ yard of dark red print for binding

6 yards of backing fabric

90×108 inches of quilt batting

Finished quilt: 75×99 inches

Each Sickle block: 16 inches square

Quantities specified are for 44/45-inch-wide,
100-percent-cotton fabrics. All measurements
include a ¼-inch seam allowance. Sew with right
sides together unless otherwise stated.

Quilt Notes

This block combines two Four-Patch squares
with two squares consisting of large pieced
triangles. The small Four-Patch units are assorted
prints, with the consistent placement of light
and dark fabrics preserving the illusion of a
continuous diagonal chain.

instructions continued on page 86

sickle
1860–1890

Cut the Fabrics

To make the best use of your fabrics, cut the pieces in the order that follows. Cut the large pieces as described below; then from those pieces, cut the smaller patches listed below them. For quick cutting, use a rotary cutter, rotary mat, and acrylic ruler.

From black print, cut:

- 5—6×70-inch strips for borders. Cut one of these strips in half resulting in two 6×35-inch strips.
- 18—8⁷/₈-inch squares. Cut each square in half diagonally to yield 35 triangles.

From white print, cut:

- 2—4¹/₂×90-inch border strips
- 2—4¹/₂×58-inch border strips
- 18—8⁷/₈-inch squares. Cut each square in half diagonally to yield 35 triangles.

From burgundy stripe, cut:

- 8—4¹/₂×42-inch strips. Cut seventy 4¹/₂-inch squares.

From each assorted print, cut:

- 2—2¹/₂×21-inch strips

Piece the Triangle-Squares

Match the long edges of one white print and one black print triangle; stitch. Press the seam allowance toward the black fabric. Make a total of 35 triangle-squares.

Piece the Four-Patch Squares

TRADITIONAL PIECING:

1 Cut the scrap fabrics into 2¹/₂-inch squares. Cut 140 light squares and 140 dark squares. Arrange light and dark fabrics in pairs. Join the 140 pairs.

2 Make 70 Four-Patch units as shown in Diagram 1.

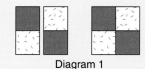

Diagram 1

Continue as described in Steps 5 and 6 below.

STRIP PIECING:

1 Match the light and dark scrap fabric strips in 18 pairs.

2 Stitch each pair together along one long edge. Press the seam allowance toward the dark fabric.

3 Cut eight 2¹/₂-inch-wide segments from each sewn strip as shown in Diagram 2.

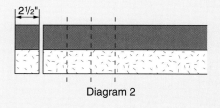

Diagram 2

4 Join pairs of these segments to make a total of 70 Four-Patch units as shown in Diagram 1, *above*.

5 Sew a burgundy stripe square to each Four-Patch unit; press the seam allowance toward the burgundy stripe square.

6 To complete the quarter block, join two of these Four-Patch/square units, positioning the Four-Patch units in opposite corners as shown in the Block Assembly Diagram. Make a total of 35 of these quarter-block squares.

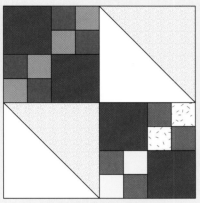

Block Assembly Diagram

Assemble the Sickle Blocks

1 Referring to the Block Assembly Diagram, join two triangle-squares and two quarter-block squares to make a Sickle block. Position light and dark fabrics as shown; press seam allowances toward the triangle-squares.

2 Make 15 Sickle blocks and five half-blocks with fabrics positioned as in the left side of the Sickle block.

Assemble the Quilt Top

1 Join five horizontal rows of three blocks each. Complete each row with a half block at the right end. Press the seam allowances toward the triangle-squares.

2 Join the rows to complete the quilt top. Press the seam allowances in one direction.

Add the Borders

1 Stitch a 58-inch-long white print border to the top and bottom edges of the quilt top. Press the seam allowances toward the border; trim excess border fabric even with the quilt sides.

2 Add the 90-inch-long white print borders to the sides.

3 Piece one 70-inch and one 35-inch black print strip, creating a border long enough for each side. Sew the black print border strips to the quilt.

Complete the Quilt

1 Layer the quilt top, batting, and backing. Baste the three layers together (see tips for completing the quilt in Quilter's Workshop beginning on *page 280*).

2 Quilt as desired. The quilt pictured on *page 84* is quilted with an overall grid of 2-inch squares.

3 Use the dark red print to make approximately 360 inches of binding (see tips for making and applying binding in Quilter's Workshop).

optical illusion

1860~1890

You'll become a pro at piecing

curved seams when you put your skills to work

on this intriguing masterpiece.

Materials

6¼ yards of solid dark green

3¾ yards *each* of solid brown and gold

1½ yards of muslin, including binding

2¾ yards of 108-inch-wide backing fabric

120-inch square of quilt batting

Finished quilt: 88×98 inches

Finished block: 10 inches square

Quantities specified are for 44/45-inch-wide, 100-percent-cotton fabrics. All measurements include a ¼-inch seam allowance. Sew with right sides together unless otherwise stated.

Quilt Notes

The real name of this block is elusive. A similar quilt, handed down in an Alabama family, was called Snail's Trail. Pattern books published in the 1930s, however, refer to the block as Broken Stone, Lover's Quarrel, or New Wedding Ring.

Because of the wonderful interplay of color and shape, the current owner of this delightful antique quilt calls it "Optical Illusion."

The quilt is made of 72 blocks in a straight set. The joined blocks form an allover pattern that obscures the definition of the blocks, creating a continuous swirl of circles and diamonds.

The slight curve of the block's seams can be sewn easily by hand or by machine.

Cut the Fabrics

Because of the curves and set-in seams of this block, window templates are recommended to create accurate pivot points on each piece for either hand or machine piecing. Make templates for Patterns A, B, C, and D on the Pattern Sheet. (See tips for making templates in Quilter's Workshop beginning on *page 280*).

From solid dark green, cut:

◆ 4—4½×94-inch border strips
◆ 288—Pattern A

From solid brown, cut:

◆ 72—Pattern D

From solid gold, cut:

◆ 288—Pattern B

From muslin, cut:

◆ 1—¾-yard piece for binding
◆ 288—Pattern C

Make the Blocks

Before you begin, see tips for piecing curved seams in Quilter's Workshop. Assemble each block as follows, referring to the Block Assembly Diagram on *page 90*.

1 For each block, use one D piece and four *each* of pieces A, B, and C.

instructions continued on page 90

2 Stitch a gold B piece to the curved edge of each A piece. Press the seam allowances toward the A pieces. Repeat to make four AB units.

3 Join an AB unit to opposite sides of the D piece, as shown in the Block Assembly Diagram. Press the seam allowances toward the B pieces.

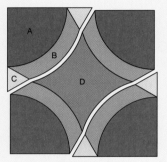

Block Assembly Diagram

4 Add C triangles to both sides of the two remaining AB units as shown in the Block Assembly Diagram. Press the seam allowances toward the triangles.

5 Join the side ABC units to the center unit, setting in the angled seam to make one block. Press the seam allowances in one direction. Make a total of 72 blocks.

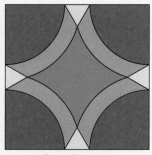

Block Diagram

Assemble the Quilt Top

1 Refer to the Quilt Assembly Diagram, *opposite*, and join the blocks into nine horizontal rows of eight blocks each. When stitching blocks together, match the seam lines of the C triangles carefully to create the illusion of a single diamond.

2 Assemble the rows in the same manner. The completed quilt top should measure $80\frac{1}{2} \times 90\frac{1}{2}$ inches.

Add the Borders

1 Stitch border strips to the $90\frac{1}{2}$-inch sides of the quilt. Press the seam allowances toward the borders; trim the border fabric even with the top and bottom edges of the quilt top.

2 Sew a border strip to the top and bottom edges in the same manner.

Complete the Quilt

1 Layer the quilt top, batting, and backing. Baste the three layers together (see tips for completing the quilt in Quilter's Workshop beginning on *page 280*).

2 Quilt as desired. The quilt shown in the photograph on *page 88* has outline quilting outside each seam and an X quilted through the center of the D pieces.

3 Use the remaining muslin to make approximately 390 inches of binding, either bias or straight-grain (see tips for making and applying binding in Quilter's Workshop).

Change the Quilt Size

The 88×98-inch finished size of this quilt is suitable for either a full- or a queen-size bed. To lengthen the quilt for a queen-size bed, make the top and bottom borders wider.

Make 54 blocks in a 6×9-block set for a 68×98-inch twin-size quilt. For a king-size bed, make 100 blocks in a 10×10-block set for a 108-inch-square quilt.

Quilt Assembly Diagram

whig's defeat

1860~1890

*The combination of pieced and
appliquéd blocks in pastel colors gives this quilt
an aged appearance.*

Materials

4$^1/_8$ yards of solid green for the patchwork,
   appliqués, borders, and binding

7$^1/_2$ yards of white print or muslin for the
   patchwork, appliquéd blocks, and borders

2$^1/_2$ yards of solid dark pink for patchwork and
   appliqués

1$^1/_4$ yards *each* of solid light pink and light green
   for patchwork

5$^1/_2$ yards of backing fabric

90×108 inches of quilt batting

Finished quilt: 80×92 inches
Finished patchwork block: 9 inches square
Finished appliquéd blocks: 9×10 inches

Quantities specified are for 44/45-inch-wide,
100-percent-cotton fabrics. All measurements
include a $^1/_4$-inch seam allowance. Sew with right
sides together unless otherwise stated.

Quilt Notes

This elegant quilt is a challenge for even
experienced quiltmakers. Tiny pieces, narrow
points, and curved edges require careful piecing.

   The quilt is made by assembling A rows and
B rows. To understand the assembly of this
quilt, refer to the Quilt Assembly Diagram on
page 97 as you cut the fabrics and assemble each
section. Four of Row A and three of Row B are
combined to create an alternating design of
patchwork and appliqué. Row A consists of four
pieced blocks alternating with three appliquéd
blocks, with appliquéd half blocks at each end.

Each B row is a single panel with alternating
appliquéd motifs. The outer border is appliquéd
wedges that form a scalloped edge for the quilt.

Cut the Fabrics

To make the best use of your fabrics, cut the
pieces in the order that follows. Cut the large
pieces first; then cut each piece into the smaller
pieces listed after it.

   Prepare templates for Patterns A through J on
Pattern Sheet (see tips for making and using
templates for patchwork and appliqué in
Quilter's Workshop beginning on *page 280*).

   For Patterns E and I, trace the pattern four
times to make the complete templates. Make a
separate template of Pattern I for the half blocks,
tracing the pattern only two times.

From solid green, cut:

◆ 1—1-yard piece for the binding

◆ 1—16×42-inch piece. From this piece cut nine
   of Pattern I, adding a $^3/_{16}$-inch seam allowance
   around each complete motif when cutting.

◆ 1—8×42-inch piece. Cut six of Pattern I for the
   half blocks, adding a $^3/_{16}$-inch seam allowance
   around the appliqué edges and a full $^1/_4$-inch
   seam allowance at the straight edge.

◆ 1—12×42-inch piece. Cut 64 of Pattern A.

◆ 224—Pattern J. Because the wedges are both pieced
   and appliquéd, add a $^1/_4$-inch seam allowance
   on the straight sides of each J wedge, but only
   a $^3/_{16}$-inch seam allowance on the curved edges.

instructions continued on page 94

whig's defeat

1860–1890

From solid white fabric, cut:

◆ 1—98×42-inch piece. From this piece
cut two 9×98-inch borders and two
9×86-inch borders.

◆ 1—76×42-inch piece. From this piece cut three
$9^1/_2×75^1/_2$-inch panels for Row B.

◆ 1—32×42-inch piece. Cut this piece into twelve
$9^1/_2×10^1/_2$-inch blocks for the Row A appliqués.

◆ 1—12×42-inch piece. From this piece cut eight
$9^1/_2×5$-inch half blocks for the A rows.

◆ 16—Pattern E

From solid dark pink, cut:

◆ 384—Pattern B

◆ 56—Pattern F

◆ 112—*each* of Patterns G and H

From solid light pink, cut:

◆ 448—Pattern C

From solid light green, cut:

◆ 384—Pattern D

Make the Patchwork Blocks

Sixteen patchwork blocks are combined with
appliquéd blocks to make four of Row A (see
Quilt Assembly Diagram on *page 97*).

1 Assemble four quarter-circle units for each
block. Each unit consists of one A piece,
seven B pieces, six C pieces, and seven D pieces.
Referring to Diagram 1, make five BCD units as
shown. Join these units, carefully setting in the

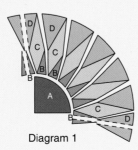

Diagram 1

angle of each adjacent unit. Complete the
quarter circle by adding a B and D piece to each
end as shown.

2 Add the A corner piece to the bottom of the
quarter circle (see Diagram 1). Leave the
fabric on each side extending over the edge.

3 Complete four quarter-circle units. Stitch
these units into the curves of one E piece to
complete the patchwork block (see tips for
stitching curved seams in Quilter's Workshop
beginning on *page 280*). Trim the excess fabric
from the quarter-circle units even with the sides
of the block. Make 16 patchwork blocks.

Make the Appliquéd Blocks

Each of the four A rows includes three blocks
and two half blocks that are appliquéd with the
F, G, and H teardrop-shape pieces.

1 To prepare the appliqués, turn under and
baste the seam allowances on the curved
edges only; leave the straight edges flat.

2 Position five teardrop pieces on one $9^1/_2$-inch
side of a $9^1/_2×10^1/_2$-inch block of solid white

Patchwork Block Diagram

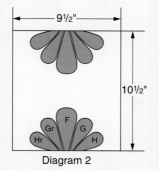

Diagram 2

as shown in Diagram 2, aligning the straight edges of the appliqués with the edge of the block. Match the center of the F teardrop with the center of the block side. Pin one G and H teardrop on each side of the F piece, placing them as close together as possible without the edges touching. Position teardrops on the opposite side of the block in the same manner.

3 Appliqué the teardrops in place (see Diagram 2); then press the block flat. Complete 12 appliquéd blocks, three for each Row A.

4 In the same manner, appliqué two half blocks for the ends of each A row, positioning the teardrops on a 5×9¹/₂-inch piece of solid white (see Diagram 3).

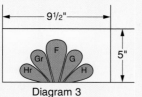

Diagram 3

Assemble the A Rows

Construct one A row by joining the half blocks, patchwork blocks, and appliquéd blocks as shown in the Quilt Assembly Diagram on *page 97*. Make four of Row A.

Make the B Rows

To prepare the three Row B panels, refer to the Quilt Assembly Diagram on *page 97*.

1 On a 9¹/₂×75¹/₂-inch strip of solid white, make horizontal guidelines as indicated by dashed lines on the diagram. (*Note:* Diagram shows finished measurements.) First, measure 4³/₄ inches

from each end of the strip; mark a horizontal line across the 9¹/₂-inch width of the fabric, using a fabric marker or pins. Then mark six more lines that are alternately spaced 9 inches and 10 inches apart as shown.

2 Referring to the diagram for placement, position three I appliqués, two half I appliques, and eight FGH teardrop appliqué units on each panel.

3 Stitch the appliqués in place. Complete three of Row B; then press the appliqués. Leave the marked lines in place to help you match them with the seam lines of the adjacent A rows.

Assemble the Quilt Top

Sew together the seven completed vertical rows as shown in the Quilt Assembly Diagram. The quilt top should measure 63¹/₂×75¹/₂ inches.

Add the Wedge Borders

1 Stitch the 9-inch-wide borders to the sides and ends of the quilt top, mitering the corners (see tips for mitering border corners in Quilter's Workshop beginning on *page 280*).

2 Join four green J pieces as shown in Diagram 4, sewing the straight edges of adjacent pieces together with a ¹/₄-inch seam allowance. Start and stop the stitching line

Diagram 4

instructions continued on page 96

approximately ³/₁₆ inch from each end of the seam. Do not baste under the curved edges of the wedge pieces yet. Make 56 four-wedge units.

3 Join the straight edges of 13 wedge units in a row for each of the two end borders, with the wider edge of the units alternating turned down then up as shown in Diagram 4 on *page 95*. Refer to the Quilt Assembly diagram, *opposite*, for the corner wedge positions.

4 Assemble 15 wedge units for each side border, referring to the diagram for positioning.

5 Turn under and baste the curved raw edges on both sides of each wedge strip.

6 Pin the wedge strips in place on the borders of the quilt, aligning the seam allowance at the end of each wedge strip with the mitered seams of the borders. The last J wedge in each row should overlap the last wedge in the adjacent row.

7 Appliqué the basted edges of the wedge strips onto the borders.

8 At the corners, baste under the raw edge of one of the two end wedges. Overlap the wedge with the basted edge on the other wedge and appliqué in place.

Do not cut scallops in the outer edge of the border yet.

Add the Quilting

1 Mark quilting as desired on the quilt top (see tips for marking quilting designs in Quilter's Workshop beginning on *page 280*). The quilt shown has outline quilting around the patchwork, the appliquéd teardrops, and the border wedges. The quilting on the I appliqués resembles leaf veins. Grid quilting covers the white background.

2 Layer the quilt top, batting, and backing. Baste the three layers together (see tips for completing the quilt in Quilter's Workshop).

3 Quilt as desired. Complete the quilting all the way to the edge of the borders.

4 When quilting is complete, remove all basting except around the outside edge of the quilt. Do not cut the scallops until the binding is sewn onto the quilt.

Bind the Scalloped Edge

1 Measure out ³/₄ to 1 inch from the appliquéd wedges all the way around the quilt, making small marks on the quilt top. Connect the marks to make a placement line for the binding.

2 See tips for making continuous bias binding in Quilter's Workshop beginning on *page 280*. Following those instructions, cut at least 390 inches of 1¹/₄-inch-wide bias from the 1-yard piece of green fabric. This binding is narrower than usual so it will lie flat on the curves.

3 See tips for applying bias in Quilter's Workshop. Fold and press the binding strip in half as directed.

4 Align the raw edge of the binding with the marked placement line. Pin the binding around the quilt, easing the fullness of the binding around each curve. Machine-sew the binding to the quilt top.

5 When stitching is complete, trim the excess border fabric at the raw edge of the binding.

6 Turn the binding over the edge, one scallop at a time, and hand-stitch it in place on the back of the quilt. Clip the binding seam allowance as necessary to smooth the binding over the curves.

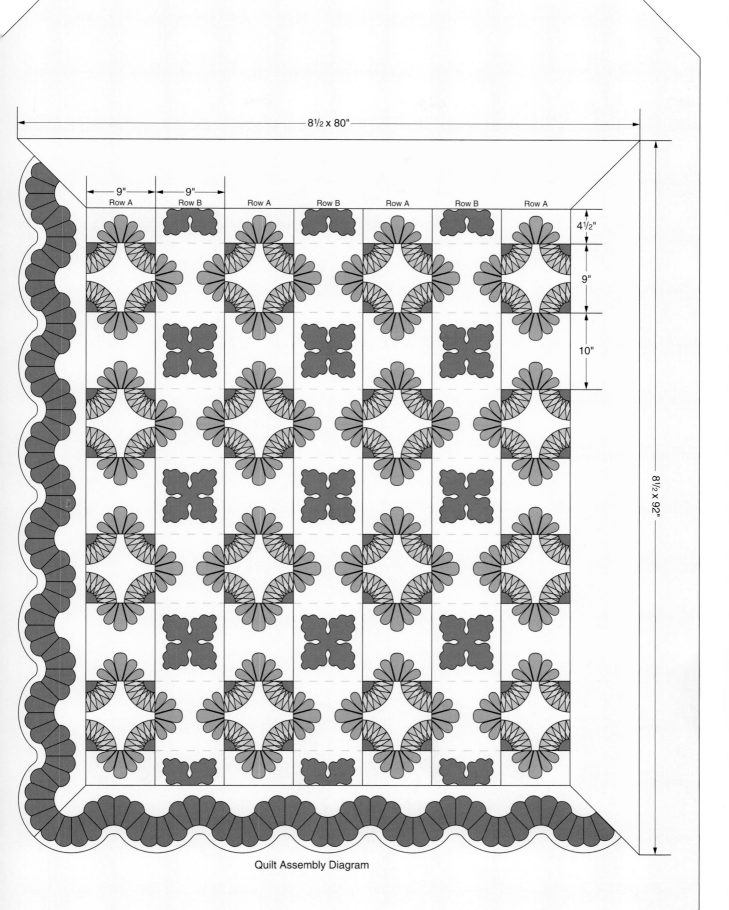

8½ x 80"

9" 9"
Row A Row B Row A Row B Row A Row B Row A

4½"

9"

10"

8½ x 92"

Quilt Assembly Diagram

straight furrows
1860-1890

Positioning the light and dark fabrics in each

Log Cabin block is key to the success of this quilt. Arrange the blocks

to create obvious furrows diagonally across the quilt.

Materials

$2^3/8$ yards of red print with black dots for
    the border

$3/4$ yard of yellow print for patchwork

$3/8$ yard of solid red for block centers

16—$1/8$-yard pieces or scraps of assorted light
    prints for patchwork

24—$1/8$-yard pieces or scraps of assorted dark
    prints for patchwork

1 yard of beige print for binding

6 yards of backing fabric (or 3 yards of
    90-inch-wide sheeting)

90×108 inches of quilt batting

Finished quilt: 80×100 inches
Finished Log Cabin block: 10 inches square

Quantities specified are for 44/45-inch-wide,
100-percent-cotton fabrics. All measurements
include a $1/4$-inch seam allowance. Sew with right
sides together unless otherwise stated.

Quilt Notes

This quilt has 48 Log Cabin blocks joined in
eight horizontal rows of six blocks each. Each
block has a center square of red. Although the
rest of the fabrics are scraps, the yellow print
consistently placed on the light side of the
Log Cabin blocks gives this quilt an especially
warm glow.

Cut the Fabrics

To make the best use of your fabrics, cut the
pieces in the order that follows. Cut cross-
grained strips for these blocks, as described
below. These strips are the width of the finished
logs plus $1/2$ inch seam allowances.

From red print with black dots, cut:
- 4—$10^1/2$×82-inch strips

From solid red, cut:
- 3—$2^1/2$×42-inch strips. From these strips, cut
   forty-eight $2^1/2$-inch A squares.

From yellow print, cut:
- 14—$1^1/2$×42-inch strips

From light scraps, cut:
- 47—$1^1/2$×42-inch strips

From dark scraps, cut:
- 69—$1^1/2$×42-inch strips

Make the Log Cabin Blocks

1 Referring to the Block Assembly Diagram on
page 100, begin each block with a red A square.
Add light-color print strips for Logs B and C and
dark-color print strips for Logs D and E, squaring
up the block as you add each pair of strips. You
may choose to use the same fabric for each pair
of logs or add variety by using different fabrics.
Always use the yellow print for Logs F and G.

instructions continued on page 100

Block Assembly Diagram

2 Continue adding strips with light colors on one side of the block and dark print strips on the other until each block is complete. Repeat to make a total of 48 Log Cabin blocks.

Assemble the Quilt Top

1 Lay out the blocks on a flat surface in eight horizontal rows of six blocks each. Referring to the Quilt Assembly Diagram, *opposite,* position the light and dark sides of the blocks as shown to achieve the illusion of diagonal lines.

2 When the blocks are arranged, join the blocks in each horizontal row. Sew the rows together to complete the quilt top. Press the seam allowances in one direction.

Add the Borders

1 Stitch a red print border strip to each long side of the quilt top. Press the seam allowances toward the borders. Trim the excess border fabric on the ends even with the quilt top.

2 Add the remaining border strips to the top and bottom edges in the same manner.

Complete the Quilt

1 Layer the quilt top, batting, and backing. Baste the three layers together (see tips for completing the quilt in Quilter's Workshop beginning on *page 280*).

2 Quilt as desired. The quilt pictured on *page 98* has diagonal lines quilted 1 inch apart through each Log Cabin block. The borders are quilted with a diagonal grid of 1-inch squares.

3 Use the beige print to make approximately 370 inches of binding (see tips for making and applying binding in Quilter's Workshop).

Quilt Assembly Diagram

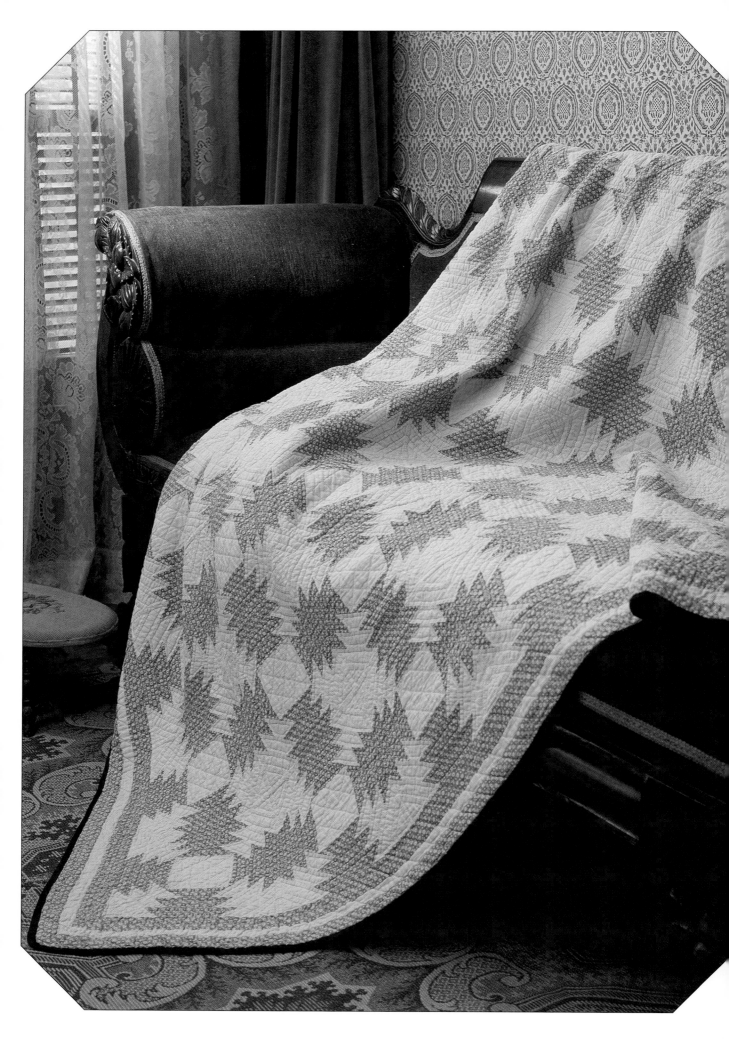

pineapple

1860–1890

Neutral muslin paired with a soft green print creates a subtle design full of movement. Choose one of the two methods to piece the Pineapple blocks.

Materials

6³/₈ yards *each* of muslin and green prints

1 yard of dark green print for binding

6 yards of backing fabric (or 3 yards of 90-inch-wide sheeting)

90×108 inches of quilt batting

Template material (for traditional piecing only)

Eighty 10-inch squares of tear-away foundation material such as tracing paper, preprinted pineapple papers, or lightweight interfacing (for strip piecing only)

Finished quilt: 80×98 inches

Finished Pineapple block: 9 inches square

Quantities specified are for 44/45-inch-wide, 100-percent-cotton fabrics. All measurements include a ¹/₄-inch seam allowance. Sew with right sides together unless otherwise stated.

Quilt Notes

The Pineapple quilt has an intriguing pattern that has possibilities that are not evident in a single block. Only when the blocks are joined does the interlocking zigzag design appear.

Here are two methods for piecing the blocks. For those who wish to sew by hand, traditional piecing is recommended; either traditional or strip piecing is appropriate for machine stitching.

Cut the Fabrics

To make the best use of your fabrics, cut the pieces in the order that follows. To piece the blocks traditionally, prepare a template for each of Patterns B through F from the Full-Size Pineapple Block Diagram on *page 105* (see tips for making and using templates for patchwork in Quilter's Workshop beginning on *page 280*). Templates are not needed for the strip-pieced method.

From muslin, cut:

◆ 10—1¹/₂×42-inch strips for the middle border

◆ 7—3¹/₂×42-inch strips. From these cut eighty 3¹/₂-inch squares for the block centers (A).

◆ 16—4×42-inch strips. From each strip cut ten 4-inch squares. Cut each square in half diagonally to get 320 G triangles.

◆ 60—1³/₄×42-inch strips. For traditional piecing only, cut 320 *each* of Patterns C and E from these strips.

From green print, cut:

◆ 8—2×42-inch strips and twelve 2×33-inch strips for the borders

◆ 110—1³/₄×42-inch strips for the patchwork. For traditional piecing only, cut 320 *each* of Patterns B, D, and F from these strips.

Make the Pineapple Blocks

Note: Press all the seam allowances toward the last piece added.

TRADITIONAL PIECING:

As you make each block, refer to the Full-Size Pineapple Block Diagram on *page 105,* and the Block Diagram on *page 104* for guidance.

instructions continued on page 104

pineapple

1860~1890

Block Diagram

1 Sew a green print B piece to opposite sides of the A square. Press; then add two more B pieces to the remaining sides of the A square.

2 Center a muslin C piece on two adjacent B pieces, matching right sides and raw edges. Stitch through all layers. Finger-press the C piece to the right side; check to see that the seam line goes neatly across the corner of the A square. Repeat, adding a C piece to the opposite corner. Press both C pieces; then add two more C pieces to the remaining corners.

3 Working in rounds add D, E, and F pieces in the same manner. Always work on opposite sides of the block and press those pieces before adding the remaining pieces in that round.

4 When the F round is complete, the resulting block is an octagon. Add the G triangles to make the block square as shown. Repeat to make 80 Pineapple blocks.

STRIP PIECING:

In this technique, fabric strips are machine-sewn to the underside of a marked 10-inch square of tearaway foundation material. The visibility of the sewing lines on the top of the foundation material simplifies this technique. After stitching a block or two, you will overcome the initial confusion caused by sewing in what seems to be an unnatural manner.

Use a lightweight material that is easily torn such as thin tracing paper, tearaway interfacing, or preprinted pineapple papers. (Do not use muslin.) The foundation will be removed to eliminate the bulk for quilting.

1 Using a ruler and a sharp pencil, trace the Full-Size Pineapple Block (One-Half) Diagram, *opposite*, on one square of foundation material. Rotate the foundation square and trace the other half to obtain a complete block. Make 80 copies using carbon paper, needle perforations, or heat transfer.

2 With the drawn side of the foundation faceup, pin a muslin A square to the *underside* of the foundation. Align the fabric with the drawn center square, wrong side of the fabric against the foundation. If the foundation is transparent, you can see the outline of the fabric in place as shown in Photo 1 on *page 106*.

3 On the underside of the foundation material, place a green print strip on one side of the muslin square, right sides of the fabrics together. To position the strip accurately, poke a pin through the foundation at each end of the drawn line as shown in Photo 1.

4 Check that the strip is straight and that the seam allowance is ample. Adjust the strip if necessary. Pin it in place on the fabric side as shown in Photo 2 on *page 106*. Cut the strip even with the sides of the A square.

5 The stitching must stay in place when the foundation is torn away, so set the machine at 12 stitches per inch. On the drawn side of the foundation, start sewing one stitch ahead of the drawn line. Stitch the strip in place, sewing right on the drawn line as shown in Photo 3. Stop one stitch beyond the end of the drawn

instructions continued on page 106

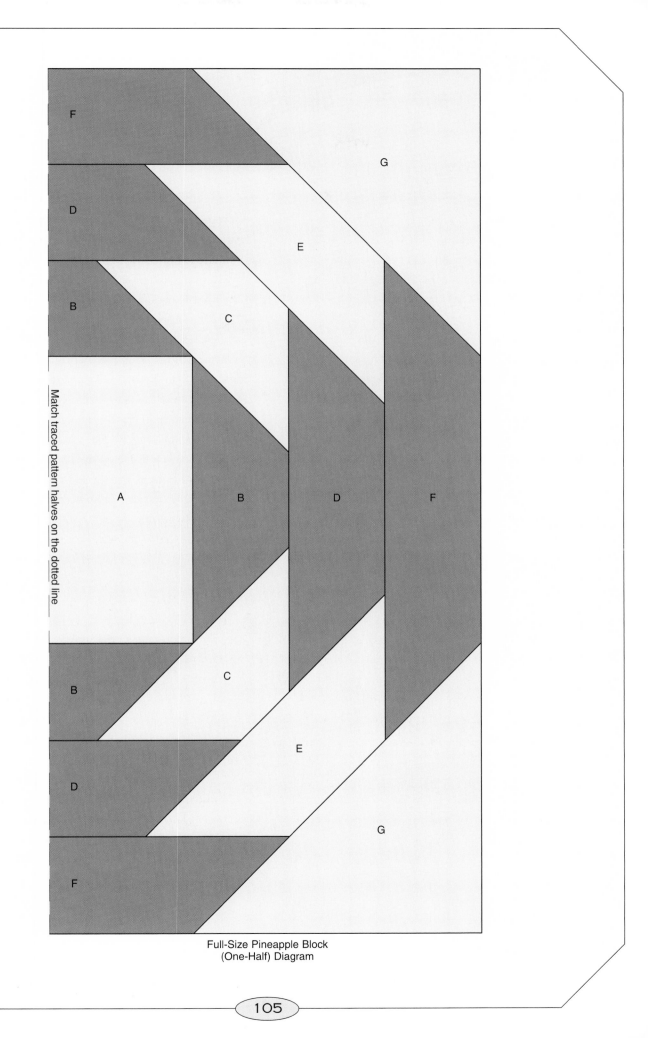

Match traced pattern halves on the dotted line

Full-Size Pineapple Block
(One-Half) Diagram

line. There is no need to backstitch because the next seam will cross and lock each line of stitching.

6 Check to see that the strip is sewn straight. Trim the seam allowance to a scant ¼ inch if necessary. Flip the strip to the right side, finger-press, and pin it to the foundation as shown in Photo 4, *below.*

7 Repeat steps 3 through 6 on the opposite side of the center square, leaving the pin in the first strip to keep it flat. Sew strips on the remaining two sides of the center square to complete the first round. As each piece is sewn, it should be pressed flat and pinned to the foundation.

8 Use a muslin strip for the second round. Right sides of the fabric together, lay the strip end at a 45-degree angle across two green

print B pieces, covering the corners of the B pieces as shown in Photo 4, *below.* From the drawn side of the foundation, pin through all layers at both ends of the sewing line to aid in aligning the strip with the sewing line. Pin the strip in place; cut off the strip, leaving at least ½ inch for a seam allowance.

9 Turn the foundation over to the drawn side. Sew the muslin strip in place by stitching on the drawn line as in the first round. On the fabric side, check that the strip is sewn straight. Trim the seam allowance as necessary, cutting away the corners of the B pieces as shown in Photo 5, *below. Note:* Trim, press, and pin each strip as it is sewn. If you do not trim each seam allowance and the corners in turn, the excess fabric is trapped under the next round, causing bulk and distortion.

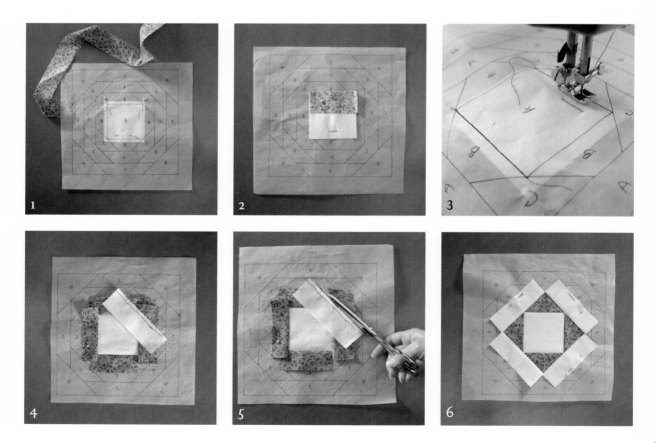

10 In the same manner, sew a strip on the opposite side of the block; then stitch the remaining two sides to complete the second round as shown in Photo 6, *opposite*.

11 Complete rounds 3, 4, and 5 in this manner, alternating colors. As the sewn pieces become longer, use more than one pin to hold them in place for sewing. Remove pins from any piece that is sewn on all sides.

12 When all the strip rounds are complete, the block is an octagon. Referring to the Block Diagram on *page 104*, sew the muslin G triangles onto the corners to make the block square. Make 80 Pineapple blocks. Do not remove the foundation material yet.

Assemble the Quilt Top

1 Sew 10 horizontal rows of eight blocks each, then join the rows.

2 To align the seams of adjacent blocks, pin through the seam lines of both blocks so the tip of the pin holds the seams together. After stitching, check the matched points. If you are not satisfied with the join, open the seam on both sides of a mismatched point; with a little judicious adjustment, you can ease into a better match.

3 Press the seam allowances open where the blocks are joined. Even if the seam lines are nicely matched, the bulk created by pressing so many seam allowances to one side makes the piecing appear inaccurate and hinders quilting.

4 To remove the foundation, make a small slit in the center of each foundation square. Slip your finger in the hole; gently tear the foundation along the seam lines and pull it away. Remove all foundation material.

Add the Borders

1 For inner border join three 2×33-inch green print strips end to end to make one border strip for each long side. Matching the center of each strip with the center point of one side, stitch border strips onto the long sides of the quilt top. Press the seam allowances toward the borders; trim excess border fabric at each end.

2 Join two 2×42-inch green print strips to make one border strip for the top edge. Repeat for the bottom border. Add borders to the quilt top as before.

3 For middle border combine three 1¹/₂×42-inch muslin strips for each side border and two strips for each end border. Add borders as before, sewing side borders first, then the end borders.

4 For outer border combine green print strips as for the inner border. Add border strips in the same manner.

Complete the Quilt

1 Layer the quilt top, batting, and backing. Baste the three layers together (see tips for completing the quilt in Quilter's Workshop beginning on *page 280*).

2 Quilt as desired. The quilt pictured on *page 102* has outline quilting in each strip of the Pineapple block. Diagonal lines, 1 inch apart, are quilted in the borders.

3 Use the dark green print to make approximately 370 inches of binding (see tips for making and applying binding in Quilter's Workshop).

railroad days
1860–1890

References to the underground railroad inspired this historical quilt. The rotation and placement of the blocks give the stitched work an interwoven appearance.

Materials

4³/₄ yards of black-and-white print for setting squares and border

¹/₈ yard *each* of 25 light and 25 medium to dark scrap fabrics for the patchwork, totaling 3¹/₈ yards *each* of light and dark fabrics

1 yard of beige print for binding

3¹/₂ yards of 108-inch-wide sheeting for backing fabric

120-inch square of quilt batting

Finished quilt: 89×107 inches

Finished block: 9 inches square

Quantities specified are for 44/45-inch-wide, 100-percent-cotton fabrics. All measurements include a ¹/₄-inch seam allowance. Sew with right sides together unless otherwise stated.

Quilt Notes

This quilt is a 9×11-block alternate straight set. Some of the 50 different blocks are made with only two fabrics, one light and one dark, while others are a jumble of colorful scraps.

In the quilt shown, the fabrics are a cheerful mix of solids, prints, stripes, and plaids. The quiltmaker was creative in the manner in which she positioned the blocks, turning them this way to suit her fancy.

Because there are only four triangle-squares in each block, quick piecing is not efficient for this scrap quilt. However, if you are making many triangle-squares with the same fabric combination, refer to the tips for making quick-pieced triangle-squares in Quilter's Workshop beginning on *page 280* before cutting the fabrics as indicated.

Cut the Fabrics

To make the best use of your fabrics, cut the pieces in the order that follows. Cutting requirements for blocks are given for one block, with the number required for the entire quilt shown in parentheses.

From black-and-white print, cut:

◆ 2—4¹/₂×100-inch strips for the side borders

◆ 6—4¹/₂×31-inch strips (cut crossgrain) for the top and bottom borders

◆ 49—9¹/₂-inch squares

From each light and dark scrap fabric, cut:

◆ 4—(200) 4-inch squares. Cut each square in half diagonally to yield eight triangles of each fabric for the triangle-squares.

◆ 2—(50) 2×21-inch strips for the Four-Patch units

Make the Blocks

1 Choose the fabrics for each block: For each block, select one 2×21-inch strip of a light fabric and one of a dark color. These strips will be used to make the Four-Patch units.

instructions continued on page 110

2 For the triangle-squares, you may use the same combination of fabrics or you may change one or both fabrics to achieve a scrappy look. Select four dark and four light triangles for each block.

3 Choose fabric combinations to make a total of 50 Underground Railroad blocks.

Make the Triangle~Squares

1 Match one light and one dark triangle. Stitch the two triangles together as shown in Diagram 1. Press the seam allowance toward the darker fabric.

2 Complete four triangle-squares for each of 50 blocks.

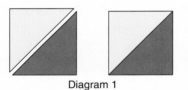

Diagram 1

Make the Four~Patch Units

Make five Four-Patch units for each block, using one of the methods described here.

TRADITIONAL PIECING:

1 Cut ten 2-inch squares from each 2×21-inch strip. Stitch one light square onto one side of each dark square; press the seam allowances toward the dark fabric.

2 Join two of these assembled units into a Four-Patch as illustrated in Diagram 2, rotating one unit to position the fabrics as shown.

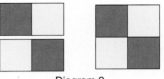

Diagram 2

STRIP PIECING:

1 For tips on strip piecing, refer to the Quilter's Workshop beginning on *page 280*.

2 For each block sew two 2×21-inch strips together, creating one 3¹/₂×21-inch strip. Press the seam allowance toward the dark fabric.

3 Cut 2-inch-wide segments from the 3¹/₂×21-inch pieced strip. Rotate one unit and join two units in a four-patch as illustrated in Diagram 2, *above*.

Assemble the Blocks

1 Press each assembled unit. Identify the five Four-Patch units and four triangle-squares for each block. All the units should measure 3¹/₂ inches square.

2 Referring to the Block Assembly Diagram, assemble the nine units in three horizontal rows of three squares each. Press the seam allowances in the first and third rows in the same direction; for the middle row, press the seam allowances in the opposite direction.

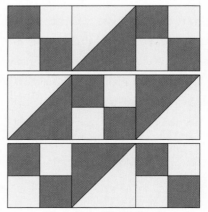

Block Assembly Diagram

3 Join the three rows to complete the Underground Railroad block. Make a total of 50 Underground Railroad blocks.

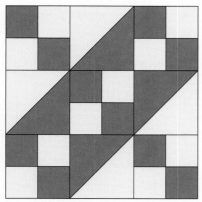

Block Diagram

Assemble the Quilt Top

1 On a flat surface arrange the blocks in 11 horizontal rows with nine squares in each row, alternating patchwork blocks with black-and-white print setting squares.

Rows 1, 3, 5, 7, 9, and 11 will alternate five pieced blocks and four setting squares, with a patchwork block at both ends. Rows 2, 4, 6, 8, and 10 will alternate four pieced blocks and five setting squares, with a setting square at both ends.

2 Join the blocks in each row, keeping all the squares in their correct positions. Press the seam allowances toward the setting squares.

3 Assemble the rows, alternating rows with patchwork blocks at each end with rows that have setting squares at the ends. Press the seam allowances in one direction. When the 11 horizontal rows are joined, the assembled quilt top should measure $81\frac{1}{2} \times 99\frac{1}{2}$ inches.

Add the Borders

1 Stitch a 100-inch-long black-and-white print border strip to each long side of the quilt. Press the seam allowances toward the borders; trim excess border fabric.

2 Join three 31-inch-long strips of black-and-white print end to end to make a border strip for the top edge of the quilt. Repeat for the bottom border.

3 Stitch the border strips to the top and bottom edges of the quilt. Press the seam allowances toward the border fabric; trim excess border fabric even with the sides.

Complete the Quilt

1 Layer the quilt top, batting, and backing. Baste the three layers together (see tips for completing the quilt in **Quilter's Workshop** beginning on *page 280*).

2 Quilt as desired. The quilt shown has diagonal lines of quilting over the entire quilt top.

3 Use the beige print to make approximately 410 inches of binding (see tips for making and applying binding in **Quilter's Workshop**).

lightning streak

1860–1890

Set in a zigzag, these pieced
triangles give the appearance of streaks of
lightning against a dark sky.

Materials

3 yards of black print

$2^{1}/_{4}$ yards of muslin

12—18×22-inch pieces of assorted prints

$^{5}/_{8}$ yard of black check fabric for binding

$2^{1}/_{8}$ yards of 90-inch-wide sheeting for
   backing fabric

72×90 inches of quilt batting

Finished quilt: $67^{1}/_{2}$×$82^{1}/_{2}$ inches

Quantities specified are for 44/45-inch-wide,
100-percent-cotton fabrics. All measurements
include a $^{1}/_{4}$-inch seam allowance. Sew with right
sides together unless otherwise stated.

Quilt Notes

Most of the scrap fabrics in this quilt are black,
gray, and blue prints. Randomly placed triangles
of pink, red, and gold add sparkle to the dark
colors. Instructions are given below for making
triangle-squares traditionally or with quick-
piecing techniques.

Cut the Fabrics

To make the best use of your fabrics, cut the
pieces in the order that follows. For tips on
diagonally cutting triangles from squares, refer to
Quilter's Workshop beginning on *page 280*. To cut
the small triangles traditionally, make a template
of the triangle pattern on *page 115*.

From black print, cut:

◆ 12—$16^{3}/_{8}$-inch squares. Cut each square
   diagonally into quarters to obtain a total of
   48 triangles. (You will have 3 triangles left over.)

◆ 5—$8^{3}/_{8}$-inch squares. Cut each square
   diagonally in half to obtain 10 corner triangles;
   set aside the one extra triangle.

From muslin, cut:

◆ 4—18×42-inch strips. Cut each strip in three
   14×18-inch pieces for the triangle-squares.

From each *assorted prints*, cut:

◆ 1—14×18-inch piece for the triangle-squares

◆ 10—$3^{1}/_{2}$-inch squares. Cut each square
   diagonally in half for a total of 240 triangles.

Make the Triangle-Squares

TRADITIONAL PIECING:

1 Use the small triangle template to make 24
triangles on each 14×18-inch piece of muslin
and assorted print. Cut 288 muslin triangles and
288 triangles of assorted print fabrics.

2 Join a muslin triangle to each print triangle.
Make 288 triangle-squares. Press the seam
allowances toward the darker fabric.

QUICK PIECING:

1 On the wrong side of *each* 14×18-inch muslin
piece, mark a 3×4-square grid of $3^{1}/_{2}$-inch squares
as shown in Diagram 1. Draw diagonal lines as
shown through the squares. Layer each muslin

instructions continued on page 114

lightning streak

1860-1890

piece, marked side up, on top of a matching piece of print fabric.

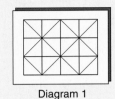

Diagram 1

2 Machine-stitch exactly ¼ inch from both sides of all diagonal lines. Pivot the fabric at corners without lifting the needle. When stitching is done, trim the excess fabric around the grid. Cut on all *horizontal* and *vertical* grid lines, cutting the fabric into squares. Next, cut on the *diagonal lines between the stitching*, cutting each square into two triangle-squares.

3 Each grid makes 24 triangle-squares. Complete 12 grids to make a total of 288 triangle-squares. Press all the seam allowances toward the darker fabric.

Make the Lightning Triangles

1 For each of the large triangles, select six random triangle-squares and four print triangles. Assemble each triangle in four rows as shown in Diagram 2. Join the rows to finish the triangle. Make 45 large triangles.

Diagram 2

2 For each corner triangle, select two different triangle-squares and four print triangles.

3 Sew a single triangle to two adjacent sides of each triangle-square as illustrated in Diagram 3, making a larger triangle. Matching seam lines carefully, join the two triangles to make one corner triangle. Make nine corner triangles.

Diagram 3

Assemble the Quilt Top

1 Join five pieced triangles and five triangles of black print in a row as shown in Diagram 4. End the row with a pieced corner triangle at the left end and a black print corner triangle at the right end, as shown in Diagram 4. Press the seam allowances toward the black triangles. Make nine vertical rows in this manner.

Diagram 4

2 Referring to the Quilt Assembly Diagram, *opposite*, lay all the assembled rows on the floor, each with the black print corner triangle at the top. Leave rows 1, 3, 5, 7, and 9 in place; rotate rows 2, 4 6, and 8 so the pieced corner triangle is at the top. When the rows are in place, a zigzag pattern emerges. Stitch together the vertical rows to complete the quilt top.

Complete the Quilt

1 Layer the quilt top, batting, and backing. Baste the three layers together (see tips for completing the quilt in Quilter's Workshop beginning on *page 280*).

Quilt Assembly Diagram

2 Quilt as desired. A grid of 1-inch squares is quilted in the black print triangles of the quilt shown on *page 112*; the pieced triangles are outline quilted.

3 Use the black check fabric to make approximately 308 inches of binding, either bias or straight-grain (see tips for making and applying binding in Quilter's Workshop).

Make a Larger Quilt

Making more rows and/or adding more triangles in each row will enlarge the finished size of this quilt. Add two more rows to make a full-size quilt; three rows for a queen-size; or five rows for a king-size quilt.

To make the quilt longer, add one or two of both pieced and plain large triangles to each vertical row. For each additional row, you'll need at least ¹/₂ yard each of black print fabric and muslin, as well as two additional 18×22-inch pieces of scrap print fabrics.

Lightning Streak
Full-Size Pattern

flying geese

1860–1890

Varied geese "fly" across this quilt in a tidy pattern. Wide sashing strips divide the rows of orderly geese and provide borders.

Materials

3¹/₄ yards of red print for sashing

1 yard of the same or coordinating red print for top and bottom borders

¹/₈ yard *each* of 10 medium or dark fabrics for the Flying Geese triangles

¹/₈ yard *each* of seven light fabrics for background

1 yard of red-and-black print for binding

6 yards of backing fabric (or 3 yards of 90-inch-wide sheeting)

90×108 inches of quilt batting

Finished quilt: 78×100 inches

Each Flying Geese block: 3×6 inches

Quantities specified are for 44/45-inch-wide, 100-percent-cotton fabrics. All measurements include a ¹/₄-inch seam allowance. Sew with right sides together unless otherwise stated.

Quilt Notes

This quilt gets its name from the triangular "geese" that "fly" up the quilt. The Flying Geese blocks are assembled in vertical rows that are joined with alternating sashing.

Cut the Fabrics

To make the best use of your fabrics, cut the pieces in the order that follows. For tips on making and using templates for patchwork, see Quilter's Workshop beginning on *page 280*. Prepare templates for Patterns A and B on *page 119*. Square the corners of the templates as indicated on the patterns.

From red print, cut:

◆ 4—8¹/₂×85-inch strips for sashing

◆ 6—8¹/₂×29-inch strips for the borders. Add the remaining red print fabric to the assorted dark prints.

From red print for top and bottom borders, cut:

◆ 4—8¹/₂×42-inch strips

From light fabrics, cut:

◆ 140—Pattern A. Place the template grainline on the crosswise fabric grain. Turn the template up and down to make common cutting lines for adjacent triangles and to maximize fabric.

From medium and dark fabrics, cut:

◆ 280—Pattern B, aligning lengthwise grain

instructions continued on page 118

flying geese
1860~1890

Make the Flying Geese Blocks

1 For each block, match one A triangle with a pair of B triangles. Sort the cut triangles into sets for 140 blocks, varying the fabric combinations as much as possible.

2 Matching both triangle sides, sew a B triangle to one side of the A triangle. Press the seam allowance toward the B triangle.

3 In the same manner, stitch the second B triangle to the remaining side of the A triangle. Make a total of 140 Flying Geese blocks.

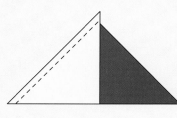
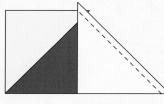

Flying Geese Block
Assembly Diagram

Make Rows of Flying Geese

1 Before sewing the blocks together, lay them out on the floor or another flat surface. Arrange the blocks in five vertical rows with 28 blocks in each row. Be sure the geese in each row point in the same direction.

2 Lay the sashing strips between the Flying Geese rows to help you see the effect. Move the Flying Geese blocks around to find a pleasing arrangement.

3 Join 28 blocks in a vertical row, sewing the top of one block to the bottom of the block above it. If your patchwork is precise, the seam line will cross the tip of each A triangle.

4 Press the joining seam allowances toward the A triangles. Stitch and press five rows of Flying Geese.

Assemble the Quilt Top

1 Fold each of the four 85-inch-long strips of red print in fourths, or measure $21^1/_4$-inch sections along the length of the strip. Mark each quarter-section with a pin on both edges of the strip. This is important for matching the horizontal seam lines of the Flying Geese units.

2 Sew the four sashing strips between the rows of Flying Geese, matching the marked points of each red strip with the horizontal seam line of every seventh geese unit.

3 Join three $8^1/_2 \times 29$-inch red print border strips end to end to make one strip for each outer edge. Stitch these strips to the long sides of the quilt; trim excess fabric even with the ends of the quilt top.

4 Join two $8^1/_2 \times 42$-inch strips of the red print border fabric to make one strip. On the top edge of the quilt, match the center seam of the border strip with the center of the middle row of Flying Geese. Right sides together, stitch the top border to the quilt. Press the seam allowance

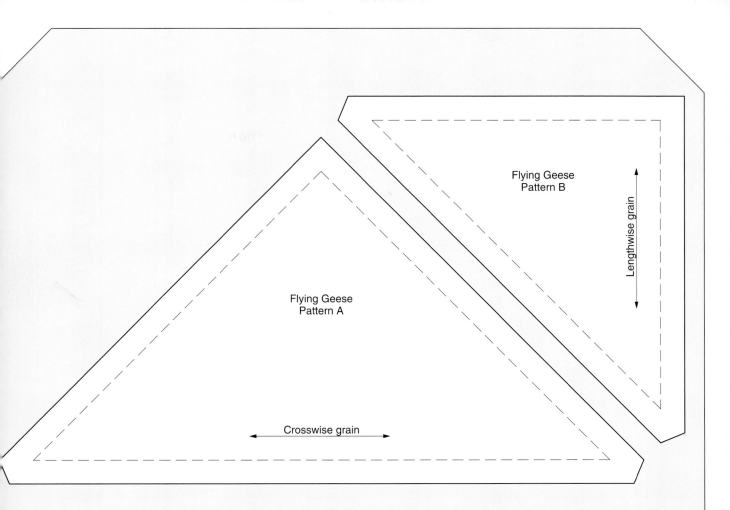

Flying Geese
Pattern B

Lengthwise grain

Flying Geese
Pattern A

Crosswise grain

toward the border fabric; trim the border fabric even with the sides of the quilt top.

5 In the same manner, make one more border strip; join it to the bottom edge of the quilt top.

Complete the Quilt

1 Layer the quilt top, batting, and backing. Baste the three layers together (see tips for completing the quilt in Quilter's Workshop beginning on *page 280*).

2 Quilt as desired. The quilt shown on *page 116* has a cable design quilted in the sashing strips and outline quilting in all the light triangles.

3 Use the red-and-black print to make approximately 370 inches of binding, either bias or straight-grain (see tips for making and applying binding in Quilter's Workshop).

Make a Larger Quilt

The size of this quilt is suitable for most twin or full-size beds.

To make a wider quilt, simply add more vertical rows. To make the quilt longer, make additional Flying Geese blocks or add wider borders to the top and bottom of the quilt.

When making a larger quilt, remember to adjust the yardage for the red print and the backing fabric. Larger batting is also necessary.

little basket

1860–1890

Simple baskets in a variety of prints are
stacked in rows amid quaint plaid triangles and stripes.
Muslin binding finishes the edges.

Materials

4 yards *each* of muslin and red plaid fabric

98—5×8-inch assorted prints for baskets, totaling
2⁷/₈ yards

1 yard of muslin for binding

6 yards of backing fabric (or 2¹/₄ yards of
108-inch-wide sheeting)

90×108 inches of quilt batting

Finished quilt: 67×98 inches
Basket block: 7 inches square

Quantities specified are for 44/45-inch-wide,
100-percent-cotton fabrics. All measurements
include a ¹/₄-inch seam allowance. Sew with right
sides together unless otherwise stated.

Quilt Notes

This quilt is set in vertical rows. Each of the
seven rows has 14 Basket blocks. Three strips of
sashing separate the vertical block rows.

Cut the Fabrics

To make the best use of your fabrics, cut the
pieces in the order that follows. For tips on
making and using templates for patchwork,
see Quilter's Workshop beginning on *page 280.*
Prepare templates for Patterns A through E
on *page 123.*

In the original quilt, the sashing strips are cut
on the straight grain of the plaid and the block
corners are cut on the bias. This makes the plaids
contrast nicely, but it also requires more yardage
and adds the difficulty of working with bias
edges on the outside of the blocks. The yardage
given below is for block corners cut on the
straight of the grain.

From muslin, cut:
- 12—1¹/₂×100-inch sashing strips
- 98—*each* of Patterns A, C, D, and D reversed

From red plaid fabric, cut:
- 6—1¹/₂×100-inch sashing strips
- 196—4¹/₂-inch squares. Cut each square
  diagonally in half to get 392 corner triangles.

From each assorted print, cut:
- 1—*each* of Patterns B and C. Add a ³/₁₆-inch
  seam allowance around the template when
  cutting the B basket handles.
- 2—Pattern E

Make the Basket Blocks

This block is a combination of patchwork and
appliqué. The curved handle is appliquéd onto
the muslin A triangle before the basket is pieced.
Plaid corner triangles, sewn onto the basket
square, complete the block.

instructions continued on page 122

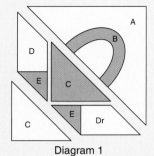

Diagram 1

1 Referring to Diagram 1, *above*, stitch an E triangle to the bottom edges of the D and D reversed pieces. Press the seam allowances toward the E triangles.

2 Sew the DE units to the short legs of the C triangle of assorted print, positioning the pieces as shown in Diagram 1. Press the seam allowances toward the C triangle.

3 Complete the bottom of the Basket block with the muslin C triangle as shown in Diagram 1; press the seam allowance toward the muslin triangle.

4 Turn under the seam allowance on the curved edges of the handle (B). Center the handle fabric on the muslin A triangle, matching raw edges. Appliqué the curved edges of the handle in place on the muslin.

5 Join the two halves of the basket block (see Diagram 2). Press the seam allowances toward the A triangle.

6 Complete the block by adding a plaid corner triangle to each side of the basket

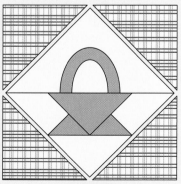

Diagram 2

block. Press the seam allowances toward the plaid fabric. Make a total of 98 Basket blocks.

Assemble the Quilt Top

1 Join the blocks end to end in seven vertical rows of 14 blocks each.

2 Stitch a plaid sashing strip between two muslin sashing strips; press the seam allowances toward the plaid fabric. Make six muslin-plaid-muslin sashings.

3 Starting 1 inch from the top of the sashing unit, measure 7-inch sections down the length of the strip. Mark each section with a pin on both sides of the strip. This is important for matching the horizontal seam lines of the Basket blocks.

4 Join the block rows with sashing strips between each row, matching the pins in each sashing unit with the block seam lines. Press the seam allowances toward the sashing. Trim the sashing even with the blocks at the top and bottom of the quilt top.

Complete the Quilt

1 Layer the quilt top, batting, and backing. Baste the three layers together (see tips for completing the quilt in Quilter's Workshop beginning on *page 280*).

2 Quilt as desired. The quilt shown on *page 120* has a diagonal grid of 1-inch squares stitched across the baskets and in the plaid corner triangles; a single line of quilting is stitched in the center of each sashing strip.

3 Use the beige print to make approximately 340 inches of binding, either bias or straight-grain (see tips for making and applying binding in Quilter's Workshop).

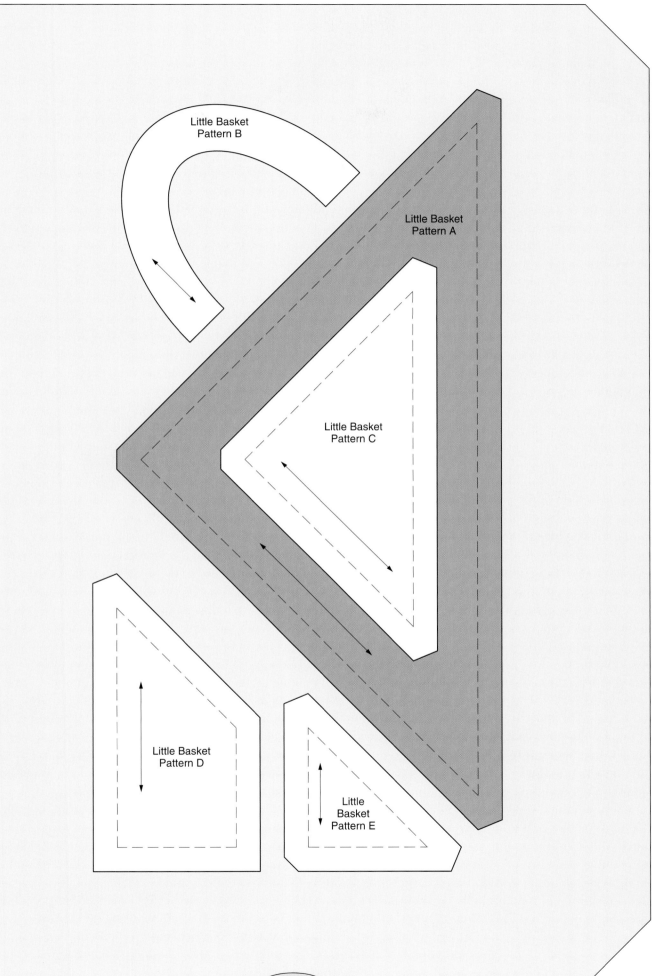

Little Basket
Pattern B

Little Basket
Pattern A

Little Basket
Pattern C

Little Basket
Pattern D

Little
Basket
Pattern E

clamshell

1860–1890

*More than 1000
fan shapes are used to create this scrappy,
hand-pieced quilt of alternating
light and dark fabrics.*

Materials

5 yards of muslin or scraps of assorted light
    prints for the clamshells

$3^{1}/_{2}$ yards or scraps of assorted medium and dark
    prints for the clamshells

$2^{3}/_{4}$ yards of blue check fabric for borders,
    binding, and shells

$5^{3}/_{4}$ yards of backing fabric

90×100 inches of quilt batting

Finished quilt: $80^{1}/_{2}×94^{1}/_{2}$ inches

Quantities specified are for 44/45-inch-wide,
100-percent-cotton fabrics. All measurements
include a $^{1}/_{4}$-inch seam allowance. Sew with right
sides together unless otherwise stated.

Quilt Notes

The Clamshell quilt is made in alternating rows
of light and dark fabrics. Our quilt has only
muslin in the light-color rows, but you may want
to add a variety of light prints and solids for a
scrappier look.

instructions continued on page 126

clamshell

1860–1890

Cut the Fabrics

To make the best use of your fabrics, cut the pieces in the order that follows.

Make a template for the clamshell pattern, *opposite*. For tips on making window templates, see Quilter's Workshop beginning on *page 280*. Mark both the cutting and sewing lines on the right side of the shell fabrics.

From blue check fabric, cut:

◆ 2—4×83-inch strips and two 4×96-inch strips for the borders
◆ 1—26×36-inch piece for binding. (Use the remaining border fabric to make shells.)

From muslin or light prints, cut:

◆ 598 clamshells

From dark prints, cut:

◆ 550 clamshells

Assemble the Quilt Top

1 Baste back the seam allowance along the top curved edge of each clamshell, leaving the lower curves and the bottom unturned.

2 Working on a flat surface (an ironing board is ideal), lay out a horizontal row of 23 light color clamshells. Referring to Diagram 1, make sure the top edges are even and the sides touch, but do not overlap.

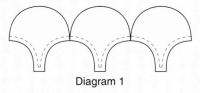

Diagram 1

3 Position a row of 22 dark shells below the first row, lapping the second row over the bottom halves of the light shells as shown in Diagram 2. Using a blind hemming stitch, appliqué the curved edges of the dark shells to the light shells.

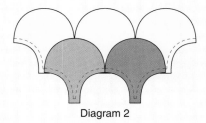

Diagram 2

4 Continue to add rows of light and dark clamshells in this manner. Join 25 rows of dark shells and 26 rows of light shells. The light rows are a half-shell wider at each end than the dark rows.

5 The quilt top should be approximately 80½×91 inches. The light shells in the top and bottom rows and at the sides can be trimmed before or after the borders are added.

To trim the top, align a ruler ¼ inch above the top row of dark shells. With a rotary cutter, carefully cut away the top of the first row of light shells. At the bottom of the quilt top, cut ¼ inch below the tip of the last dark row, removing the bottom half of the last row of light shells.

On the right edge of the quilt top, place the ruler ¼ inch to the right of the dark shells to trim the excess fabric of the light shells. Repeat on the left edge of the quilt, cutting ¼ inch from the left side of the dark shells.

Add the Borders

Center the border strips on each edge of the quilt top, mitering the borders (see tips for mitering border corners in Quilter's Workshop beginning on *page 280*).

Complete the Quilt

1 Layer the quilt top, batting, and backing. Baste the three layers together (see tips for completing the quilt in Quilter's Workshop).

2 Quilt as desired. The quilt shown on *page 125* has outline quilting inside the curves of each clamshell. The border is quilted with straight lines perpendicular to the edges of the quilt.

3 Use the remaining blue check fabric to make approximately 360 inches of binding (see tips for making and applying binding in Quilter's Workshop).

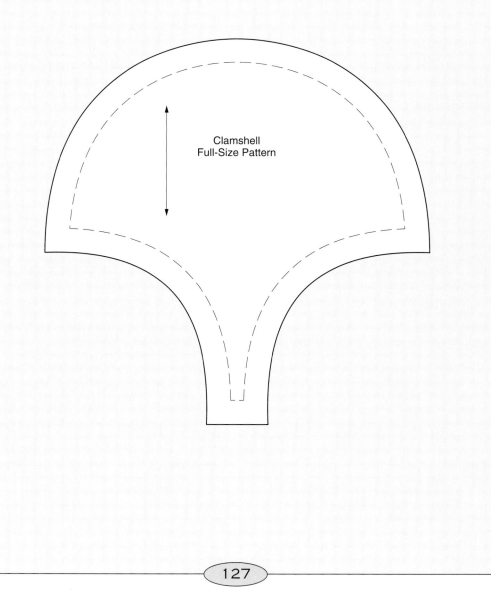

Clamshell
Full-Size Pattern

postage stamp

1860-1890

Composed of tiny pieced

squares, this masterpiece sings with color,

texture, and pattern.

Materials

4³/₄ yards of solid yellow for blocks and binding

1¹/₄ yards *each* of solid black and orange

1 yard of solid green

33—¹/₄-yard pieces or strips of assorted prints

6³/₈ yards of backing fabric (or 3³/₈ yards of
90-inch-wide sheeting)

90×108 inches of quilt batting

Finished quilt: 78×104 inches

Finished block: 26 inches square

Quantities specified are for 44/45-inch-wide,
100-percent-cotton fabrics. All measurements
include a ¹/₄-inch seam allowance. Sew with right
sides together unless otherwise stated.

Quilt Notes

This is the ultimate scrap lover's quilt. *Note:* The
quilt shown *opposite* has three blocks across and
3¹/₄ blocks down. To simplify the assembly and to
achieve a more useful length, these instructions
are for a 12-block quilt with three blocks across
and four blocks down. Refer to the Block
Assembly Diagram on *page 131* while cutting
fabrics and making the Postage Stamp blocks.

Cut the Fabrics

From solid yellow, cut:

◆ 85—1¹/₂×42-inch strips. From these strips, cut
24 pieces 1¹/₂×11¹/₂ inches and 48 *each* of the

following: 1¹/₂×9¹/₂ inches, 1¹/₂×7¹/₂ inches, 1¹/₂×5¹/₂
inches, 1¹/₂×3¹/₂ inches, and 1¹/₂-inch squares.

From solid black, cut:

◆ 29—1¹/₂×42-inch strips

From orange, cut:

◆ 25—1¹/₂×42-inch strips

From green, cut:

◆ 21—1¹/₂×42-inch strips

From each assorted print, cut:

◆ 5 or 6—1¹/₂×42-inch strips, cutting a total of
166 strips. From each strip, cut twenty-eight
1¹/₂-inch squares. Cut 386 squares of assorted
prints for each block, a total of 4,632 for the
12-block quilt.

Piece the Units

Each yellow diamond is encircled by rows of
green, orange, and black squares. Using the
following instructions, you can strip-piece these
units before assembling the block to reduce the
amount of piecing required later. If you prefer to
assemble these units traditionally, one square at a
time, you can sew them by hand or by machine.

TRADITIONAL PIECING:

1 From the 1¹/₂×42-inch strips of green, orange,
and black fabrics, cut forty-eight 1¹/₂-inch
squares of each fabric for one block.

2 Sew one orange square between a black and
a green square. Press the seam allowances
toward the orange fabric. Make 48 three-square
units for each block.

3 Make two-square units
in the same manner, using squares of black
and orange fabric. Press the seam allowances
toward the orange fabric. Make eight two-square
units for each block.

4 Cut the remaining four strips of black
fabric into ninety-six 1½-inch squares for
the block patchwork.

STRIP PIECING:

1 Machine-stitch one 1½×42-inch strip of orange
fabric between strips of green and black fabrics
as shown in the Strip Set Diagram. Press the seam
allowances toward the orange fabric.

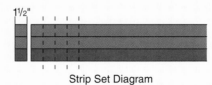

Strip Set Diagram

2 Using a rotary cutter and a ruler, measure
and cut 1½-inch-wide vertical units from the
strip set as shown in the Strip Set Diagram. Cut
28 three-square units from each strip set.

instructions continued on page 130

Each block has 48 three-square units, so make two strip sets for each block. Set aside the eight extra units from the second strip set until you have enough to use for a later block.

3 Make two-square units in the same manner, using strips of black and orange fabric. Press the seam allowance toward the orange fabric. Cut eight two-square units for each block.

4 Cut the remaining four strips of black fabric into ninety-six 1½-inch squares for the block patchwork.

Make the Horizontal Sections

The Postage Stamp block is assembled in 26 vertical rows as indicated in the Block Assembly Diagram, *opposite*. However, because some of the yellow strips are horizontal, sections of the block are preassembled, as described below, to avoid awkward corners.

At the top and bottom of the Block Assembly Diagram are center sections. Assemble these sections before joining the rest of the block. Begin with the section at the bottom of the block (see red arrow).

1 Start at the center of the section, indicated by the red arrow on the diagram. Stitch a 1½-inch square of yellow onto the green square of one three-square unit (see Diagram 1). Press the seam allowance toward the yellow.

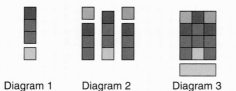

Diagram 1   Diagram 2   Diagram 3

2 Sew one assorted print square onto the black end of two other three-square units (see Diagram 2); press the seam allowance toward

the assorted print. Referring to Diagram 3, sew the three units together with the yellow square in the center between the green squares.

3 Sew a 1½×3½-inch yellow strip across the end of this assembled unit as shown in Diagram 3. Press the seam allowance toward the yellow strip.

4 Join two scrap squares onto the black end of two other three-square units. Stitch one of these onto each side of the center section, aligning the green square of each unit with the yellow strip at the bottom of the center section.

5 Sew a 1½×5½-inch yellow strip across the end of the assembled unit. Press the seam allowance toward the yellow strip. Following Diagram 4, continue assembling the bottom section in this manner until the section is complete.

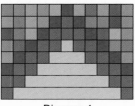

Diagram 4

6 Follow steps 1 through 5 again to make the section at the top of the block. Complete this section by adding a 1½×11½-inch solid yellow strip at the top as shown in Diagram 5.

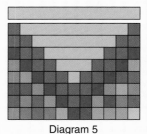

Diagram 5

Assemble the Blocks

1 Referring to the Block Assembly Diagram, *opposite*, assemble the center scrap section of rows 8 through 18, positioning black squares in rows 8 and 18 as shown. Join the squares in vertical rows,

pressing all seam allowances in the same direction. Then assemble the rows, rotating alternate rows to alternate the direction of the seam allowances.

2 Join the three sections of rows 8 through 18 to complete the center section of the block.

3 Referring to the Block Assembly Diagram, construct rows 1 through 7 by sewing scrap squares, three-square units, and yellow strips end to end in vertical rows.

4 Join rows 1 through 7, then stitch the assembled unit onto the left side of the center section.

5 Make rows 19 through 26 in the same manner; stitch this unit onto the right side of the center section.

6 Make a total of 12 Postage Stamp blocks. As you finish each block, mark the top of the block with a pin to avoid confusion later.

Assemble the Quilt Top

Join the blocks in four horizontal rows of three blocks each. Make sure the pinned side of each block is at the top. Assemble the four rows to complete the quilt top.

Complete the Quilt

1 Layer the quilt top, batting, and backing. Baste the three layers together (see tips for completing the quilt in Quilter's Workshop beginning on *page 280*).

2 Quilt as desired. The quilt shown on *page 129* has outline quilting on the yellow strips and a diagonal line quilted through each 1-inch square.

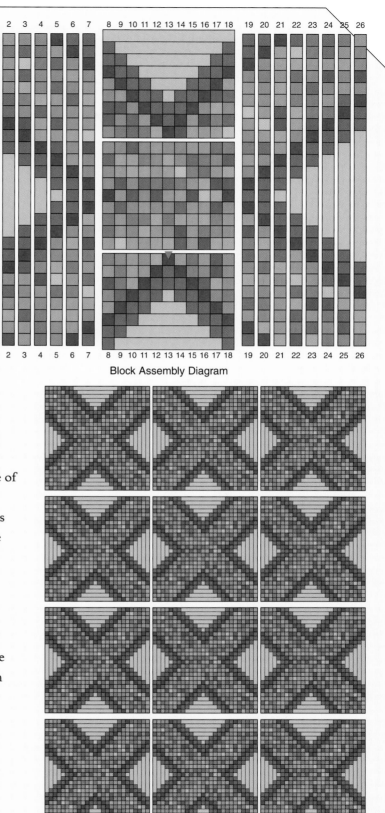

Block Assembly Diagram

Quilt Assembly Diagram

3 Use the remaining solid yellow to make approximately 375 inches of binding, either bias or straight-grain (see tips for making and applying binding in Quilter's Workshop).

hearts & gizzards

1860~1890

*Create this illusionary quilt with a combination
of appliqué and piecing. The mixture of techniques ensures precise curves
that will make your quilt resemble this antique version.*

Materials

4²/₃ yards of solid white or muslin for the
patchwork, appliqué, and binding
4 yards of solid orange for the patchwork and
appliqué
81×96 inches of quilt batting
5 yards of backing fabric

Finished quilt top: 66¹/₂×81¹/₂ inches
Finished block: 15 inches square

Quantities specified are for 44/45-inch-wide,
100-percent-cotton fabrics. All measurements
include a ¹/₄-inch seam allowance. Sew with right
sides together unless otherwise stated.

Select the Fabric

In the 1930s and 1940s, quiltmakers often selected
solid color fabric for their quilts. The orange and
white fabrics of this quilt contrast strongly. If you
want a more subtle contrast, substitute a pastel
for the orange, or choose a print with lots of
white in it. The white fabric used for the quilt
shown *opposite* has a slight sheen and actually may
be Cloth of Gold, a popular brand of fabric in
the '30s and '40s.

Cut the Fabrics

To make the best use of your fabrics, cut the
pieces in the order that follows. Pattern pieces B,
C, and D are on the Pattern Sheet. To make

templates from the patterns, see tips for making
templates in Quilter's Workshop beginning on
page 280. When using templates, always mark the
appliqué pattern pieces on the right side of your
fabric. If you prefer to use another appliqué
method, see "Learn to Needle-Turn Appliqué" on
page 135 to make freezer-paper templates.
Note: Pattern pieces B and C include seam
allowances on the two straight sides of each
pattern. The curved edges have no added seam
allowances because those edges will be appliquéd.
When cutting out the pieces, add a scant ¹/₄-inch
seam allowance beyond the curved edge.

From solid white, cut:

- 40—8³/₈-inch squares, cutting each square in
half diagonally for a total of 80 A triangles
- 3—3³/₄-inch-wide strips, cutting each strip as
shown in Diagram 1 for a total of 18 D pieces or
18 of Pattern D

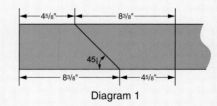

Diagram 1

- 11—4¹/₈-inch squares, cutting each square in
half diagonally for a total of 22 E triangles
- 80—Pattern B
- 120—Pattern C
- 2—21-inch-wide strips for bias binding (refer to
"Cutting Bias Strips," *opposite*)

CUTTING BIAS STRIPS

To cut bias strips, begin with a 21×42-inch strip.
Referring to the diagram below, use a large acrylic
triangle to square up the left edge of the fabric and
to draw a 45-degree angle. Then cut the fabric on
the drawn line. Handle the edges carefully to avoid
distorting the bias. Cut enough 2¼-inch-wide strips
on the bias to total 375 inches in length.

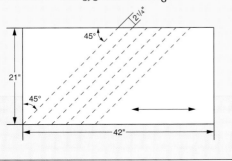

From solid orange, cut:

◆ 40—8³/₈-inch squares, cutting each square in
   half diagonally for a total of 80 A triangles

◆ 3—3³/₄-inch-wide strips, cutting each strip as
   shown in Diagram 1 for a total of 18 D pieces or
   18 of Pattern D

◆ 11—4¹/₈-inch squares, cutting each square in
   half diagonally for a total of 22 E triangles

◆ 80—Pattern B

◆ 120—Pattern C

instructions continued on page 134

hearts & gizzards

1860–1890

Make the Blocks

1 To prepare pattern pieces B and C for appliqué, baste under the seam allowance along the curved edge.

2 Position and pin one orange B piece and one orange C piece to each white A triangle (see Diagram 2). The two straight sides of B and C align with the raw edges of the A triangle. Appliqué the curved edges of pieces B and C in place. Make 80 units. Then repeat to make 80 units with one white B and one white C piece appliquéd to each orange A triangle (see Diagram 2).

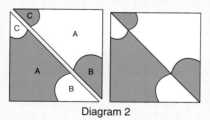
Diagram 2

3 Join a pair of contrasting A triangles to form a block quadrant (see Diagram 3). Press the seam allowances toward the orange fabric. Make 80 block quadrants.

4 Join four block quadrants to make a block (see Diagram 3). Make 20 blocks.

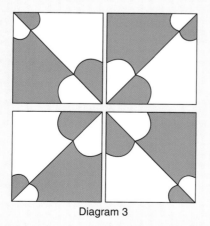
Diagram 3

Make the Border and Corner Units

1 Position and pin one orange C piece to each white D piece and one white C piece to each orange D piece (see Diagram 4). Appliqué the curved edges in place. Make 18 CD units of each color combination.

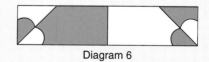
Diagram 4

2 Appliqué one orange C piece to each white E triangle and one white C piece to each orange E triangle (see Diagram 5). Make 22 CE units of each color combination. Set aside four CE units of each color combination for corner units.

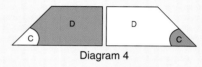
Diagram 5

3 Join one contrasting CE unit to each CD unit. Referring to Diagram 6, sew together pairs of the contrasting units to complete the border units. Make a total of 18 border units.

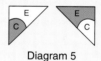
Diagram 6

4 With the remaining eight CE triangle units, make four corner units as shown in Diagram 7.

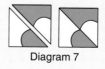
Diagram 7

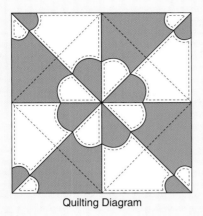

Quilting Diagram

Assemble the Quilt Top

1 Referring to the photograph on *page 133*, lay out the blocks, the border units, and the corner units in rows. The top horizontal row includes four border units with a corner unit on each end. Then there are five rows with four blocks in each row with a border unit on each end. The bottom row includes four border units with a corner unit on each end.

2 Sew together the border units and blocks in each horizontal row. Press the seam allowances in each row in the same direction, alternating the direction with each row. Join the rows.

Complete the Quilt

1 Layer the quilt top, batting, and backing. Baste the three layers together (see tips for completing the quilt in Quilter's Workshop beginning on *page 280*).

2 Quilt as desired. The antique quilt shown on *page 133* has in-the-ditch quilting along the seams and next to the curved edges, with some additional straight-lines intersecting blocks. The dashed lines in the Quilting Diagram *above* indicate stitch placement.

3 When binding the quilt, curve around the side and corner pieces to achieve the same curved edges as on this antique quilt. To cut your binding see "Cutting Bias Strips" on *page 133*. See binding tips in Quilter's Workshop to finish the bias binding.

LEARN TO NEEDLE-TURN APPLIQUÉ

Try this freezer-paper technique.

1 Make templates for pattern pieces B and C as instructed in the Quilter's Workshop beginning on *page 280*.

2 Trace around each template on the smooth side of freezer paper. You'll need a freezer-paper template for each appliqué piece. For the quilt shown on *page 133*, you'll need 160 B freezer-paper templates and 240 C freezer-paper templates.

Cut 2½-inch-wide and 3½-inch-wide strips of freezer paper with your scissors. Accordion-fold the narrow strips approximately every 3½ inches. Then accordion-fold the wider strips about every 5½ inches. On the top fold of the small strip, trace around Template C. On the top fold of the large strip, trace around Template B. Staple or pin through the center of the drawn shape to keep the layers aligned. Cut on the drawn line for multiple freezer-paper templates (see Photo 1). Repeat these steps for the number of templates.

3 Using a dry iron set on wool, press the shiny side of the freezer-paper templates to the right side of your fabric (see Photo 2). Leave ½ inch of space between the paper pieces at the curved edges. Cut out the pieces, trimming right next to the paper on the straight edges. Cut a scant ¼ inch away from the freezer paper along the curved edges.

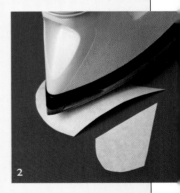

4 Position and pin pieces B and C on the A triangles as described in "Make the Blocks" *opposite*. With your needle and thread that matches the appliqués, stitch the pieces in place, turning under the seam allowances next to the curved edge of the paper templates as you stitch (see Photo 3). Remove the paper templates once you complete the stitching.

1890-1920

This was a period of transition for American quilters, who combined techniques from the past—patchwork, crazy quilting, embroidery, and appliqué.

From dark and somber fabric prints to stunning graphic Amish masterpieces in solid colors, quilts made use of a variety of fabrics and piecing methods. As the interest in quilting waned, Americans who preferred Victorian decorating styles purchased ready-made bedding from Montgomery Ward and Sears, Roebuck & Co. catalogs. This innovative way to purchase affordable goods also enabled items to reach even remote locations. With manufactured products readily available, homemade quilts lost their popularity. Although few appliquéd quilts were made, pieced ones were sewn in remote rural areas.

The Boldness of Amish Designs

Amish quilts in particular kept the art form alive. In the late 1800s and early 1900s, Amish quilts were equally utilitarian and visually dramatic. Before 1880 Amish quilts were generally black, gray, brown, or dark blue, reflecting the group's rule of dressing in somber tones and the small number of colorfast dyes available. Quilting details often featured feathered or floral designs.

As Amish communities spread beyond Pennsylvania—primarily to Ohio, Indiana, Illinois, and Iowa—each settlement set its own quilting guidelines. For example, quilts with lighter colors were most likely made in Ohio and Indiana; black and yellow showed up in Midwestern quilts. Traditionally Amish borders were not mitered because that was

BASKETS c. 1920
This quilt, probably made in Kansas, uses colors typical of most Amish quilts. Courtesy: University of Nebraska-Lincoln, No. 2000.007.0088

less frugal. Amish women often made quilts or tops to sell as a way to contribute to family incomes.

Mainstream America innovations, such as the sewing machine, provided a faster way for piecing, and mass-circulation magazines offered patterns to copy or order by mail.

continued on page 140

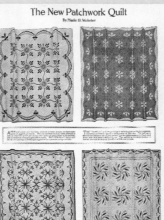

In the January 1911 issue of Ladies' Home Journal, Marie Webster's quilt designs were the first published in color. Eventually she sold her own mail-order patterns.

Fabric of the Time

During the turn of the 20th century, fabrics reflected the colors of mourning. Empress Eugénie mourned her husband, Napoleon III. Queen Victoria mourned her husband, Albert, and her mother, the Duchess of Alba. It is thought that these deaths influenced the dreary colors of the time. People in mourning were expected to wear black clothing the first year after the death of a family member. After that they might wear gray, dark purple, or dark blue.

In 1897 the Sears, Roebuck & Co. catalog offered fabrics, including shirting prints, percales, sateens, and more. Mourning prints, listed in a separate category of importance, were phased out of the catalog within the next few years.

The available colors ranged from light blue and pink to turkey red and Nile green. Faded reds, such as salmon pink, orange, and reddish brown, were prominent in quilts around the United States. These fabrics were possibly dyed with Georgia or Arkansas red clay.

Indigo blue prints were often referred to as Dutch blue or German blue for countries skilled at making blue dyes.

Another important blue was cadet blue. This misty hue, often printed in combination with black or white, was vat-dyed to be equally blue on both sides of the fabric. In the early 1900s, baby blue was created.

The Influence of Print

Farmers traded rural life for factory work in the cities, and new technologies improved the lives of the growing middle class. As art and architecture reformers rejected excessive Victorian styles, displays of wealth, and the flood of impersonal, mass-produced goods, simplicity and practicality gained in favor—a theme borrowed from the Arts and Crafts Movement in England.

With the burgeoning field of home economics, *Ladies' Home Journal* and other women's magazines offered decorating advice for bungalows and Prairie-style homes. The sanitary qualities of washable cotton quilts grew in favor, and long-forgotten heirloom quilts or newly made ones became popular. In the early 1900s, the magazines promoted simple geometric quilts in white and one other color, preferably red or blue.

Red or blue "art needlework," or primitive embroidery, which was a return to a simpler outline style, also became popular in quilts. Because colorfast turkey red thread was the choice of many needleworkers, the embroidery was known as redwork. Women

WREATH OF ROSES c. 1915
Designed by noted quilt designer Marie Webster, this quilt was originally published in Ladies' Home Journal *in October 1915. Unlike the original, this version was made without a scalloped edge.*

LADIES' HOME JOURNAL'S PREMIER QUILTER

Color pages appeared in *Ladies' Home Journal* for the first time in 1910. The January 1911 issue took full advantage of color printing for a page of quilts that changed the course of quiltmaking in the 20th century.

In "The New Patchwork Quilt," Marie Webster, *right*, presented four quilts appliquéd in solid pastel colors. The description opened with, "A new and artistic note has been achieved in these designs for handmade quilts of applied patchwork. The aim has been to make them practical as well as beautiful by the use of colorfast linens of good quality in the patterns, and a foundation of equally good white muslin." These words clearly expressed the standards of the Arts and Crafts philosophy.

In her book *A Joy Forever: Marie Webster's Quilt Patterns*, Rosalind Webster Perry shared how her grandmother's quilts reached the pages of *Ladies' Home Journal*. In 1909 the 50-year-old Indiana woman wanted a quilt for her new Colonial Revival home. Having never made one before but skilled with a needle, she restyled a traditional appliquéd pattern. Family and friends urged Marie to send her beautiful quilt to the magazine. The editor immediately recognized the artistic qualities of the design and asked for more quilts from Marie. She produced several more quilts and pillows for the magazine.

Because no patterns were available for the first series, reader letters were forwarded to Indiana, where Marie's family and friends pitched in to develop patterns. Her son had the idea to use blueprints for the patterns, and other family members cut full-size samples from tissue paper. The patterns, tissue samples, a sheet of instructions, and fabric swatches sold for 50 cents. *Ladies' Home Journal* produced 15-cent mail-order transfer patterns for some of the designs.

Not surprisingly Marie became famous as a result of the magazine's features. In 1912 Frank Doubleday asked her to write a book about quilts. Three years later *Quilts: Their Story and How to Make Them*, the first book published about quilts, was greeted with rave reviews.

also transferred designs to fabrics, tablecloths, and household linens for stitching.

Color preferences for fabrics focused on a warm pastel palette. Lighter colors, involving white backgrounds with narrow shirting stripes, pastel plaids, even-weave or printed ginghams, calicoes, and solid chambrays in muted pastel shades, were popular.

The List Grows

Vintage catalogs and swatch books of cotton fabrics that were used by manufacturers, wholesalers, and retailers are clues to the fabrics of this era. They included cotton fabrics in solids and prints, indigos, grays, chambrays, shirtings, and double

continued on page 142

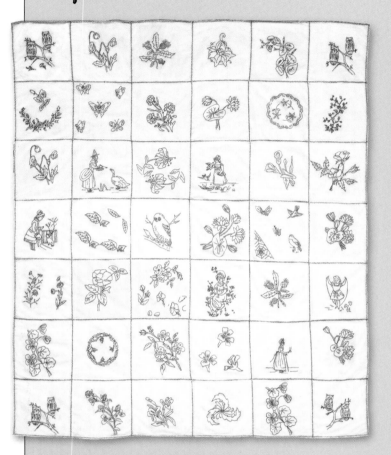

REDWORK COVERLET c. 1890

Several of the blocks of this redwork coverlet were embroidered using designs meant for linens from pre-1900 issues of Ladies' Home Journal. *Quilt patterns weren't published until after 1910.*

pinks for less than 10 cents per yard in standard goods.

"Imperiale percales" in dots, mill engravings, diagonal plaids, stripes, even-weave checks, and florals were used in home sewing projects. The remnants often went into quilts. In quiltmaking certain combinations were favored—cadet blue, claret, and Shaker gray together, and white background shirtings with indigo or cadet blue.

The Popularity of Appliqué

Women's magazines helped popularize appliquéd quilts, which dominated the quilting features in *Ladies' Home Journal* for many years. Appliqué forms and subjects were endless, and magazines could offer new and original designs to hold reader interest. Also appliqué patterns were easy to provide, either printed on paper for tracing or produced as iron-on transfers. Selling patterns was a profitable venture. In 1908, three years after the Home Pattern Co. was established to print fashion and transfer

ERA TIMELINE

1902 October: E. T. Meredith begins *Successful Farming*; 4-H organization is founded. **1903** Orville and Wilbur Wright make the first airplane flight in Kitty Hawk, North Carolina. The flight lasts 12 seconds. **1908** Henry Ford introduces the Model T.

1910 Boy Scouts and Campfire Girls organizations are founded. **1912** April 14: *Titanic*, the grandest ocean liner of the time, sinks on her maiden voyage from England to New York; 1,500 passengers and crew perish. Girl Scouts of America founded. **1913** The 16th Amendment to the Constitution is ratified,

giving Congress the power to levy income taxes. **1914** August: World War I begins in Sarajevo. **1915** *Quilts: Their Story and How to Make Them* by Marie Webster is the first quilt book published in the U.S. **1919** June 28: World War I ends; October: *Ladies' Home Journal* sells 2 million copies.

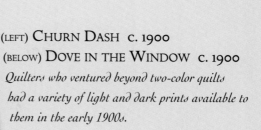

(LEFT) CHURN DASH c. 1900
(BELOW) DOVE IN THE WINDOW c. 1900
*Quilters who ventured beyond two-color quilts
had a variety of light and dark prints available to
them in the early 1900s.*

patterns for *Ladies' Home Journal,* it employed 500 people and had sold 28 million patterns.

The magazine also legitimized quilts as an art form by having five leading artists and illustrators design quilts for publication. All were complicated appliqué style. In 1911 the magazine used the new technique of color printing to feature a page of quilts by Marie Webster. Her designs, primarily florals, were published in the magazine for 15 years. She also showed how to use part of a quilt design in decorative home accents, such as pillows. Later Frank Doubleday published a book of her work, the first book ever published about quilts.

During the years of World War I, magazine coverage of quilting diminished as publications focused on knitting for the Red Cross and on conserving food staples. There was little mention of quilting pursuits.

By the end of World War I, the country was headed for prosperity and equality, and the American way of life was changing.

lattice

1890–1920

The careful arrangement of white and red gives

this quilt top the look of a woven lattice. This design could also be used as

a signature quilt by asking people to sign the larger white spaces.

Materials

3⅝ yards *each* of solid red and solid white

⅝ yards of binding fabric

4⅞ yards of backing fabric

78×87 inches of quilt batting

Finished quilt: 72×81 inches

Finished block: 9 inches square

Quantities specified are for 44/45-inch-wide, 100-percent-cotton fabrics. All measurements include a ¼-inch seam allowance. Sew with right sides together unless otherwise stated.

Cut the Fabrics

To make the best use of your fabrics, cut the pieces in the order that follows. Prepare templates for Patterns A and B on the Pattern Sheet (see tips for making and using templates in Quilter's Workshop beginning on *page 280*).

From solid red, cut:

◆ 288—Pattern A

◆ 144—Pattern B

From solid white, cut:

◆ 288—Pattern A

◆ 144—Pattern B

From binding fabric, cut:

◆ 8—2½×42-inch strips

Make the Blocks

1 Sew a red A to a white B. Add a red A. Repeat to make two red ABA units.

2 Join a white A to a red B. Add a white B. Repeat to make two white ABA units.

3 Referring to a block in the Quilt Assembly Diagram and noting color placement, join the four units to make one Lattice block. Repeat to make 72 red and white Lattice blocks.

Assemble the Quilt Top

1 Referring to the Quilt Assembly Diagram, lay out the Lattice blocks in nine horizontal rows containing eight blocks each. Sew the blocks together in each row. Press the seam allowances in one direction, alternating the direction with each row.

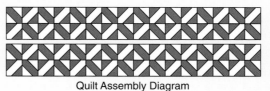

Quilt Assembly Diagram

2 Join the rows. Press the seam allowances in one direction. The pieced quilt top should measure 72½×81½ inches, including the seam allowances.

Complete the Quilt

1 Layer the quilt top, batting, and backing. Baste the three layers together (see tips for completing the quilt in Quilter's Workshop beginning on *page 280*). Quilt as desired.

2 Use the 2½×42-inch strips to bind the quilt (see binding tips in Quilter's Workshop).

goose tracks

1890–1920

This block has several names—Pride of Italy,
The Crossroads, Blue Birds Flying, and Fancy Flowers—
because the placement provides a variety of images.

Materials

4½ yards of pink print for blocks, setting blocks, and borders

2½ yards of cream print for block background and binding

1½ yards of black print for blocks

5 yards of backing fabric

76×90 inches of quilt batting

Finished quilt: 70×84¼ inches
Finished block: 10 inches square

Quantities specified are for 44/45-inch-wide, 100-percent-cotton fabrics. All measurements include a ¼-inch seam allowance. Sew with right sides together unless otherwise stated.

Cut the Fabrics

To make the best use of your fabrics, cut the pieces in the order that follows. Prepare templates for Patterns A through E on *page 149* (see tips for making and using templates in Quilter's Workshop beginning on *page 280*).

Cut the border strips the length of the fabric (parallel to the selvage). The measurements are mathematically correct. You may wish to cut your border strips longer than specified to allow for possible sewing differences. Trim the strips to the lengths needed before joining them to the quilt top.

From pink print, cut:

♦ 2—7×84¾-inch border strips

♦ 2—7×57½-inch border strips

♦ 4—15½-inch squares, cutting each diagonally twice in an X for a total of 16 setting triangles (you will have 2 leftover triangles)

♦ 2—8-inch squares, cutting each in half diagonally for a total of 4 corner triangles

♦ 12—10½-inch squares for setting squares

♦ 80—*each* of Patterns A and A reversed

From cream print, cut:

♦ 8—2½×42-inch binding strips

♦ 80—Patterns D and E

♦ 160 of Pattern C

From black print, cut:

♦ 80—*each* of Patterns A, A reversed, and B

♦ 20 of Pattern D

Make the Blocks

1 Referring to the Block Assembly Diagram, join a pink print A and black print A reversed. Join a pink print A reversed and a black print A. Join the two units. Set in two cream print C triangles; then set in a cream print D square to make a pieced unit (see tips for setting

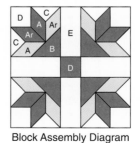

Block Assembly Diagram

instructions continued on page 148

in seams in Quilter's Workshop beginning on *page 280*). Repeat to make four pieced units.

2 Lay out the four pieced units, four cream print E rectangles, and a black print D square in three rows. Join the pieces in each row; join the rows to make one Goose Tracks block. Press the seam allowances in one direction.

3 Repeat steps 1 and 2 to make a total of 20 Goose Tracks blocks.

Assemble the Quilt Center

1 Referring to the Quilt Assembly Diagram, lay out the twenty $10\frac{1}{2}$-inch Goose Tracks blocks,

12 pink print $10\frac{1}{2}$-inch setting squares, and 14 pink print setting triangles in diagonal rows.

2 Sew together blocks in each diagonal row. Press seam allowances toward pink print setting squares and triangles. Join the rows. Add the four pink print corner triangles to make the quilt center. Press the seam allowances in one direction.

Add the Borders

1 Sew a pink print $7\times57\frac{1}{2}$-inch border strip to the top and bottom of the quilt center.

2 Sew a pink print $7\times84\frac{3}{4}$-inch border strip to each side of the quilt center. Press the seam allowances toward the borders.

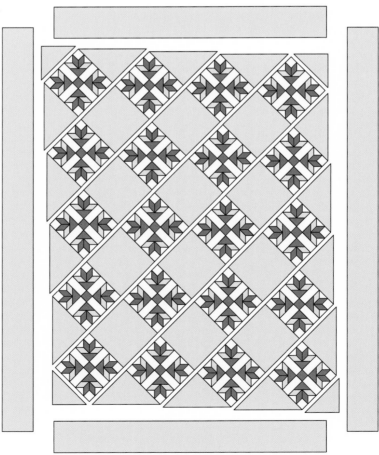

Quilt Assembly Diagram

Complete the Quilt

1 Layer the quilt top, batting, and backing. Baste the three layers together (see tips for completing the quilt in Quilter's Workshop beginning on *page 280*). Quilt as desired.

2 Use the cream print 2¹⁄₂×42-inch strips to bind the quilt (see binding tips in Quilter's Workshop).

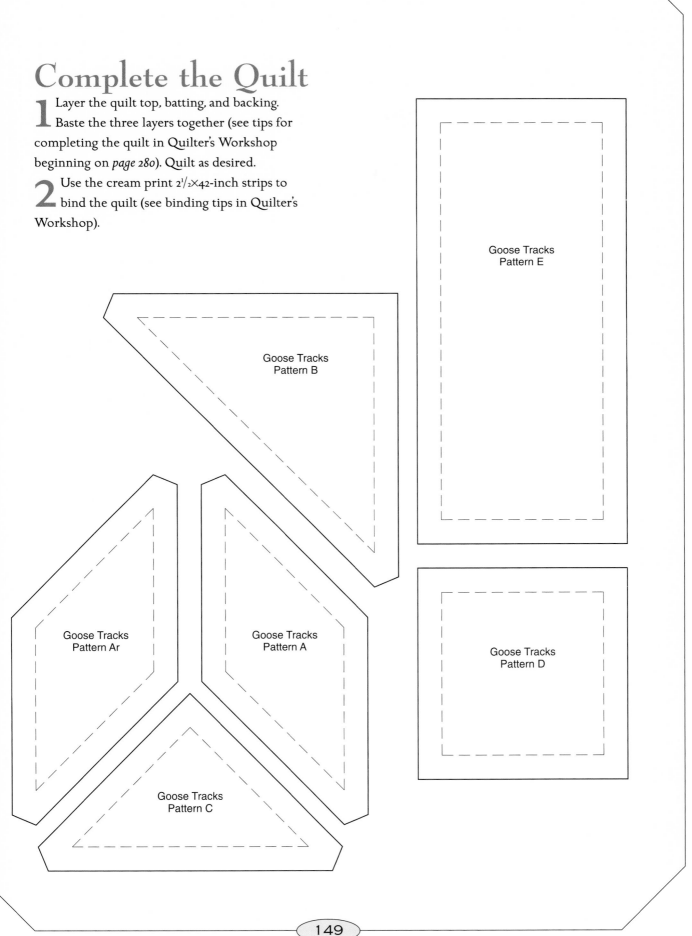

Goose Tracks
Pattern E

Goose Tracks
Pattern B

Goose Tracks
Pattern Ar

Goose Tracks
Pattern A

Goose Tracks
Pattern D

Goose Tracks
Pattern C

windmill

1890–1920

In 1903, two-color quilts of red and white were
highly prized. Instead of using solid white, the red whirligigs are offset
with cream-and-black shirting prints.

Materials

6¹/₂ yards total of assorted cream-and-black
   shirting prints for blocks, setting squares and
   units, and borders
1³/₄ yards of red print for blocks and
   pieced border
⁵/₈ yard of red-and-black print for binding
5 yards of backing fabric
72×89 inches of quilt batting

Finished quilt: 65¹/₄×82¹/₈ inches
Finished block: 12 inches square

Quantities specified are for 44/45-inch-wide,
100-percent-cotton fabrics. All measurements
include a ¹/₄-inch seam allowance. Sew with right
sides together unless otherwise stated.

Cut the Fabrics

To make the best use of your fabrics, cut the
pieces in the order that follows. Cut the border
strips the length of the fabric (parallel to the
selvage). There are no pattern pieces for
this project; the letter designations are for
placement only.

From assorted cream-and-black prints, cut:
- 4—2×88-inch border strips
- 4—2×72-inch border strips
- 12—12¹/₂-inch setting squares

THE WINDMILL PATTERN

- 11—7-inch squares, cutting each diagonally
  twice in an X for a total of 44 C triangles
  (you'll have 2 leftover triangles)
- 48—4¹/₂-inch B squares
- 25—4¹/₈-inch squares, cutting each diagonally
  twice in an X for a total of 100 E triangles
- 2—3³/₄-inch squares, cutting each in half
  diagonally for a total of 4 D triangles
- 164—2⁷/₈-inch squares, cutting each in half
  diagonally for a total of 328 A triangles

From red print, cut:
- 24—4¹/₈-inch squares, cutting each diagonally
  twice in an X for a total of 96 E triangles
- 164—2⁷/₈-inch squares, cutting each in half
  diagonally for a total of 328 A triangles

From red-and-black print, cut:
- 8—2¹/₂×42-inch binding strips

instructions continued on page 152

Assemble the Pinwheel Units

1 Sew together one cream-and-black print A triangle and one red print A triangle to make a triangle-square (see Diagram 1). Press the seam allowance toward the red triangle. The pieced triangle-square should measure 2$\frac{1}{2}$ inches square, including the seam allowances. Repeat to make a total of 328 triangle-squares.

Diagram 1

2 Referring to Diagram 2 for placement, sew together four triangle-squares in pairs. Press the seam allowances toward the red triangles. Then join the pairs to make one Pinwheel unit. Repeat to make a total of 82 Pinwheel units.

Diagram 2

Assemble the Windmill Blocks

1 Referring to Diagram 3 for placement, lay out five Pinwheel units and four cream-and-black print B squares in three rows.

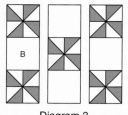

Diagram 3

2 Sew together the pieces in each row. Press the seam allowances toward the cream-and-black squares. Then join the rows to make a Windmill block. Press the seam allowances in one direction. The pieced Windmill block should measure 12$\frac{1}{2}$ inches square, including the seam allowances.

3 Repeat steps 1 and 2 to make a total of six Windmill blocks.

Assemble the Side Setting Units

1 Referring to Diagram 4 for placement, sew together four Pinwheel units, two cream-and-black print B squares, and three cream-and-black print C triangles in diagonal rows. Press the seam allowances in one direction, alternating the direction with each row.

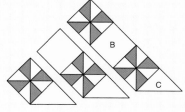

Diagram 4

2 Join the rows to make a side setting unit A. Press the seam allowances in one direction.

3 Repeat steps 1 and 2 to make a total of six of side setting unit A.

4 Referring to Diagram 5 for placement, sew together four Pinwheel units, two

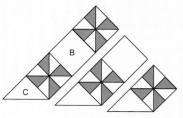

Diagram 5

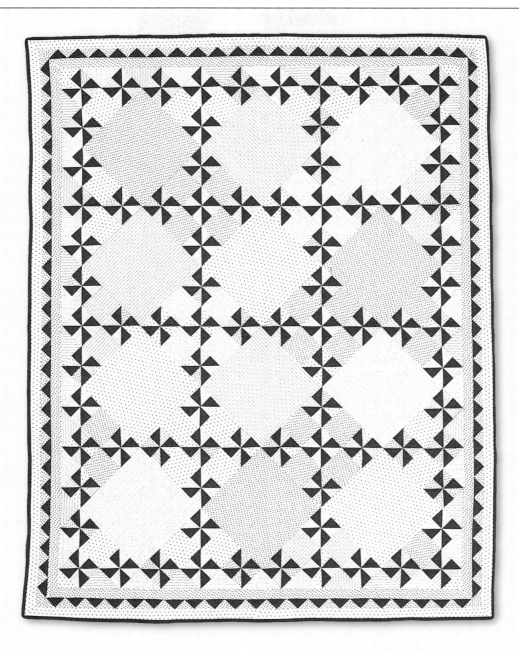

Assemble the Corner Setting Units

cream-and-black print B squares, and three cream-and-black print C triangles in diagonal rows. Press the seam allowances in one direction, alternating the direction with each row.

5 Join the rows to make a side setting unit B. Press the seam allowances in one direction.

6 Repeat steps 4 and 5 to make a total of four of side setting unit B.

1 Referring to Diagram 6 for placement, sew together three Pinwheel units, one

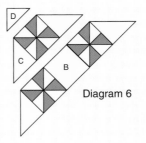

Diagram 6

instructions continued on page 154

cream-and-black print B square, four cream-and-black print C triangles, and one cream-and-black print D triangle in diagonal rows. Press the seam allowances toward the cream-and-black print square and triangles.

2 Join the rows to make a corner unit A. Press the seam allowances in one direction.

3 Repeat steps 1 and 2 to make a total of two of corner unit A.

4 Referring to Diagram 7 for placement, join three Pinwheel units, one cream-and-black print B square, two cream-and-black print C triangles, and one cream-and-black print D triangle in diagonal rows. Press the seam allowances toward the cream-and-black print square and triangles.

Diagram 7

Quilt Assembly Diagram

5 Join the rows to make a corner unit B. Press the seam allowances in one direction.

6 Repeat steps 4 and 5 to make a total of two of corner unit B.

Assemble the Quilt Center

1 Referring to the Quilt Assembly Diagram, *opposite*, for placement, lay out the six Windmill blocks, 12 cream-and-black print 12$\frac{1}{2}$-inch setting squares, the side setting units, and the corner units in diagonal rows.

2 Sew together the pieces in diagonal rows; do not add the corner unit As. Press the seam allowances toward the setting squares. Join the rows. Press the seam allowances in one direction. Add the corner units to complete the quilt center. The pieced quilt center should measure 56$\frac{3}{4}$×73$\frac{5}{8}$ inches, including the seam allowances.

Assemble and Add the Borders

1 Referring to Diagram 8, sew together 21 red print E triangles and 22 cream-and-black print E triangles to make a pieced top border strip. Press the seam allowances toward the red triangles. Repeat to make a pieced bottom border strip.

Diagram 8

2 Center and sew a cream-and-black print 2×72-inch strip to each long edge of the pieced top border strip (see Diagram 9). Press the seam allowances toward the cream-and-black print strips. Trim the edges for making mitered corners. Repeat to make the bottom border.

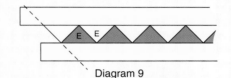
Diagram 9

3 Sew together 27 red print E triangles and 28 cream-and-black print E triangles to make a pieced side border strip. Repeat to make a pieced second side border strip.

4 Center and sew a cream-and-black print 2×88-inch strip to each long edge of the pieced side border strips. Press the seam allowances toward the cream-and-black print strips. Trim edges for making mitered corners.

5 Add the pieced borders to the pieced quilt center, mitering the corners to complete the quilt top (see tips for mitering border corners in Quilter's Workshop beginning on *page 280*).

Complete the Quilt

1 Layer the quilt top, batting, and backing. Baste the three layers together (see tips for completing the quilt in Quilter's Workshop beginning on *page 280*).

2 Quilt as desired. Machine quilted variations of feathered stars in the cream-and-black print areas of the quilt and inside each of the red print triangles are stitched on the quilt shown.

3 Use the red-and-black print 2$\frac{1}{2}$×42-inch strips to bind the quilt (see binding tips in Quilter's Workshop).

crazy quilt

1890–1920

Lavish Victorian style is the influence for this intricate crazy quilt constructed using a multitude of fabrics and embroidery stitches.

Crazy Quilting Techniques

The charm of crazy quilting is that there is no set pattern, thus no two quilts are the same. A crazy quilt grows as it is worked—too much planning rarely produces the satisfactory results achieved by spontaneity.

In addition to the construction techniques described here, see *pages 160–161* for ideas on embellishing crazy quilts with embroidery, buttons, appliqués, and other items. For illustrations on how to make basic embroidery stitches, see Stitch Diagrams on *page 181*.

Finished size of quilt, *opposite:* 74 inches square

Working on a Foundation

Like string piecing, crazy quilting is stitched onto a base fabric that serves as a foundation. For a large quilt, it is practical to make small units that are then joined.

To make small units from a pattern, such as a square or diamond shape, begin with foundation pieces that are slightly larger than the corresponding pattern piece; once the foundation pieces are covered with crazy quilting, cut them to the size and shape of the pattern.

Victorian Construction Techniques

Victorian crazy quilters nearly always appliquéd the fabric pieces onto the foundation in a random fashion. In some cases, a large piece was basted onto the foundation and then smaller pieces were stitched on or around it.

In some quilts, construction units remain defined in the finished work and appear more planned, as in rows of diamond-shape pieced blocks set on point. In others, pieces at the edges of adjacent blocks are appliquéd over each other to obscure the joining line.

Modern Construction Techniques

Crazy quilting can be stitched by machine. The two techniques described here are similar to string piecing. Steps 1A through 1D on *page 158* describe the Fan Method. Steps 2A through 2C on *page 159* explain the Center Method. Steps 3 through 5 on *pages 159–160* cover a combination of techniques.

When the crazy-quilted piece is completely assembled, layer it on backing fabric and bind the edges (few crazy quilts have batting between the layers). Tying the top and backing fabric together is optional.

instructions continued on page 158

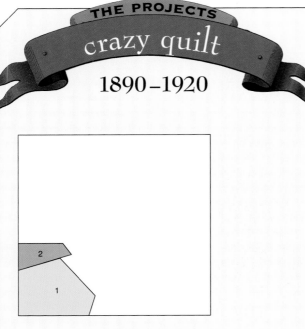

With the Fan Method, start in a corner and build outward, fanning back and forth from one side of the foundation to the other. Begin by placing Piece 1 flush with one corner of the foundation, *above*. Piece 1 should have four or five sides. Place Piece 2 on the top side of Piece 1 with right sides together; machine-stitch through the pieces and the foundation. Flip the second piece to the right side and press.

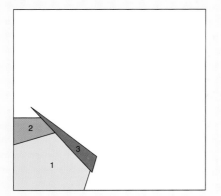

Align Piece 3 with the second side of the corner piece, making sure it extends over both of the previously sewn pieces, *above*. Stitch it down in the same manner as before. Trim any excess fabric from the seam allowance, then flip Piece 3 to the right side and press the piece flat.

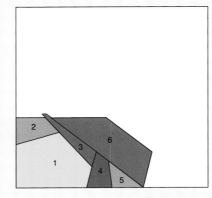

Cover the third side of the corner piece with Piece 4 in the same manner—sew it down, flip it over, and press. When all the sides of Piece 1 are stitched, start working back in the opposite direction to lay down the next level, as indicated by Pieces 5 and 6, *above*.

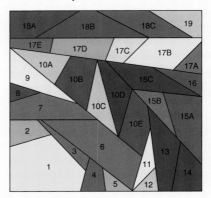

Fan back and forth from right to left, then left to right, adding pieces until the foundation is filled. If you encounter an awkward angle, it is easiest to appliqué the edges in place. To fill in a long edge, piece a separate unit that can be stitched in place as one piece (see pieces 10, 15, 17, and 18 *above*). Trim each seam allowance and press each piece flat before adding the next piece.

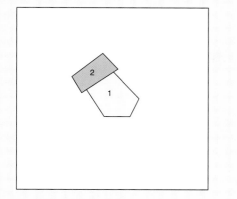

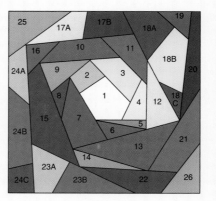

2A Begin the Center Method by placing Piece 1 at the approximate center of the foundation. If this is dark fabric, it will appear to recede, bringing attention to the center; a light fabric will have the opposite effect. Piece 1 should have five or six sides. With right sides together, sew the next fabric piece onto any side of Piece 1 using a standard ¼-inch seam allowance. Flip Piece 2 over to right side, then press it flat, *above*.

2C Continue adding fabric pieces in this manner, working outward from the center. To fill in a long edge, piece a separate unit that can be sewn in place as one piece (see pieces 17, 18, 23, and 24, *above*). Once the foundation is filled, trim all pieces even with the edges of the foundation. If you are working with separate blocks, stitch embroidery designs on each block as desired before joining them.

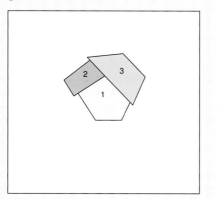

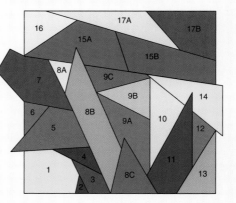

2B Stitch Piece 3 onto the next side of the center piece, making sure it completely covers the edges of pieces 1 and 2, *above*. Trim excess fabric from the seam allowance, then press Piece 3 to the right side. The work can go clockwise or counterclockwise, but maintain the same direction throughout construction of the block.

3 Combine techniques for added interest. As you sew, leave some points and angles unstitched so they can be appliquéd over an adjacent piece later (see pieces 8B, 8C, and 11, *above*). Overlapping pieces break up long seam lines. Leave some pieces at the block edges untrimmed (pieces 5, 7, and 14) so they can be appliquéd onto the adjacent block to obscure the joining seam.

instructions continued on page 160

4 Appliqués cover seam lines and trouble spots, and their varied shapes add charm to a crazy quilt. Hearts, crescent moons, bows, and flowers are some appliqué motifs that work nicely in crazy quilting. When the piecing is complete, hand-stitch appliqués over the seams to interrupt straight lines.

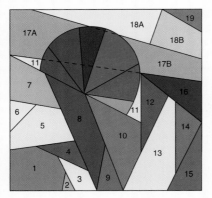

5 Pieced fans are frequently seen in antique crazy quilts. A fan can be appliquéd onto the crazy quilt piecing or stitched into a seam, *above*. The curved edge is left loose as you add more pieces, then it is appliquéd over the completed patchwork. This is an excellent way to introduce curves and other shapes that break up long straight seam lines.

Embellishments For Crazy Quilts

Unrestrained profusions of varied fabrics and personalized decorative details make antique crazy quilts interesting to examine and new crazy quilts fun to piece.

Fabric stores stock myriad lush fabrics, delectable laces, buttons, and ribbons that offer great possibilities for crazy quilting.

Select the Fabrics

Because crazy quilts are rarely used and washed in the same manner as other quilts, any fabric can be used—even those considered too fragile or impractical for traditional quilts.

For elegance, experiment with velvet, velveteen, moiré, satin, and silk. For a more informal look, use cotton, wool, and thin-wale corduroy. The remnant table at any fabric store is a wonderful hunting ground for small pieces of exotic fabrics suitable for crazy quilting.

Scraps of ribbon, clothing, handkerchiefs, neckties, upholstery, and leftover fabrics are fun to use, especially if they have sentimental value.

Mix Textures, Patterns, and Solids

Use different fabric textures and patterns to achieve the integrated mix that makes a crazy quilt so delightful.

A solid fabric without nap shows embroidery to its best advantage, but a quilt made with just solids requires a lot of embellishment to be interesting—add random pieces of brocade or paisley print to balance the solids. In the same way, napped fabrics, such as velvet, will add interesting texture when mixed with other fabrics.

Embroidery

Embroidery is to crazy quilting as frosting is to a cake. The basic embroidery stitches found in Stitch Diagrams on *page 181* are just a few that can be used to cover seam lines or embellish a narrow fabric strip or ribbon. Victorian crazy quilts are rich tapestries of embroidered animals, flowers, and Oriental motifs. Outlines of a baby's hands or feet frequently appear.

Stitch embroidery motifs and pictures onto large fabric pieces, which can be trimmed to fit into the patchwork or onto a pieced block before the quilt is assembled.

Any drawing or photograph you can trace can become an embroidery motif. Victorians perforated magazine pictures with large needles so the printed image could be outlined on the fabric with powder, such as talcum or cinnamon. Since powder rubs off as a piece is handled, lightly trace the outlined shape in pencil.

Spiders and Webs

Victorian crazy quilts frequently feature an embroidered spider and a web. According to European folklore, spiders in needlework are a symbol of good fortune.

A spiderweb is easy to stitch (see Stitch Diagrams on *page 181*). The spokes and concentric rings of the web are couched in place. Use metallic threads to make a web shimmer. A web is most effective when it is stitched in a light-color thread on a dark background.

Use beads for the spider's body; make lazy daisy or straight stitches for the legs.

Other Embellishments

Once the foundation is completely filled, add trims such as lace, ribbon, and appliqués. Small doilies and lacy handkerchiefs add interest.

Cover seam lines and appliqués with embroidery, then add beads and buttons as desired. Clusters of buttons create interesting shapes. Novelty buttons, such as flowers, stars, and animals, add a touch of whimsy.

sunshine & shadow

1890–1920

Careful placement of light and dark fabric strips creates the look of highlights and shadows in this intricate quilt. Each Log Cabin block is created with a different combination of four fabrics.

Materials

⅛ yard *each* of solid medium red and dark red fabrics for the block centers

½ yard *each* of 13 light, 13 dark, and 26 medium-value fabrics in solids, prints, and plaids for the blocks

1 yard of tan print for binding

5 yards of backing fabric

81×96 inches of quilt batting

Assorted colors of embroidery floss or perle cotton, and an embroidery needle for tying (optional)

Finished quilt: 77×82½ inches

Finished Log Cabin block: 5½ inches square

Quantities specified are for 44/45-inch-wide, 100-percent-cotton fabrics. All measurements include a ¼-inch seam allowance. Sew with right sides together unless otherwise stated.

Quilt Notes

The quilt *opposite* is made of a medley of silk fabrics. Silk has a rich luster, but it is fragile and difficult to wash; quiltmakers may find cotton easier to work with.

The dark sides of the blocks are made from a variety of prints, solids, and plaids in black, dark gray, brown, royal blue, hunter green, purple, and burgundy. The light fabrics are ivory, gold, light gray, peach, yellow, and aqua. Medium tones of all these colors also are widely used.

Each of the 210 Log Cabin blocks has a red center square. The light side of each block is made by alternating light and medium fabric strips; the dark side is made by alternating dark and medium strips.

Although no two blocks are made with the same four fabrics, the same two light or dark fabrics must be present in four adjacent blocks for the contrasting diamond pattern to appear when the blocks are joined. The instructions and diagrams that follow clarify the requirements of the fabric positioning. Study these carefully before you begin.

Cut the Fabrics

To make the best use of your fabrics, cut the pieces in the order that follows. Cut cross-grained strips for the Log Cabin blocks as described. These strips are the width of the logs plus ¼ inch on both sides for seam allowances. It is not necessary to make templates or to cut pieces to the length of each log.

From each scrap fabric, cut:

◆ 17—1×42-inch strips

From each red fabric, cut:

◆ 105—1-inch squares for the block centers

instructions continued on page 164

Selecting Fabric Combinations for the Blocks

This quilt is not difficult to make, but it requires careful planning of the fabric placement. As you read these instructions, refer to the photograph of the quilt on *page 162* for guidance. We also suggest that you make a schematic drawing of the quilt to assist you in positioning the fabrics.

1 Divide your fabric strips into four tonal groups: light, medium-light, medium-dark, and dark.

2 Divide the dark and medium-dark fabrics in the same manner, selecting 42 dark/medium-dark combinations consisting of four strips of each fabric. Choose 21 dark/medium-dark combinations with just two strips of each fabric.

3 Select 49 light/medium-light fabric combinations, with four strips of each fabric in each group. Choose seven more light/medium-light combinations with two strips of each fabric in each combination.

4 As you make blocks, pull strips from these fabric combinations as described in the following steps. Each block will require a four-fabric set—a light/medium-light combination and one dark/medium-dark combination.

Make the Log Cabin Blocks

Note: Each block is constructed counterclockwise. Once you understand how to make one block, lay out the fabrics and arrange them in the correct order for each subsequent block.

1 To make Block 1, refer to Diagram 1. Begin each block with a red No. 1 square. Add logs No. 2 and No. 3, using a light fabric. Add logs No. 4 and No. 5, using a medium-dark fabric.

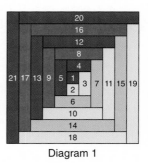

Diagram 1

2 Using a medium-light fabric, add logs No. 6 and No. 7. Then use the darkest fabric in the set for logs No. 8 and No. 9.

3 Continue adding light and dark logs in sequence as shown until Block 1 is complete. Continue using the same fabric for each adjacent pair of logs as shown in Diagram 1.

4 Make Block 4 in the same manner using the same light and medium-light fabrics in the same positions as in Block 1, but using a different combination of dark fabrics.

5 Referring to Diagram 2, *opposite*, make Block 2 and Block 3 using the same two light fabrics, but reversing the positions of the light and medium-light fabrics. Note that the dark fabrics are different in each of the four blocks.

6 Continue making blocks in groups of four in this manner. To assist you in positioning the fabrics correctly, lay the blocks on the floor in rows as illustrated in the Quilt Assembly Diagram, *opposite*.

Select the fabrics for each block carefully as you work. The same dark fabrics should meet at the intersections of each four-block group just as the light fabrics do.

Use the eight-strip fabric sets to make the four blocks of the same combination. Use the four-strip sets where only two blocks of a color combination are needed around the outside edge of the quilt.

Make a total of 210 Log Cabin blocks. You should have enough fabric strips left over to make additional blocks if you want to make a larger quilt.

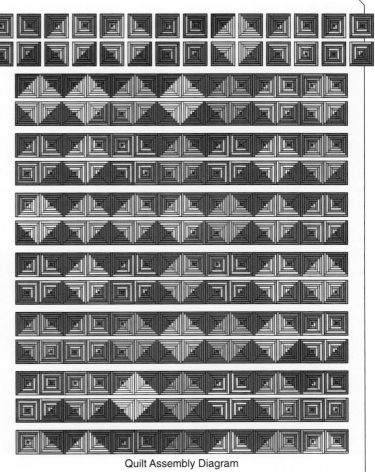

Quilt Assembly Diagram

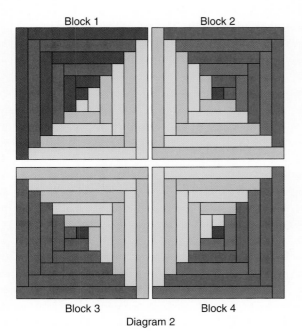

Block 1   Block 2

Block 3   Block 4
Diagram 2

Assemble the Quilt Top

1 Lay the blocks out on the floor or another flat surface in 15 horizontal rows of 14 blocks each. Referring to the photograph on *page 162*, and the Quilt Assembly Diagram, *right*, position the light and dark sides of the blocks as shown to achieve the alternating light and dark diamonds.

2 When the blocks are arranged as desired, join the blocks in each horizontal row. Sew the rows together to complete the quilt top. Press the seam allowances in one direction.

Complete the Quilt

1 Layer the quilt top, batting, and backing. Baste the three layers together (see tips for completing the quilt in Quilter's Workshop beginning on *page 280*).

2 Quilt as desired. The quilt pictured on *page 162* is not quilted but is tacked, or tied, at the corner of each block with embroidery floss.

3 Use the tan print to make approximately 330 inches of binding, either bias or straight-grain (see tips for making and applying binding in Quilter's Workshop).

diamond-in-the-square

1890–1920

*Large blocks of color are set in a graphic
background for highly detailed basket, star, feather,
and floral quilting designs.*

Materials

3 yards of solid turquoise

1⁵/₈ yards of solid purple

2 yards of solid dark red

1¹/₄ yards of dark green print for binding

2¹/₂ yards of 90-inch-wide sheeting for backing

90×108 inches of quilt batting

Finished quilt: 82×82 inches square

Quantities specified are for 44/45-inch-wide,
100-percent-cotton fabrics. All measurements
include a ¹/₄-inch seam allowance, except for the
border strips (see Cut the Fabrics, *right*). Sew with
right sides together unless otherwise stated.

Quilt Notes

The quilt *opposite* is made of lightweight wool in
classic Amish colors of purple, red, and
turquoise. The graphic effect of the bold solid
colors is enhanced by the elaborate quilting in
black thread.

The pumpkin seed quilting design in the
purple border is frequently found in Amish
quilts, as are the diamond star and feather wreath
in the center square. The floral quilting design in
the red triangles is often found in Diamond-in-
the-Square quilts made in Lancaster County,
Pennsylvania, as are the glass fruit bowls quilted
in the corners.

Patterns for the center motifs, the pumpkin
seed border, and the fruit bowl quilting designs
are found on the Pattern Sheet.

Cut the Fabrics

To make the best use of your fabrics, cut the
pieces in the order that follows. Measurements
stated for the turquoise border strips allow a
¹/₂-inch seam allowance for the binding.

From solid turquoise, cut:

◆ 4—15³/₄×53-inch strips for outer border

From solid purple, cut:

◆ 1—30¹/₂-inch square

◆ 4—5¹/₂×42¹/₂-inch strips for inner border

From solid dark red, cut:

◆ 1—15³/₄×64-inch strip. Cut into four 15³/₄-inch
squares for the outside corners.

◆ 4—5¹/₂-inch squares for inner border corners

◆ 2—22-inch squares. Cut each square in
half diagonally for four triangles for the
quilt center.

From dark green print, cut:

◆ 8—4¹/₂×42-inch strips

Assemble the Quilt Top

1 Referring to the Quilt Assembly Diagram on
page 169, stitch a red triangle onto opposite
sides of the purple square; press the seam
allowances toward the center. Join a red triangle
to each remaining side of the square.

2 Stitch a purple border strip to the top and
bottom edges of the center section; press
the seam allowances toward the borders.

instructions continued on page 168

3 Sew a red corner square to each end of the remaining purple border strips; press seam allowances toward the purple fabric. Add these borders to the sides of the center section, matching the seam line of each corner square with the seam line of the horizontal border. Press the seam allowances toward the border strips.

4 Join the turquoise outer borders to the quilt top in the same manner, stitching the top and bottom borders first, then adding the side borders with the red corner squares.

Mark the Quilting Designs

Extensive quilting of the kind featured on this quilt requires careful marking. See tips for marking designs on quilt tops in Quilter's Workshop beginning on *page 280*. Use a nonpermanent fabric marker to draw quilting designs on the top.

1 Make a tracing of the feather wreath pattern on the Pattern Sheet, marking the dots indicated on the pattern. Make one more tracing in the same manner. Tape the tracings together, overlapping them by matching the dots. The resulting curve is one-fourth of the feather wreath. Make a stencil of the design if desired.

2 Make tracings or stencils for the quilting patterns on the Pattern Sheet. The star and the floral bouquet quilting designs are used in the center purple square, and the pinwheel motif is used in the small border corners. Trace the pumpkin seed border and fruit bowl patterns on Pattern Sheet. Make or purchase additional quilting designs for the red setting triangles and the outer border.

3 Start marking in the center of the quilt. Using a yardstick for a straight-edge, draw a horizontal line from corner to corner of the center purple square. Draw another line to mark the vertical center. These lines will be erased later, but are important guidelines for placing the quilting motifs. The intersection of the two lines indicates the center of the square.

4 Measure $11^{1}/_{4}$ inches from the center of the center purple square along both vertical and horizontal placement lines. Mark these four points for placement of the spine of the feather wreath.

5 Align your stencil or tracing for the feather wreath with two placement points. If you have made a quarter section of the wreath, the dot at each end should align with a marked point. Mark this quarter section on the quilt top. Move the stencil to the next quadrant, again aligning the dots on the design with two placement points. Mark all four quadrants of the feather wreath in this manner.

6 Position one point of the star diamond on the intersection of the placement lines; place the opposite point on the vertical line. Mark quilting lines for that diamond. Move the stencil to the same position on the opposite side of the horizontal placement line; mark a second diamond.

7 Mark two more diamonds on each side of the first two, making a six-pointed star.

8 The floral design on the Pattern Sheet fits in the corners of the purple center square. Mark one design in each corner, aligning the stem of the design on the placement lines.

9 If desired, remove the markings for the placement lines so you won't quilt them. Be careful not to erase markings for the quilting motifs.

10 Align the pumpkin seed motif with the center of each purple border strip. Mark pumpkin seed squares along the length of the border in both directions. Fill in the triangular spaces as shown on the pattern. At the end of each border, fill in the space between the last pumpkin seed square and the red corner with echo quilting as shown on the pattern.

11 Center and mark a pinwheel in each small red corner square.

12 Center the fruit bowl in each of the outer border corners; mark the design on each red square.

13 Mark the setting triangles and outer border strips as desired. The quilt shown on *page 166* has a floral bouquet quilted in each red triangle and elaborate undulating feathers quilted in the turquoise borders.

Complete the Quilt

1 When the marking is complete, layer the quilt top, batting, and backing. Baste the three layers together (see tips for completing the quilt in Quilter's Workshop beginning on *page 280*). Quilt on all the marked lines. When the quilting is complete, remove the markings and basting.

2 Use dark green print 4¹/₂×42-inch strips to bind the quilt (see making and applying binding tips in Quilter's Workshop). Stitch the binding to quilt top with a ¹/₂-inch seam allowance. The finished binding on this quilt is ⁷/₈ inch wide.

Quilt Assembly Diagram

ocean waves

1890–1920

Triangle-squares of varied color fabrics parade around bold star blocks. The arrangement of the multicolor blocks set against a black background creates visual movement.

Materials

2¼ yards of solid black

¾ yard *each* of solid light yellow and lavender

Scraps or approximately ⅝ yard *each* of six different solid fabrics

¾ yard of binding fabric

4½ yards of backing fabric

81-inch square of quilt batting

Finished quilt: 70 inches square

Quantities specified are for 44/45-inch-wide, 100-percent-cotton fabrics. All measurements include a ¼-inch seam allowance, except for binding. Sew with right sides together unless otherwise stated.

Quilt Notes

The eight-pointed stars in the setting squares of this quilt set it apart from the ordinary. The center section is surrounded by a strip-pieced "piano key" border that repeats the scrap fabrics used in the center. There are 864 small triangles in this quilt; most are joined to make 384 triangle-squares.

Cut the Fabrics

See tips for making templates for hand or machine piecing and for cutting triangles from squares in Quilter's Workshop beginning on *page 280*. Prepare a template for Pattern X on the Pattern Sheet.

From solid black, cut:

◆ 2—8½×73-inch strips and two 8½×58-inch strips for outer border

◆ 1—13¼-inch square. Cut this square in quarters diagonally for four setting triangles.

◆ 2—7-inch squares. Cut each square in half diagonally to yield four corner triangles.

◆ 20—3-inch squares (Y)

◆ 5—4¾-inch squares. Cut each square in quarters diagonally to obtain 20 Z triangles.

From each of the solid yellow and lavender, cut:

◆ 2—2×38-inch strips for pieced border

◆ 3—14-inch squares for the triangle patchwork

◆ 20—Pattern X diamonds

From each of the six scrap fabrics, cut:

◆ 3—14-inch squares for triangle-squares

◆ 2—2×38-inch strips for pieced border

◆ 8—2⅞-inch squares. Cut each square in half diagonally to create 16 triangles of each fabric.

Make the Triangle-Squares

TRADITIONAL PIECING:

1 To make a template for the patchwork triangles, draw a 2⅞-inch square on template material; draw a diagonal line through the square; cut out triangles. Use these templates to mark 32 triangles on each 14-inch fabric square; cut 768 triangles.

2 Join two triangles to make one triangle-square; press the seam allowances toward the darker fabric. Make 384 triangle-squares.

QUICK PIECING:

See tips for quick-piecing triangle-squares in Quilter's Workshop beginning on *page 280*. Refer to these instructions to mark and stitch the grids described here.

1 On the wrong side of one light-color 14-inch fabric square, mark a 4×4-square grid of $2^{7}/_{8}$-inch squares (see Diagram 1). Layer this square, marked side up, on one matching square of another scrap fabric.

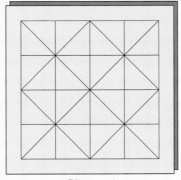

Diagram 1

instructions continued on page 172

2 Machine-stitch the grid exactly ¹/₄ inch from both sides of all diagonal lines, then cut on all the drawn lines. Each grid makes 32 triangle-squares. Stitch 12 grids to make a total of 384 triangle-squares. Press all the seam allowances toward the darker fabric.

Assemble the Blocks

Use the assembled triangle-squares to make Blocks A, B, and C.

1 Select nine triangle-squares for one of Block A, avoiding similar fabric combinations. Referring to Diagram 2, assemble these triangle-squares in three rows of three squares each, then join the rows. Be sure the seam lines in all the squares are angled in the same direction as shown in Diagram 2. Make 16 of Block A.

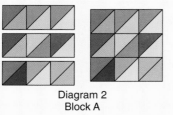

Diagram 2
Block A

2 Make four more of Block A. Join them to make one of Block B (see Diagram 3, *top right*). See how the seam lines are angled in each quadrant of the assembled block. Make four of Block B.

3 Referring to Diagram 4, *top right*, combine three triangle-squares with three individual triangles of scrap fabric to make Block C. Make 32 of Block C.

Make the Star Blocks

1 Join eight X diamonds to make each star, alternating yellow and lavender diamonds.

Diagram 3
Block B

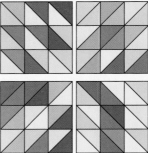

Diagram 4
Block C

2 Referring to Diagram 5, set a Z triangle into alternate openings around the star (see tips for setting in pieces in Quilter's Workshop). Set a Y square into the remaining openings. Make five star blocks.

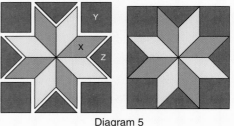

Diagram 5
Star Block

3 Stitch a completed C block onto opposite sides of each star block; press the seam allowances toward the star. Add a C unit onto the remaining block sides in the same manner.

Assemble the Quilt Top

1 Referring to the Quilt Assembly Diagram, *opposite*, join the units in five horizontal rows. For rows 1, 3, and 5, join C units onto the black setting triangles as shown.

Quilt Assembly Diagram

2 Join the rows to complete the quilt top. Press the seam allowances in one direction.

Add the Borders

1 Join five 2×38-inch strips of scrap fabric as shown in Diagram 6. Press the seam allowances to one side. Make three strip sets.

2 Cut nine 4-inch-wide units from each strip set as shown in Diagram 6.

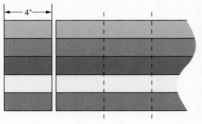

Diagram 6

3 Cut eight 2×4-inch pieces from the one remaining 2×38-inch strip.

4 Sew one 2×4-inch piece onto both ends of one pieced unit. Add five more pieced units end to end to make one border strip. Compare the border strip to one side of the quilt top. Add or subtract 2×4-inch segments to the border strip

to match the length of the side, then stitch the border onto the quilt top. Repeat to add a border strip to the opposite side of the quilt top.

5 Join seven pieced units and two 2×4-inch units to make a border for each of the remaining sides. Adjust the length of the border strip as before, if necessary. Stitch these borders onto the quilt top.

6 Stitch the 8½×58-inch black borders onto opposite edges of the quilt. Press the seams toward the black fabric; trim excess border fabric even with the sides. Add the 73-inch-long strips onto the remaining edges.

Complete the Quilt

1 Layer the quilt top, batting, and backing. Baste the three layers together (see tips for completing the quilt in Quilter's Workshop beginning on *page 280*). Quilt as desired.

2 Cut seven 3½×42-inch strips of bias binding fabric. Stitch the strips together end to end to make about 290 inches of straight-grain binding (see tips for making and applying binding in Quilter's Workshop). To fill out the binding, take a ½-inch seam when sewing binding onto quilt top.

Making a Larger Quilt

The size of this quilt is ideal for a large wall hanging or a short twin-size coverlet (without a pillow tuck). To make a 94×94-inch quilt, make the center area of the quilt with five rows of five blocks each. Draw an assembly diagram similar to the one *above* before starting.

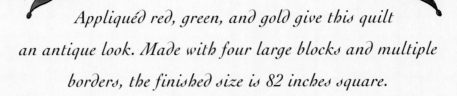

princess feathers

1890–1920

*Appliquéd red, green, and gold give this quilt
an antique look. Made with four large blocks and multiple
borders, the finished size is 82 inches square.*

Materials

6½ yards of solid gold for the blocks, borders,
   and binding
3½ yards of solid green
2¼ yards of solid red
2½ yards of 90-inch-wide sheeting for backing
90×108-inch precut quilt batting

Finished quilt: 82 inches square
Finished Princess Feathers block: 33 inches square

Quilt Notes

Elaborate appliquéd quilts, such as this one, are
rare in Amish country. Red, green, and gold were
popular colors among Amish and Mennonite
colonies at the turn of the century, but the
predominance of gold and the appliqués used
in this quilt are somewhat unusual. Since the
quilt originated in Pennsylvania, it was most
likely made either by a Mennonite woman or a
quilter influenced by Pennsylvania Dutch
colors and motifs.

   The same fabrics are used to piece the quilt
backing in the traditional Amish Bars pattern on
page 178, making it a reversible quilt.

Cut the Fabrics

See tips for making templates for appliqué in
Quilter's Workshop beginning on *page 280*. Make
a template for each of Patterns A through I on
the Pattern Sheet.

For the center daisy (A) and the tulip petals
(D, E, and F), either make a template of the
complete shape by joining the two halves of the
pattern or a template of half of the pattern. Place
the half on the fold of the fabric. Add a ³/₁₆-inch
seam allowance around each piece.

From solid gold, cut:
- 4—34-inch squares
- 2—5½×74-inch strips and two 5½×84-inch
   strips for outer border
- 4—1½×72-inch strips for inner border
- 5—2½×72-inch strips for straight-grain binding
- 32—Pattern B
- 16—Pattern F

From solid green, cut:
- 4—1½×74-inch strips for the third inside border
- 1—17½×42-inch piece. From this piece, cut
   sixteen 1¾×10-inch strips for long stems and
   thirty-two 1¾×7½-inch strips for short stems.
- 16—*each* of patterns C, D, and G
- 64—Pattern I

From solid red, cut:
- 4—1½×70-inch strips for the first inside border
- 4—Pattern A
- 16—Pattern E
- 32—Pattern H

Prepare Stems for Appliqué

1 Fold one stem piece in half lengthwise.
   Machine-stitch ¼ inch from the raw edge.

Press the seam allowance open, centering the seam line in the middle of the strip. Turn the strip right side out and press again.

2 Seam all the stem strips in this manner. The ends will be covered by appliqué pieces, so it is not necessary to finish those edges.

Position the Appliqués

1 Fold each 34-inch background square in half vertically, horizontally, and diagonally; lightly press the folds to establish placement guidelines for the appliqués. If desired, trace the complete design on the background fabric with an erasable fabric marker.

2 Prepare the appliqué pieces for each block by basting back the seam allowances. It is not necessary to turn under edges that will be covered by other pieces, such as the bottom edge of the feathers that meet with the daisies. Clip seam allowances as necessary to achieve crisp points and curves. Cut out the center of each H rose, trimming the seam allowance to 1/8 inch. Do not turn under this edge yet.

instructions continued on page 176

3 Appliqué the eight petals (B) onto the center daisy (A), positioning the petals as indicated on the A pattern on the Pattern Sheet.

4 Referring to the Appliqué Placement Diagram, *right,* pin or baste all pieces in place on the background square before appliquéing them. Start by positioning the daisy in the center of the block. Slip one end of a long stem under the daisy at each diagonal placement line. Center a feather (C) over each vertical and horizontal placement line, slipping the bottom of each feather under the daisy.

5 Position petals (D, E, F, and G) for each tulip at the end of each long stem. The tip of the G diamond should be aligned with the diagonal placement line. Working out from the center of the flower, pin the F petals in place and then the E petals. The straight edges of the D piece will cover the raw edges of the E petals and the top of the stem.

6 Referring to the Appliqué Placement Diagram, position a short stem on both sides of each long stem approximately halfway between the daisy and the tulip. Tuck the ends of the short stems under the long stems. Pin a rose (H) in place at the end of each short stem.

7 Position pairs of small leaves (I) in place as shown in the Appliqué Placement Diagram, slipping the blunt end of each leaf under the long stem piece.

Appliqué the Blocks

1 Stitch all leaf and stem pieces in place first to anchor the other pieces.

2 Appliqué the feathers (C) in place next, then stitch the center daisy (A) over the ends of all the long stems and feathers.

Appliqué Placement Diagram

3 Stitch the roses in place. In the center of each rose, use your needle to turn back and appliqué the edge of the red rose fabric, revealing the gold base fabric underneath. Appliqué the four tulips.

4 Make a total of four Princess Feathers blocks. Press each appliquéd block. Trim each block to 33½ inches square.

Assemble the Quilt Top

1 Join the four blocks in two rows of two blocks each; join the rows into a 66½-inch square. Press the seam allowance to one side.

2 Sew a 1½×70-inch red border strip to the side of the quilt top that you've designated as the top; add a second red strip to the opposite side. Press the seam allowances toward the borders, then trim the border fabric even with the sides of the quilt top.

3 Stitch the remaining red border strips to the sides of the quilt top. Press the seam allowances toward the border; trim excess border fabric.

4 Add the gold and green narrow borders in the same manner, sewing the border strips to the top and bottom edges of the quilt first and then stitching the side borders.

5 Stitch the $5^1/_2 \times 74$-inch strips of gold fabric to the green borders at the top and bottom edges of the quilt. Press the seam allowances toward the gold fabric. Complete the quilt top by adding the $5^1/_2 \times 84$-inch gold borders to the sides.

Complete the Quilt

1 Layer the quilt top, batting, and backing. Baste the three layers together (see tips for completing the quilt in Quilter's Workshop beginning on *page 280*).

2 Quilt as desired. The quilt pictured on *page 175* has outline quilting around each appliquéd shape and in the narrow borders. A diagonal grid of $^1/_2$-inch squares is quilted in the background of the appliqué. A pattern for the cable design quilted in the outer border is at *right*.

3 Use the solid gold $2^1/_2 \times 72$-inch strips to make approximately 340 inches of straight-grain binding (see binding tips in Quilter's Workshop).

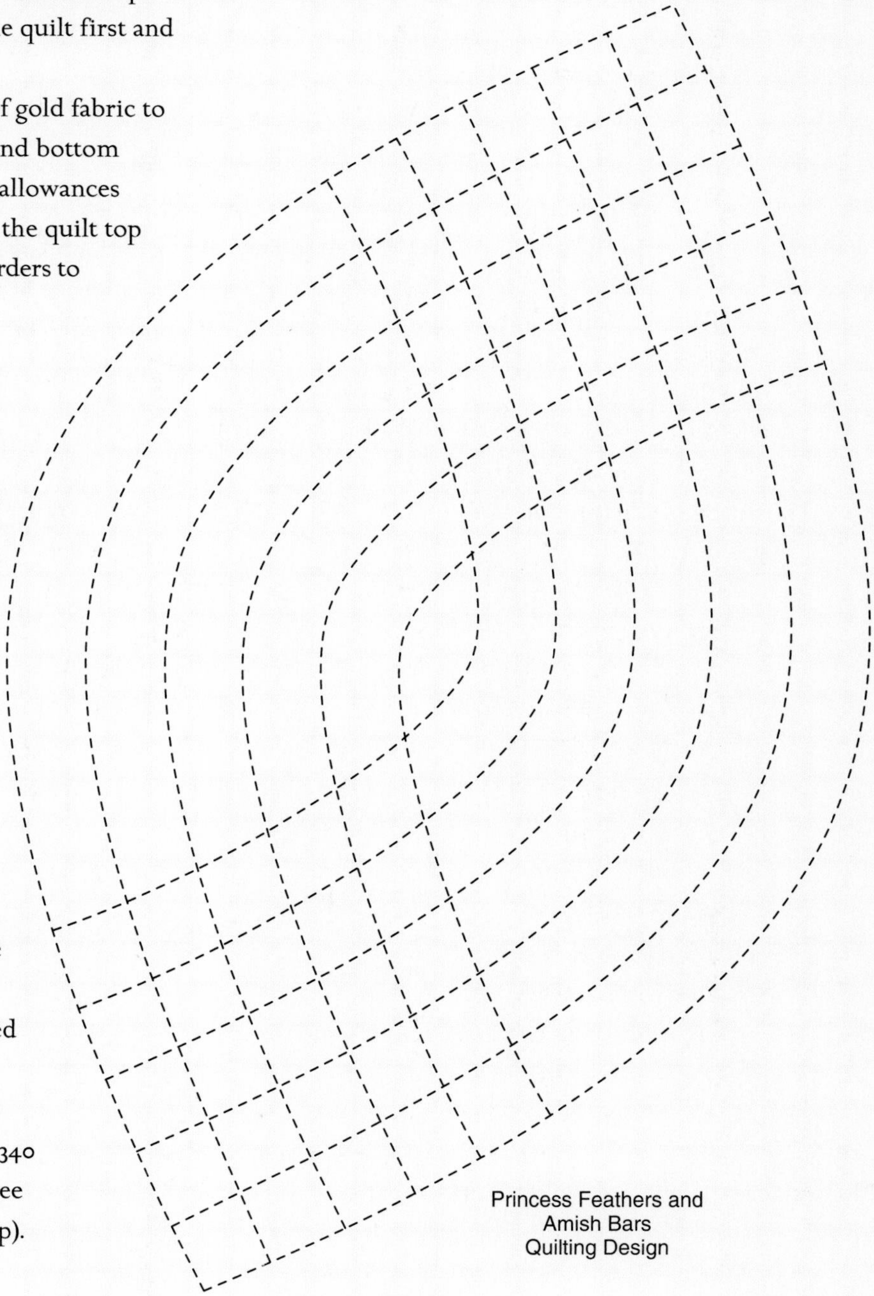

Princess Feathers and
Amish Bars
Quilting Design

amish bars

1890–1920

The back of this bar quilt features
the Princess Feathers appliquéd quilt design on
page 175, making it reversible.

Materials

2³/₄ yards of solid red

2¹/₈ yards *each* of solid gold and green (includes binding)

2¹/₂ yards of 90-inch-wide sheeting for backing

90×108 inches of quilt batting

Finished quilt: 82 inches square

Quantities specified are for 44/45-inch-wide, 100-percent-cotton fabrics. All measurements include a ¹/₄-inch seam allowance. Sew with right sides together unless otherwise stated.

Quilt Notes

Bar quilts were popular among Amish colonies because they were practical—they required little sewing time and could use scraps, so they cost little to make. The Amish Bars quilt *opposite* is the back of the Princess Feathers quilt on *page 175*.

Cut the Fabrics

From solid red, cut:

◆ 4—5¹/₂×71-inch strips for bars

◆ 3—6¹/₂×71-inch strips for the outer bars and bottom border

◆ 2—6¹/₂×36-inch cross-grained strips for the top border

From solid gold, cut:

◆ 5—5¹/₂×71-inch strips for bars

◆ 5—2¹/₂×71-inch strips for binding

From solid green, cut:

◆ 5—5¹/₂×71-inch strips for bars

◆ 4—6¹/₂-inch squares for border corners

Assemble the Quilt Top

This quilt is assembled in two halves, then the top border is added to each half so the center seam is continuous from the top of the quilt to the bottom border.

1 Referring to the Quilt Assembly Diagram on *page 180*, assemble the left half of the quilt top. Begin with a 6¹/₂-inch-wide strip of red fabric, and add a strip of gold fabric to one long side.

2 Add a strip of green fabric to the gold strip. Continue adding strips in a red-gold-green sequence as shown until eight strips are joined, ending with a gold strip. Press all seam allowances toward the red or green strips.

3 Join the remaining strips in this manner to complete the right half of the quilt top. Start with a green strip, then add strips in a red-gold-green sequence, ending with a 6¹/₂-inch-wide red strip.

4 Stitch a green corner square to one end of each 36-inch-long red border strip. Press the seam allowances toward the red fabric.

instructions continued on page 180

5 Matching the seam lines of the corner square and the outer red bar, stitch one border strip onto the top edge of both quilt halves. Press the seam allowances toward the borders; trim excess border fabric even with the sides of the quilt top.

6 Join the two quilt halves, stitching from the top border down to the bottom of the bars. Press the seam allowance to one side.

7 Sew a green square to each end of the remaining red border strip. Matching the seam lines of the squares with the outer red bars, stitch the border strip to the bottom edge of the quilt. Press the seam allowance toward the border fabric.

Complete the Quilt

1 Layer the quilt top, batting, and backing. Baste the three layers together (see tips for completing the quilt in Quilter's Workshop beginning on *page 280*).

2 Quilt as desired. The quilt shown on *page 178* is quilted to accommodate the Princess Feathers design on the reverse. The cable design quilted in the border is centered in each bar (the pattern is on *page 177*).

3 Use the solid gold 2½×71-inch strips to make approximately 340 inches of straight-grain binding (see binding tips in Quilter's Workshop beginning on *page 280*).

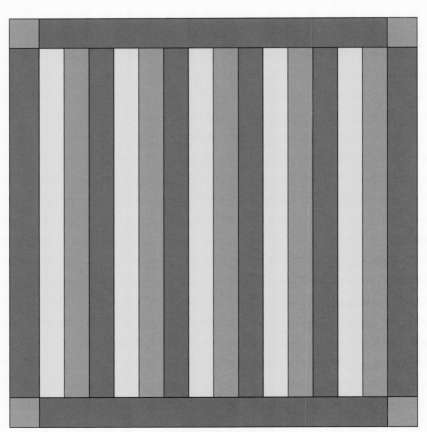

Quilt Assembly Diagram

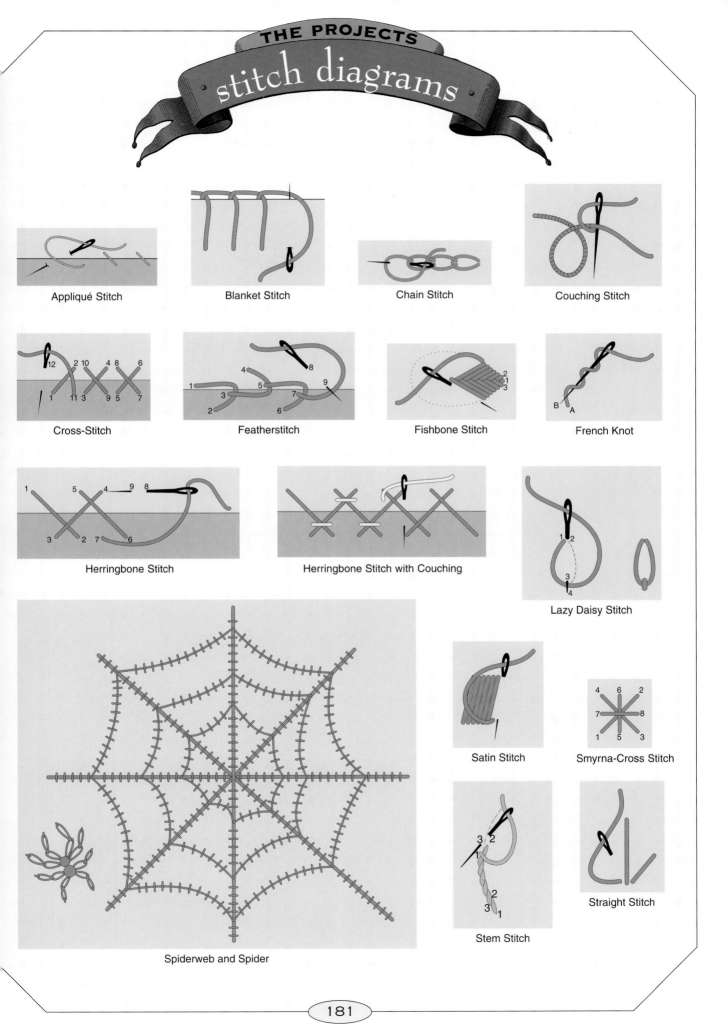

Appliqué Stitch

Blanket Stitch

Chain Stitch

Couching Stitch

Cross-Stitch

Featherstitch

Fishbone Stitch

French Knot

Herringbone Stitch

Herringbone Stitch with Couching

Lazy Daisy Stitch

Satin Stitch

Smyrna-Cross Stitch

Stem Stitch

Straight Stitch

Spiderweb and Spider

1920-1950

Reflecting the prosperity of the 1920s, quilts from this era were made from lovely and lively colors.

Prosperity and change earmarked the 1920s. By 1921 women had the right to vote and a somewhat easier time at home. As electricity, gas, water lines, automobiles, telephones, and new washing and sewing machines effected major household changes, women experienced renewed interest in quiltmaking. Many newspapers and magazines printed quilting articles and patterns. A Gallup survey in 1930 indicated that quilting columns were the most popular feature in six major city newspapers.

The crash of Wall Street in 1929 and the Great Depression of the 1930s meant hard economic times. As a contrast, most quilted projects of the decade were pretty, pastel, and sophisticated. Fabrics for quilts were too expensive for many people, so some used printed feed and grain sacks, recycled clothing, and fabric scraps to make quilts.

Combination Quilts

Quilters during the Great Depression incorporated old and new techniques and fabrics. Quilts were made with traditional patterns and strong colors; pastel fabrics with patterns reflecting Art Deco and Art Nouveau styles; black and white circles and squares, and pinks—particularly dusty rose, in gingham checks and reproduction calicoes. Soft sky blue was popular in juvenile prints.

As dyes improved, colorfast hues—mint green, bright purple, and true orange—were introduced.

continued on page 186

FAN STAR c. 1935
This quilt appeared in the November 1935 issue of Better Homes and Gardens *magazine.*

Fabric of the Time

An abundance of pastel solids and multicolor small floral print fabrics fostered a growing interest in the scrap look that would soon dominate quiltmaking.

Soft pink paired with green was popular for making appliqué quilts. Replicating classic quilt styles led to the reproduction of double pinks, and green and yellow calicoes. In solids, turkey red gave way to soft light reds, and pastel blues supplanted indigoes and cadet blues.

Supple, lustrous cotton sateen was marketed in solid pastels, and it was often used in wholecloth and pieced quilts. Also new was rayon, which substituted for more expensive silk or satin wholecloth boudoir quilts and occasionally was used in pieced quilts.

The influence of Art Deco is obvious in fabrics of the 1920s, with black and white squares and circles common. Unlike earlier fabrics, backgrounds were mostly white.

During the early 1900s, red with a slightly bluish overtone was introduced and often was used with white for embroidered blocks that featured flowers, children, or animals. This fabric was often the "dark spot" on an otherwise pastel quilt.

Pinks regained popularity, especially dusty rose, with gingham checks and reproduction calicoes as favorites. In juvenile prints, soft sky blue was indicative of the time.

As fabric dyes improved, reliable, colorfast hues were introduced, including mint green and bright purple. In the late 1920s, a true orange appeared on the fabric scene.

Although fabrics remained thin at the turn of the century, the quality improved during the 1920s, with many of the fabrics finished with a glaze to provide sheen to the surface.

The most recognizable fabrics from the 1930s are printed, heavy-threaded feed sacks.

The variety of fabrics available opened the door for more creativity in quilting.

(LEFT) *Novelty cotton prints sometimes featured characters from popular animated films.*

Prints of the era gave quilters more design options. There were dots, wavy lines, leaves, flowers, and novelty prints.

Besides *Ladies' Home Journal,* other magazines, such as *Successful Farming, Better Homes and Gardens,* and *Good Housekeeping,* began offering quilt, needlework, and home decorating patterns as well. Designers Ruby Short McKim, Florence La Ganke Harris,

Emma S. Tyrrell, Carlie Sexton, Laura Holmes, and Fleeta Brownell Woodroffe gathered numerous followers of their patterns and their thoughts. McKim's full-size pattern pieces also appeared for 33 years in the *Kansas City Star* newspaper.

continued on page 188

FEED-SACK FRENZY

In the mid-1920s, Gingham Girl Flour was sold in red-and-white gingham bags, perhaps the first time that reusable print fabric appeared as packaging for flour, sugar, salt, grains, seeds, and feed. Husbands who bought feed or seeds in 98-pound sacks were admonished by their wives to search for matching bags, as it took four bags, measuring approximately 36×42 inches when opened, to make a woman's dress.

Designs ranged from small florals to bold plaids, stripes, novelty designs, and figures in vivid, sometimes garish colors. Feed sacks were made in at least five fabric qualities, some with a lower thread count than domestic yard goods. The fabric was serviceable for clothing, kitchen curtains, slipcovers, and quilts. For the next 40 years, printed cotton bags, or feed sacks, were a staple for home sewing.

SNAIL'S TRAIL c. 1930–1940

RUBY SHORT MCKIM

In December 1922 *Successful Farming* debuted the first contribution by Ruby Short McKim. She was a designer who had studied at a New York art school and taught in Missouri schools. Ruby's ideas for needlework and decorating projects reached a wide audience through the magazine pages in the 1920s and led her to be an editor at *Better Homes and Gardens* in 1928.

Ruby's talents included capturing characters with a few essential lines. In 1916 she drew Art Deco-style figures for the *Kansas City Star.* These designs, intended for outline embroidery on quilt blocks, may be the earliest quilt patterns published in a newspaper.

In 1917 Ruby married Arthur McKim. They settled in Missouri, where Arthur ran their mail-order business for products Ruby designed.

Ruby sold transfer patterns for the first time in her November 1928 article for *Successful Farming.* Her career reached a new plateau when she wrote the "Adventures in Home Beautifying" column for *Better Homes and Gardens.* The quality of the designs and easy directions set a high standard for the magazine's decorating stories.

In September 1928 her full-size pattern pieces appeared in the *Kansas City Star* and were the beginning of a 33-year offering of full-size quilt patterns by the paper. The clippings from the newspaper are hoarded, bought, and sold even today.

In her October 1929 feature for *Better Homes and Gardens,* Ruby introduced two series of full-size patterns collected into 15-cent booklets titled *Patchwork Patterns,* shown *right.* Ruby's remark, "Hundreds of you sent for our pieced flower blocks last fall," indicates that reader response may have prompted her to prepare several pattern collections.

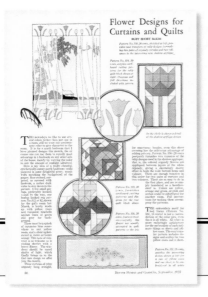

The blocks of GEOMETRIC ROSE, below, *are based on a Ruby McKim pattern featured in the September 1928 issue of* Better Homes and Gardens, *shown at* left.

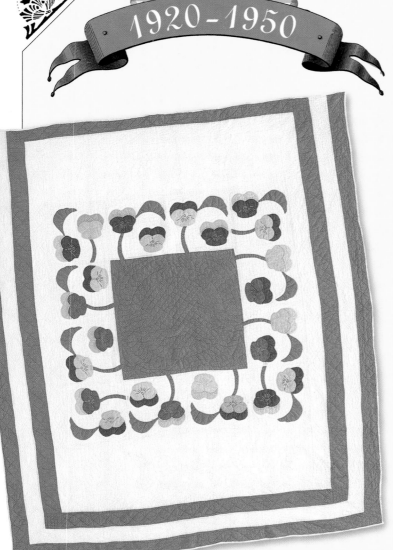

PANSY QUILT c. 1930

Ruby Short McKim described her Pansy quilt as "…an appliqué pattern using that gentle favorite, the pansy, conventionalized somewhat to form a central border, which is really just 12 blocks, each 12 inches square."

Tools of the Trade

Two cooks who were also devoted to quilting, Carrie Hall and Rose Kretsinger, documented a creative period in quilting history by writing *The Romance of the Patchwork Quilt in America.*

Women in the 1930s quilted using a sewing machine for piecing. Writers and designers often paired old and new designs for interest. Time-saving quilting tools, popular for busy homemakers, included precut templates, quilt kits, and stamped embroidery blocks.

Highs and Lows

Although 1933 was the worst year of the Depression, it was a milestone for quilters. Sears, Roebuck & Co. sponsored a quilt contest to coincide with the 1933 Chicago World's Fair. The grand prize was $1,000, and there were nearly 25,000 quilts entered.

When the United States entered World War II in 1941, quilting again declined. With many men gone to war, women joined the workforce. After the war they returned to

ERA TIMELINE

1920 E. T. Meredith serves Woodrow Wilson's cabinet as Secretary of Agriculture; the 19th Amendment is ratified, giving women the right to vote; and Prohibition takes effect. 1923 The Charleston becomes a popular dance. 1927 *The Jazz Singer* is the first talking movie; the first television transmission occurs; and Charles Lindbergh completes the first solo flight across the Atlantic in the *Spirit of St. Louis* airplane. 1929 Announcement of the first *Academy Awards* at a banquet at the Hollywood Roosevelt Hotel declares the movie *Wings* as movie of the year; the first car radio is produced; and the stock market crashes. 1930 *Better Homes and Gardens* introduces its cookbook, designed as a loose-leaf notebook. 1932 Franklin Delano Roosevelt is elected president during the Great Depression. 1933 *Ladies' Home Journal* celebrates its 50th

raising families. Everything new and modern had strong appeal over anything antique or traditional. Magazines featured cooking, parenting, and decorating. Fortunately, quilting didn't die entirely, but it was nearly 30 years before it became popular again.

(RIGHT) Dahlia c. 1934
Although yellow was the favorite color of quilters who ordered Hubert Ver Mehren's medallion kits, the kits were also available in pink, blue, and orchid.

(BELOW) *Manufacturers promoted colors and designs by sending swatch books, such as this one from 1938, to retailers.*

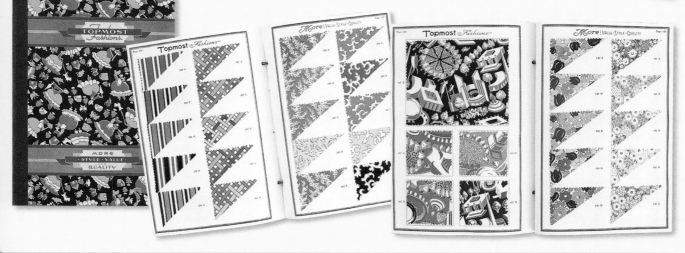

Anniversary; Singer Sewing Machine Co. introduces the Featherweight sewing machine at the Chicago World's Fair; Prohibition ends. 1934 The Dionne Quintuplets are born in Canada. 1935 *The Romance of the Patchwork Quilt in America*, by Carrie Hall and Rose Kretsinger, is published.

1936 The Golden Gate Bridge in San Francisco is completed. 1937 The first feature-length Disney movie, *Snow White and the Seven Dwarfs*, premieres. 1939 Major motion pictures *Gone with the Wind* and *The Wizard of Oz* are released; September 1: Germany invades Poland. 1941 December 7: Japan

attacks the United States naval base at Pearl Harbor, and the U.S. enters World War II. 1943 The Jitterbug is a popular dance. 1944 June 6: The Allies invade Europe on D-Day. 1945 World War II ends. 1949 The Pillsbury Bake-Off begins as the Great National Recipe and Baking Contest.

crazy ann

1920 – 1950

Two-color quilts were again popular, with the blue and white combination the No. 1 choice. The Crazy Ann block, also called Pinwheel, has a whimsical sense of movement.

Materials

6 yards of solid white
$3\frac{1}{4}$ yards of solid blue
$5\frac{1}{3}$ yards of backing fabric
77×105 inches of quilt batting

Finished quilt: $70\frac{5}{8}$×$98\frac{7}{8}$ inches
Finished quilt block: 10 inches square

Quantities specified are for 44/45-inch-wide, 100-percent-cotton fabrics. All measurements include a $\frac{1}{4}$-inch seam allowance. Sew with right sides together unless otherwise stated.

Cut the Fabrics

To make the best use of your fabrics, cut the pieces in the order that follows.

From solid white, cut:

- 70—8-inch squares, cutting each in half diagonally for a total of 140 setting triangles
- 210—$3\frac{3}{8}$-inch squares, cutting each in half diagonally for a total of 420 large triangles, or 420 of Pattern B
- 140—$2\frac{5}{8}$-inch squares, cutting each in half diagonally for a total of 280 small triangles, or 280 of Pattern A

instructions continued on page 192

From solid blue, cut:

- 74—3³⁄₈-inch squares, cutting each in half diagonally for a total of 148 large triangles, or 148 of Pattern B
- 136—3-inch squares, or 136 of Pattern C
- 140—2⁵⁄₈-inch squares, cutting each in half diagonally for a total of 280 small triangles, or 280 of Pattern A
- 9—2¹⁄₂×42-inch binding strips

Make the Crazy Ann Blocks

1 For one Crazy Ann block you will need 8 white A triangles, 12 white B triangles, 8 blue A triangles, 4 blue B triangles, and 4 blue C squares.

2 Referring to the Block Assembly Diagram, sew a white A triangle to each short side of a blue B triangle to make Flying Geese unit 1. Repeat to make four of Flying Geese unit 1.

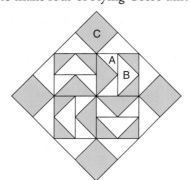

Block Assembly Diagram

3 Sew a blue A triangle to each short side of a white B triangle to make Flying Geese unit 2. Repeat to make four of Flying Geese unit 2.

4 Join Flying Geese units 1 and 2, noting placement of B triangles, to make four pieced squares.

5 Referring to the Block Assembly Diagram, sew together two pieced squares to make a pieced unit. Press the seam allowance toward the large blue triangle. Repeat to make a second pieced unit.

6 Sew the two pieced units together to make a center unit. Press the seam allowance in one direction.

7 Sew a white B triangle to two adjoining sides of a blue C square to make a pieced corner unit. Repeat to make four pieced corner units.

8 Sew a pieced corner unit to opposite sides of the center unit. Sew a pieced corner to each of the remaining sides of the center unit to make a Crazy Ann block. Make a total of 33 Crazy Ann blocks.

Make the Half Blocks

1 For one Crazy Ann half block, you will need 4 white A triangles, 6 white B triangles, 4 blue A triangles, 4 blue B triangles, and 1 blue C square.

2 Follow steps 1 through 7 in "Make the Crazy Ann Blocks" to make a 9-inch Crazy Ann block, completing the construction layout as shown in Diagram 1. Trim the half block to measure 10¹⁄₂ inches on the short sides and 14¹⁄₂ inches on the long side, including the seam allowances. Repeat to make four half blocks.

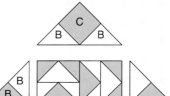

Diagram 1

Add the Setting Triangles

1 Sew a white setting triangle to opposite sides of a block (see Diagram 2, *opposite*). Press seam allowances toward the triangles. Sew a white setting triangle to the remaining sides of the block to complete the full-size block. Repeat to make a total of 33 blocks. Press seam allowances

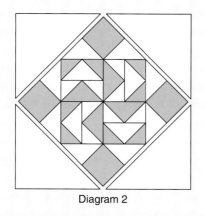

Diagram 2

Quilt Assembly Diagram

toward the triangles. The block should measure 14⅝ inches square, including the seam allowances.

2 Sew a white setting triangle to the short sides of each Crazy Ann half block to complete the four half-blocks. Press the seam allowance toward the triangles.

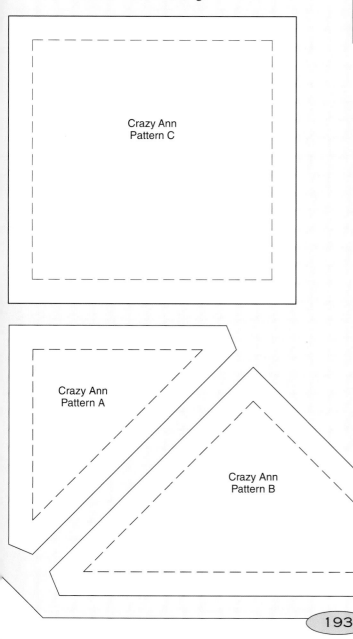

Crazy Ann
Pattern C

Crazy Ann
Pattern A

Crazy Ann
Pattern B

Assemble the Quilt Top

Referring to the Quilt Assembly Diagram, lay out the 33 Crazy Ann blocks and the four half blocks in five vertical rows. Sew together the blocks in each vertical row. Press the seam allowances in alternating directions in each row. Join the rows to complete the quilt top. Press all seam allowances in one direction.

Complete the Quilt

1 Layer the quilt top, batting, and backing. Baste the three layers together (see tips for completing the quilt in Quilter's Workshop beginning on *page 280*). Quilt as desired.

2 Use the blue 2½×42-inch strips to bind the quilt (see binding tips in Quilter's Workshop).

The crib-size Butterfly quilt, opposite, far left, *uses two patterns for the appliquéd butterflies. The quiltmaker of the antique Churn Dash quilt,* opposite, near right, *probably constructed the blocks from scraps.*

Materials for the Butterfly Quilt

5—9-inch squares of assorted prints

1¼ yards of white print for blocks, setting squares, and inner border

1½ yards of blue-and-white print for outer border and backing

¼ yard of solid blue for binding

39×43 inches of quilt batting

Embroidery floss

Finished quilt: 32½×37 inches

Butterfly block: 9½ inches square

Quantities specified are for 44/45-inch-wide, 100-percent-cotton fabrics. All measurements include a ¼-inch seam allowance. Sew with right sides together unless otherwise stated.

Cut the Fabrics

To make the best use of your fabrics, cut the pieces in the order that follows. Patterns for the Resting Butterfly and Butterfly in Flight blocks are on the Pattern Sheet. See tips for making templates for appliqués in Quilter's Workshop beginning on *page 280*.

From white print, cut:

◆ 5—10-inch foundation squares

◆ 4—9½-inch squares

◆ 2—2×32½-inch border strips (#2)

◆ 2—3×27½-inch border strips (#1)

From blue-and-white print, cut:

◆ 2—1¾×37½-inch border strips (#4)

◆ 2—3×30½-inch border strips (#3)

◆ 1—39×43-inch backing

From solid blue, cut:

◆ 4—2×42-inch strips for binding

Appliqué the Butterfly Blocks

1 For each butterfly block, you will need one white print 10-inch foundation square and one 9-inch piece of assorted prints. For this quilt you will need two Resting Butterfly blocks and three Butterfly in Flight blocks.

2 Cut out the appliqué pieces for the Resting Butterfly and the Butterfly in Flight blocks.

3 To make a Resting Butterfly block, fold a 10-inch foundation square in quarters; press. Position A and B pieces from Resting Butterfly pattern on the background square and appliqué using contrasting embroidery floss and blanket stitch (see Blanket Stitch diagram on *page 181*). Appliqué C piece. Trim the foundation square to 9½ inches. Stem-stitch the antennae and work French knots at the ends (see Stem Stitch and French Knot diagrams on *page 181*).

4 To make a Butterfly in Flight block, fold a 9½-inch foundation square diagonally twice in an X; press. Position A piece from Butterfly in Flight pattern on the background square; appliqué using contrasting embroidery floss and

instructions continued on page 196

blanket stitches. Appliqué B piece over A piece, using matching embroidery floss. Stem-stitch the wings and antennae. Blanket-stitch around the wings to complete the block.

5 Make two Resting Butterfly blocks and three Butterfly in Flight blocks. Each block should measure 9½ inches square, including the seam allowances.

Assemble the Quilt Center

1 Referring to the Quilt Assembly Diagram, *right*, lay out the five completed blocks and four setting squares in three horizontal rows. Sew together the blocks in each row.

2 Join the rows. The pieced quilt center should measure 27½ inches square.

Add the Inner Border

Sew one white print 3×27½-inch border (#1) to the top and bottom of the quilt center. Sew a white print 2×32½-inch border (#2) to each side of the quilt center. Press the seam allowances toward the inner border.

Border Corner Cutting Guide

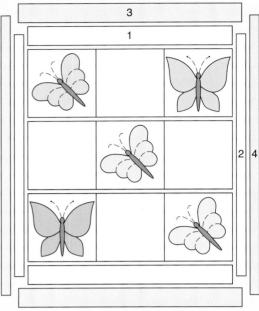

Quilt Assembly Diagram

Add the Outer Border

Sew one blue-and-white print 3×30½-inch border (#3) to the top and bottom of the quilt center. Sew a blue-and-white print 1¾×37½-inch border (#4) to each side of the quilt center. Press the seam allowances toward the outer border.

Complete the Quilt

1 This quilt has rounded corners. To duplicate this look, use the pattern, *left*, or trace around a plate and then mark and cut the curve on the borders.

2 Layer the quilt top, batting, and backing. Baste the three layers together (see tips for completing the quilt in Quilter's Workshop beginning on *page 280*).

3 Quilt as desired. This quilt was quilted by machine, using 1-inch-wide squares nested inside one another in the setting squares and 1¼ inches in around butterfly squares. Diagonal lines from corner to corner and on the borders were machine-stitched with straight lines.

4 Use the solid blue 2×42-inch strips to bind the quilt (see binding tips in Quilter's Workshop).

churn dash
1920 – 1950

Materials for the Churn Dash Quilt

$^3/_8$ yard *each* of gold check, solid light green, and
  blue check for blocks

$^1/_4$ yard *each* of pink check and solid dark blue,
  peach, tan, and pink for blocks

$3^1/_8$ yards of white print for setting squares and
  side and corner triangles

$2^3/_8$ yards of solid light peach for borders
  and binding

4 yards of backing fabric

72×83 inches of quilt batting

Finished quilt: 66×77 inches

Churn Dash block: $7^3/_4$ inches square

Cut the Fabrics

To make the best use of your fabrics, cut the
pieces in the order that follows. Patterns A–D are
on *page 199*. Cut the border and binding strips the
length of the fabric (parallel to the selvage). The
measurements are mathematically correct. You
may wish to cut the border strips longer than
specified to allow for possible sewing
differences. Trim the strips to the lengths needed
before joining them to the quilt top. For this
project, the setting and corner triangles are cut
larger than necessary to allow for sewing
differences. After assembling the quilt center,
trim them to fit.

From each *gold check* and *solid light green*, cut:

◆ 12—$4^1/_8$-inch squares, cutting each in half
  diagonally for a total of 24 triangles, or 24 of
  Pattern A

◆ 24—$1^3/_4$×$2^1/_8$-inch rectangles, or 24 of Pattern C

From *blue check*, cut:

◆ 10—$4^1/_8$-inch squares, cutting each in half
  diagonally for a total of 20 triangles, or 20 of
  Pattern A

◆ 20—$1^3/_4$×$2^1/_8$-inch rectangles, or 20 of Pattern C

From *pink check*, cut:

◆ 8—$4^1/_8$-inch squares, cutting each in half
  diagonally for a total of 16 triangles, or 16 of
  Pattern A

◆ 16—$1^3/_4$×$2^1/_8$-inch rectangles, or 16 of Pattern C

From each *solid dark blue* and *peach*, cut:

◆ 6—$4^1/_8$-inch squares, cutting each in half
  diagonally for a total of 12 triangles, or 12 of
  Pattern A

◆ 12—$1^3/_4$×$2^1/_8$-inch rectangles, or 12 of Pattern C

From *solid tan*, cut:

◆ 4—$4^1/_8$-inch squares, cutting each in half
  diagonally for a total of 8 triangles, or 8 of
  Pattern A

◆ 8—$1^3/_4$×$2^1/_8$-inch rectangles, or 8 of Pattern C

From *solid pink*, cut:

◆ 2—$4^1/_8$-inch squares, cutting each in half
  diagonally for a total of 4 triangles, or
  4 of Pattern A

◆ 4—$1^3/_4$×$2^1/_8$-inch rectangles, or 4 of Pattern C

From *white print*, cut:

◆ 5—$12^1/_2$-inch squares, cutting each diagonally
  twice in an X for a total of 18 setting triangles
  (you will have 2 leftover)

◆ 20—$8^1/_4$-inch squares for setting squares

◆ 2—$6^1/_2$-inch squares, cutting each in half
  diagonally for a total of 4 corner triangles

◆ 60—$4^1/_8$-inch squares, cutting each in half
  diagonally for a total of 120 triangles, or 120 of
  Pattern A

instructions continued on page 198

- 120—1³/₄×2¹/₈-inch rectangles, or 120 of Pattern B
- 30—1³/₄-inch squares, or 30 of Pattern D

From solid light peach, cut:

- 2—6×77¹/₂-inch border strips (#2)
- 2—6×55¹/₂-inch border strips (#1)
- 4—2×78-inch strips for binding

Assemble the Blocks

1 For one block you will need four white A triangles, four white B rectangles, and one white D square. You'll also need four A triangles and four C rectangles in the same color.

2 Referring to the Block Assembly Diagram, sew a white A triangle to a color A triangle to make a triangle-square. Using matching colors, repeat to make four triangle-squares.

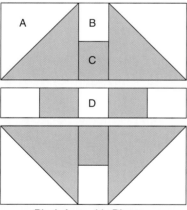

Block Assembly Diagram

3 Join a white B rectangle to a matching color C rectangle. Repeat to make four BC units.

4 Referring to the Block Assembly Diagram, lay out the pieces in three horizontal rows. Sew together the pieces in each row. Join the rows to make one Churn Dash block. Make a total of 30 Churn Dash blocks.

Assemble the Quilt Top

1 Referring to the Quilt Assembly Diagram, *opposite*, lay out the Churn Dash blocks, 20 white print 8¹/₄-inch setting squares, and 18 white print setting triangles in diagonal rows. The corner triangles will be added later.

2 Sew together the pieces in each diagonal row. Press the seam allowances toward the white print setting squares and triangles. Join the rows. Add the four white print corner triangles. Press all seam allowances in one direction.

3 Trim the setting and corner triangles to leave a ¹/₄-inch seam allowance beyond the block corners. The pieced quilt center should measure 55¹/₂×66¹/₂ inches, including the seam allowances.

Add the Borders

Before cutting borders measure the quilt top and adjust the lengths to fit. Sew one solid light peach 6×55¹/₂-inch border strip (#1) to the top and bottom edges of the pieced quilt center. Add one solid light peach 6×77¹/₂-inch border strip (#2) to each side edge of the quilt top. Press the seam allowances toward the borders.

Complete the Quilt

1 Layer the quilt top, batting, and backing. Baste the three layers together (see tips for completing the quilt in Quilter's Workshop beginning on *page 280*).

2 Quilt as desired. The original quiltmaker hand-quilted the setting blocks with a feathered wreath, outlined the pieces in the quilt block ¹/₄ inch in from the seams, and used an oval interlocking chain pattern for the borders.

3 Use the solid light peach 2×78-inch strips to bind the quilt (see binding tips in Quilter's Workshop).

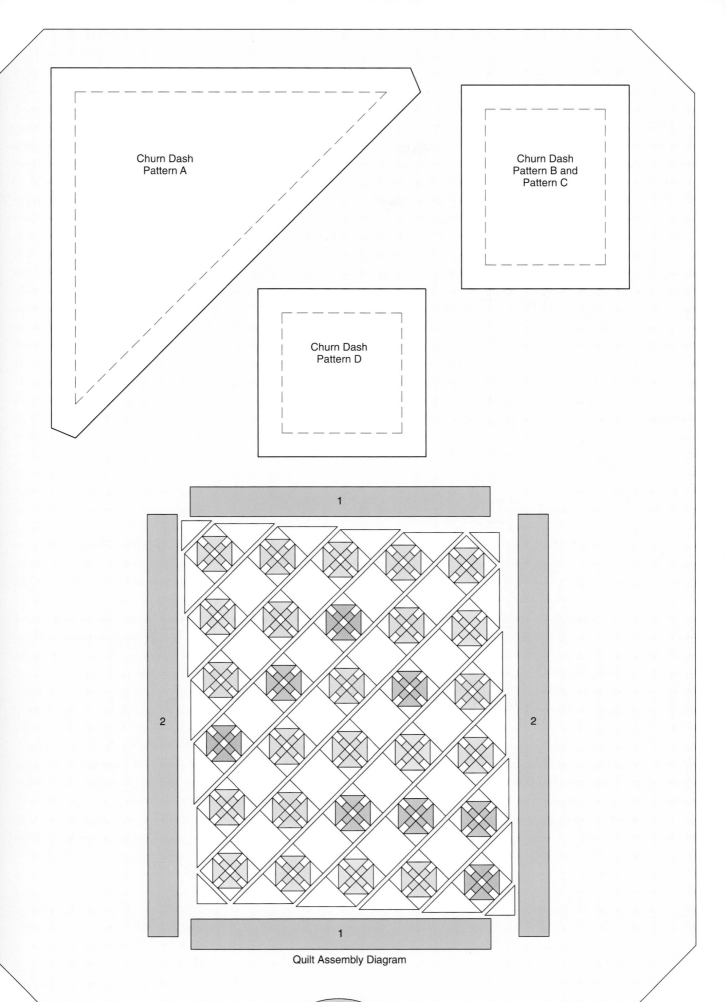

Churn Dash
Pattern A

Churn Dash
Pattern B and
Pattern C

Churn Dash
Pattern D

1

2

2

1

Quilt Assembly Diagram

carpenter's square

1920 – 1950

*Use rotary cutting and strip
piecing to create this handsome design of
graphic interwoven lines.*

Materials

7 yards of solid white fabric for patchwork,
   border, and binding
5 yards of solid blue fabric
3¼ yards of 90-inch-wide sheeting for backing
120-inch square of quilt batting

Finished quilt: 86×109 inches
Finished Carpenter's Square block:
   23 inches square

Quantities specified are for 44/45-inch-wide,
100-percent-cotton-fabrics. All measurements
include a ¼-inch seam allowance. Sew with right
sides together unless otherwise stated.

Quilt Notes

The Carpenter's Square block has hidden
potential. A single block is interesting, but when
the 12 blocks are joined in a straight set, the
contrasting fabrics create an illusion of
intricately interwoven strips.

   This block looks more complex to make
than it is. It is so well suited to rotary cutting
and strip piecing that traditional methods are
not recommended.

   Referring to the Block Assembly Diagram,
above right, identify the diagonal rows that are the
basic units of the Carpenter's Square block. Rows
1, 2, and 3 are white strips. Rows A, B, and C are
cut from one strip set. The corners (Unit D) are
made separately.

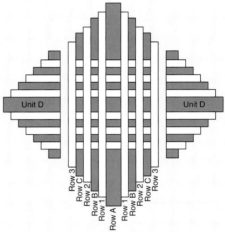

Block Assembly Diagram

Cut the Fabrics

To make the best use of your fabrics, cut the
pieces in the order that follows. Cut all 42½-inch-
wide strips cross-grain to make efficient use of
the fabric. Narrower strips can be cut from the
width remaining after the side borders are cut.

From solid white fabric, cut:

- 1—30×42½-inch piece for the binding
- 2—5½×102-inch strips and six 5½×30-inch strips
  for the outer border
- 24—1¾×31-inch strips for Row 1
- 24—1¾×26-inch strips for Row 2
- 1—24×42½-inch piece. From this piece, cut
  twenty-four 1¾×21-inch strips for Row 3.
- 1—32×42½-inch piece. From this piece, cut
  eighteen 1¾×42½-inch strips for the ABC
  strip set.

instructions continued on page 202

- 1—18×42$\frac{1}{2}$-inch piece. From this piece, cut ten 1$\frac{3}{4}$×42$\frac{1}{2}$-inch strips. Cut each strip into five 8$\frac{1}{2}$-inch-wide segments to obtain forty-eight 1$\frac{3}{4}$×8$\frac{1}{2}$-inch pieces for Unit D.

- 1—14×42$\frac{1}{2}$-inch piece. From this piece, cut seven 1$\frac{3}{4}$×42$\frac{1}{2}$-inch strips. Cut each strip into seven 6-inch wide segments to obtain forty-eight 1$\frac{3}{4}$×6-inch pieces for Unit D.

- 1—7×42$\frac{1}{2}$-inch piece. From this piece, cut four 1$\frac{3}{4}$×42$\frac{1}{2}$-inch strips. Cut each strip into twelve 3$\frac{1}{2}$-inch-wide segments to obtain forty-eight 1$\frac{3}{4}$×3$\frac{1}{2}$-inch pieces for Unit D.

From blue fabric, cut:

- 4—4×42$\frac{1}{2}$-inch strips and two 4×95-inch strips for the inner border

- 12—1$\frac{3}{4}$ ×42$\frac{1}{2}$-inch strips for the ABC strip set

- 3—3×42$\frac{1}{2}$-inch strips for the ABC strip set

- 16—3×34-inch strips. From these strips, cut forty-eight 3×9$\frac{3}{4}$-inch pieces for Row A and Unit D.

- 24—1$\frac{3}{4}$×34-inch strips. From these strips, cut ninety-six 1$\frac{3}{4}$×7$\frac{1}{4}$-inch pieces for Row B and Unit D.

- 15—1$\frac{3}{4}$×42$\frac{1}{2}$-inch strips. From these strips, cut ninety-six 1$\frac{3}{4}$×4$\frac{3}{4}$-inch pieces for Row C and Unit D, plus forty-eight 1$\frac{3}{4}$×2$\frac{1}{4}$-inch pieces for Unit D.

Make the ABC Strip Sets

See strip piecing tips in Quilter's Workshop beginning on *page 280. Note:* Throughout the assembly of rows A, B, and C, press the seam allowances toward the white fabric.

1 Begin with a 3×42$\frac{1}{2}$-inch strip of blue fabric for the center of the strip set (see Diagram 1). Stitch a 1$\frac{3}{4}$×42$\frac{1}{2}$-inch strip of white fabric onto both long sides of the center strip.

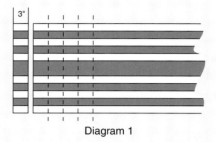

Diagram 1

2 Select four more 1$\frac{3}{4}$×42$\frac{1}{2}$-inch strips of each fabric. Sew the strips together in blue-white pairs, matching the 42$\frac{1}{2}$-inch lengths.

3 Add these units to the center strip to assemble the strip set as illustrated. The completed strip set measures 15$\frac{1}{2}$×42$\frac{1}{2}$ inches.

4 Cut twelve 3-inch-wide units from this strip set for the center portion of Row A.

5 Make two more ABC strip sets. From these strip sets, cut forty-eight 1$\frac{3}{4}$-inch-wide units for the center portions of Rows B and C (see Diagram 2).

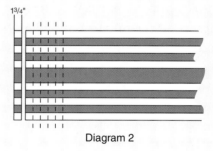

Diagram 2

Complete Rows A, B, and C

1 To complete Row A, stitch a 3×9$\frac{3}{4}$-inch strip of blue fabric onto both ends of each of the twelve 3-inch-wide units.

2 To complete Row B, add one 1$\frac{3}{4}$×7$\frac{1}{4}$-inch strip of blue fabric onto both ends of each of 24 of the 1$\frac{3}{4}$-inch-wide units.

3 To complete Row C, stitch a 1$\frac{3}{4}$×4$\frac{3}{4}$-inch blue strip onto the 24 remaining 1$\frac{3}{4}$-inch-wide units.

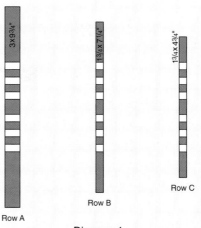

Row A

Row B

Row C

Diagram 4

Make the Corners (Unit D)

One corner unit is made with 13 fabric strips (see Diagram 3). *Note:* Throughout the construction of the corner unit, press all seam allowances toward the blue fabric.

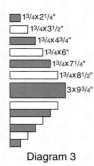

13/4x21/4"
13/4x31/2"
13/4x43/4"
13/4x6"
13/4x71/4"
13/4x81/2"
3x93/4"

Diagram 3

1 Begin with a 3×9³/₄-inch strip of blue fabric for the center of the strip set. Stitch a 1³/₄×8¹/₂-inch strip of white fabric onto both long sides of the center strip, aligning all three strips at one end. Because the strips are not the same length, the center blue strip extends beyond the two white ones. Do not trim the excess fabric.

2 Add a 1³/₄×7¹/₄-inch strip of blue fabric onto each side of the unit, keeping all the strips aligned at one end.

3 Continue adding strips to both sides of the unit, alternating white and blue strips of decreasing length. The last strips on the outside of the unit are 1³/₄×2¹/₄-inch strips of blue fabric. Make a total of 24 corner units.

Assemble the Blocks

Note: Throughout the assembly of the blocks, press each new seam allowance toward the unpieced strip of fabric (Row 1, 2, or 3).

1 Lay out the assembled A, B, and C rows with the white strips cut for Rows 1, 2, and 3 (see Diagram 4, *above,* and the Block Assembly Diagram on *page 201*).

2 Sew the Row 3 strip onto the pieced Row C, matching the centers of both strips. The strips are not the same length so there is excess fabric at both ends of the longer Row C (see Diagram 5). Wait until the blocks are assembled before trimming these irregular ends of fabric to minimize the risk of stretching the bias edges.

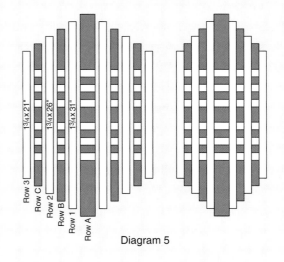

13/4x21"
13/4x26"
13/4x31"

Row 3
Row C
Row 2
Row B
Row 1
Row A

Diagram 5

3 Add Row 2 onto Row C, matching the centers of both rows as before.

4 Stitch Row B onto Row 2 in the same manner, then add Row 1 and Row A, which forms the diagonal center of the block.

instructions continued on page 204

5 For the other side of the block, join Rows 1, B, 2, C, and 3 in succession. If the centers of each row are carefully matched, the piecing in Rows A, B, and C will align and create the illusion of interwoven strips.

6 Add a D corner unit to opposite sides of the block (see Diagram 6). Align center of each corner unit as you did for the previous rows.

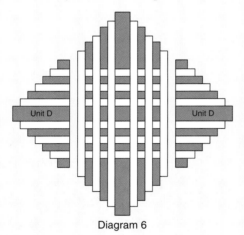

Diagram 6

7 Make a total of 12 Carpenter's Square blocks. Do not trim the edges of the blocks until after they are joined.

Join the Blocks

Use an acrylic ruler and a fabric marker to draw seam lines around the edges of each block before joining the blocks (see Diagram 6). Mark the sewing lines on the wrong side of each block. Do not cut excess fabric from the block edges until the blocks are joined and you are sure the seam is acceptable.

1 Make a mark in the center of the wide middle strip of one corner unit, ³/₄ inch from the unstitched end of the strip. This mark pinpoints the corner of the block.

2 On each seam line of that corner unit, measure ³/₄ inch from the unstitched

bottom edge of each of the 12 narrow strips. Make a mark at each of these points.

3 Draw a line on each side of the corner unit connecting the marks and extending across the adjacent block rows to the next corner.

4 Repeat Steps 1, 2, and 3 on the opposite corner unit, then measure the square defined by these drawn lines. It should be a precise 23-inch square. However, it is unlikely that anyone's cutting and sewing will result in absolute precision. As you mark each block, you may find your marked squares are slightly larger or smaller—that is fine as long as they are consistent. The borders are cut long enough to accommodate a reasonable variance.

5 Mark sewing lines on all the blocks in this manner.

6 With right sides together and matching seam lines, pin two blocks together. Each row should align with the matching row in the adjacent block. Stitch the blocks together on the marked sewing line.

7 Check the seam on the right side of the joined blocks. The adjacent rows should match nicely. The small blue square formed in the center of the two blocks should be approximately 1¹/₄ inches square.

8 When you are satisfied with the stitched seam, use a rotary cutter and the acrylic ruler to trim the excess fabric from the seam allowance. Press the remaining ¹/₄-inch seam allowance open if there is too much bulkiness to press it to one side.

9 In this manner, join the blocks in four horizontal rows of three blocks each. Join the rows to complete the quilt top, aligning the seam lines of adjacent blocks carefully. Around the outside of the quilt top, leave the jagged edges of the blocks untrimmed until the inner borders are added.

Add the Borders

1 Stitch one 4×95-inch strip of blue fabric to each long side of the quilt top, using the marked lines on the blocks as a sewing line. When you are satisfied with the seam, trim the excess fabric of the blocks from the seam allowance. Press the remaining $1/4$-inch seam allowances toward the border fabric.

2 Join two 4×42$1/2$-inch strips of blue fabric to make one 84$1/2$-inch-long border strip. Matching the center seam of the border with the center of the bottom edge of the quilt, stitch the border onto the quilt. In the same manner, add a blue border strip to the top edge. Trim excess fabric from the seam allowances and press.

3 Sew one 5$1/2$×102-inch strip of white fabric onto each long side of the quilt. Trim excess border fabric even with the ends of the quilt top.

4 Join three 5$1/2$×30-inch white strips to make a border for each of the two remaining sides. Matching the center of the border strip with the center of the quilt edge, stitch the borders onto the top and bottom of the quilt.

Mark the Quilt

Mark the desired quilting design on the quilt top. The quilt shown on *page 200* has simple outline quilting around the block patchwork and a small cable quilted in the narrow border. The outer border is quilted with diagonal lines spaced 1$1/4$ inches apart.

You can leave the borders straight or make a scalloped edge similar to the one pictured. If you want a scalloped edge, use a saucer or small bowl as a template and trace gentle curves along the outer edge of the quilt. Do not cut the scallops until after the quilting is complete.

Complete the Quilt

1 Layer the quilt top, batting, and backing. Baste the three layers together (see tips for completing the quilt in Quilter's Workshop beginning on *page 280*). Quilt as desired.

2 Use the white fabric 30×42$1/2$-inch strip to make approximately 410 inches of binding (see tips for making and applying binding in Quilter's Workshop).

If you are making a scalloped edge, see tips on preparing continuous bias binding in Quilter's Workshop; stitch the binding onto the quilted top before cutting the scallops from the outer border fabric.

Quilt Assembly Diagram

star diamond

1920 – 1950

Noted quilt designer Emma Tyrrell shared

this classic quilt block with Ladies' Home Journal *magazine*

readers in the April 1933 issue.

Materials

7 yards of solid off-white for blocks and borders
$1^1/_2$ yards of solid blue for blocks and binding
$2^3/_4$ yards of blue floral for blocks and border
$7^1/_4$ yards of backing fabric
86×106 inches of quilt batting

Finished quilt top: 80×100 inches
Finished block: 18 inches square

Quantities specified are for 44/45-inch-wide,
100-percent-cotton fabrics. All measurements
include a $^1/_4$-inch seam allowance. Sew with right
sides together unless otherwise stated.

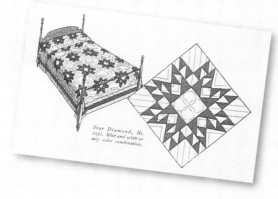

Star Diamond, No.
1051. Blue and white or
any color combination.

Cut the Fabrics

To make the best use of your fabrics, cut the
pieces in the order that follows. Cut the
border strips the length of the fabric (parallel
to the selvage). There are no pattern pieces for
this project; the letter designations are for
placement only.

From solid off-white, cut:

◆ 2—$3^1/_2$×$100^1/_2$-inch outer border strips
◆ 2—$3^1/_2$×$74^1/_2$-inch outer border strips
◆ 2—$5^1/_2$×$88^1/_2$-inch inner border strips
◆ 2—$5^1/_2$×$58^1/_2$-inch inner border strips
◆ 3—$2^1/_2$×$58^1/_2$-inch sashing strips
◆ 12—$7^1/_4$-inch squares, cutting each diagonally
  twice in an X for a total of 48 triangles for
  Position F
◆ 12—$6^1/_2$-inch squares for Position H
◆ 48—$4^1/_2$-inch squares for Position C

◆ 24—$4^1/_4$-inch squares, cutting each diagonally
  twice in an X for a total of 96 triangles for
  Position D
◆ 96—$2^7/_8$-inch squares, cutting each in half
  diagonally for a total of 192 triangles for
  Position A
◆ 48—$2^5/_8$-inch squares for Position E
◆ 48—$2^1/_2$-inch squares for Position B
◆ 8—$2^1/_2$×$18^1/_2$-inch sashing strips

From solid blue, cut:

◆ 9—$2^1/_2$×42-inch binding strips
◆ 48—$3^7/_8$-inch squares, cutting each in half
  diagonally for a total of 96 triangles for
  Position G

From blue floral, cut:

◆ 2—$3^1/_2$×$94^1/_2$-inch middle border strips
◆ 2—$3^1/_2$×$68^1/_2$-inch middle border strips
◆ 48—$4^1/_4$-inch squares, cutting each diagonally
  twice in an X for a total of 192 triangles for
  Position D
◆ 96—$2^7/_8$-inch squares, cutting each in half
  diagonally for a total of 192 triangles for
  Position A

instructions continued on page 208

Assemble Unit 1

1 For one Unit 1, you will need four solid off-white A triangles, four blue floral A triangles, one solid off-white B square, and one solid off-white C square.

2 Sew together one solid off-white A triangle and one blue floral A triangle to make a triangle-square (see Diagram 1). Press the seam allowance toward the blue floral triangle. The pieced triangle-square should measure 2¹⁄₂ inches square, including the seam allowances. Repeat to make a total of four triangle-squares.

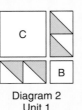

Diagram 1

3 Referring to Diagram 2, lay out the four triangle-squares, one B square, and one C square in two rows. Sew together the pieces in each row. Press the seam allowances toward the B and C squares. Then join the rows to make Unit 1. Press the seam allowances in one direction. Pieced Unit 1 should measure 6¹⁄₂ inches square, including the seam allowances.

Diagram 2
Unit 1

4 Repeat steps 1–3 to make a total of 48 of Unit 1.

Assemble Unit 2

1 For one Unit 2 you will need four blue floral D triangles, two solid off-white D triangles, one solid off-white E square, one solid off-white F triangle, and two solid blue G triangles.

2 Sew together one solid off-white D triangle and one blue floral D triangle to make a triangle-square. The triangle-square should measure 2⁵⁄₈ inches square, including seam allowances. Repeat to make a second triangle-square.

3 Referring to Diagram 3, lay out the two triangle-squares, two blue floral D triangles, one solid off-white E square, and one solid off-white F triangle in diagonal rows. Sew together the pieces in each row. Press the seam allowances toward the off-white E and F pieces. Then join the rows. Press seam allowances in one direction.

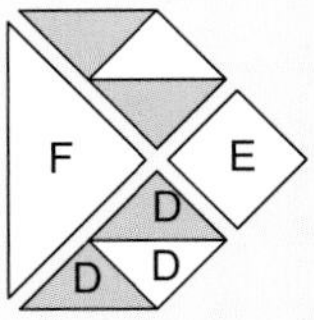

Diagram 3

4 Referring to Diagram 4, join the two solid blue G triangles to adjoining side edges of the Step 3 unit to make Unit 2. Press the seam allowances toward the large triangles. Pieced Unit 2 should measure 6¹⁄₂ inches square, including the seam allowances.

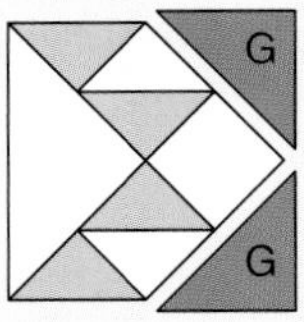

Diagram 4
Unit 2

5 Repeat steps 1–4 to make a total of 48 of Unit 2.

Assemble the Star Diamond Blocks

1 Referring to Diagram 5 for placement, lay out four of Unit 1, four of Unit 2, and one solid off-white H square in three horizontal rows of three units each.

Diagram 5

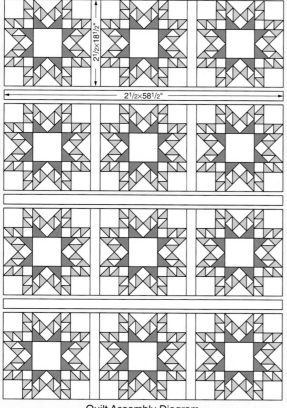

$21/2 \times 181/2"$

$21/2 \times 581/2"$

Quilt Assembly Diagram

2 Sew together the units in each row. Press the seam allowances in one direction, alternating with each row. Then join the rows to make a Star Diamond block. Press the seam allowances in one direction. The pieced Star Diamond block should measure 18½ inches square, including the seam allowances.

3 Repeat steps 1 and 2 to make a total of 12 Star Diamond blocks.

Assemble the Quilt Center

1 Referring to the Quilt Assembly Diagram for placement, lay out the 12 Star Diamond blocks, the eight off-white 2½×18½-inch sashing strips, and the three off-white 2½×58½-inch sashing strips in seven horizontal rows.

2 Sew together the pieces in each row. Press all seam allowances toward the sashing strips. Then join the rows to make the quilt center. Press the seam allowances in one direction. The pieced quilt center should

measure 58½×78½ inches, including the seam allowances.

Add the Borders

1 Sew the solid off-white 5½×58½-inch inner border strips to the top and bottom edges of the pieced quilt center. Add a solid off-white 5½×88½-inch inner border strip to each side edge of the pieced quilt center. Press the seam allowances toward the solid off-white border.

2 Sew the blue floral 3½×68½-inch middle border strips to the top and bottom edges of the pieced quilt center. Then add a blue floral 3½×94½-inch middle border strip to each side edge of the pieced quilt center. Press the seam allowances toward the blue print border.

3 Sew the solid off-white 3½×74½-inch outer border strips to the top and bottom edges of the pieced quilt center. Then add a solid off-white 3½×100½-inch outer border strip to each side edge of the pieced quilt center. Press the seam allowances toward the blue print border.

Complete the Quilt Top

1 Layer the quilt top, batting, and backing. Baste the three layers together (see tips for completing the quilt in Quilter's Workshop beginning on *page 280*).

2 Quilt as desired. The quilt shown is machine-quilted around each piece in the Star Diamond block and diagonally in the center. In the center of each large off-white area there are stitched overlapping circles. The outer off-white border has quilted half circles.

3 Use the solid blue 2½×42-inch strips to bind the quilt (see binding tips in Quilter's Workshop).

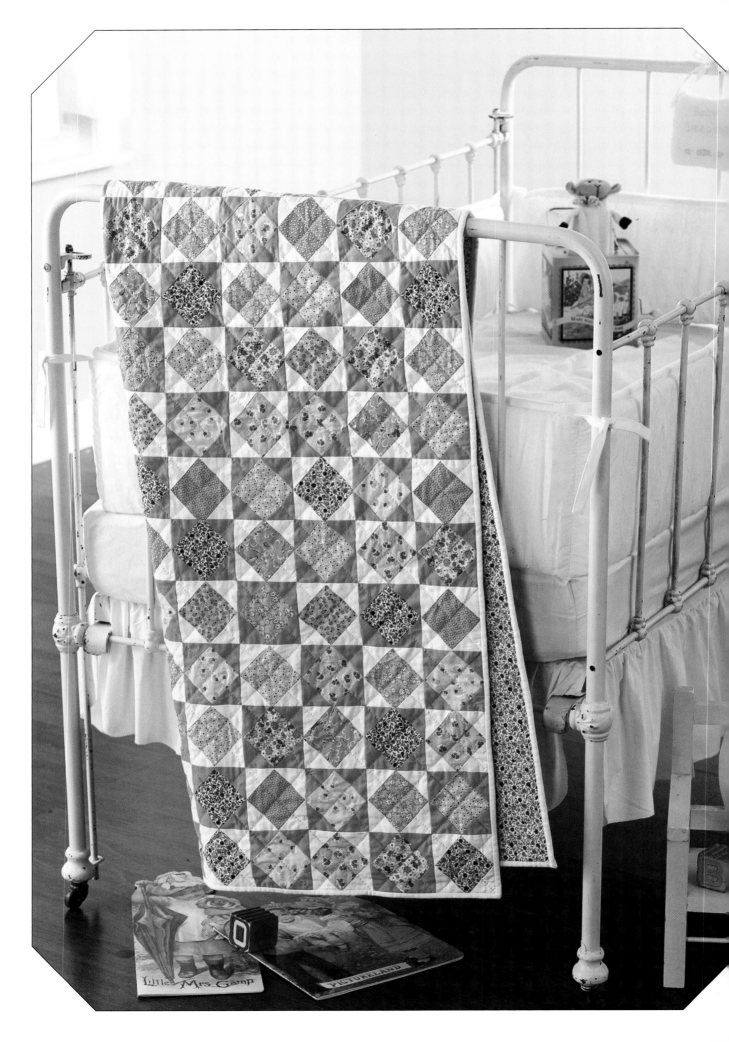

8-point all over

1920 - 1950

This crib quilt is based on a design popular

in the late 1800s. The easy-to-piece block was introduced to

Better Homes and Gardens *readers in 1932.*

Materials

1¹/₂ yards assorted pink prints for blocks

1¹/₂ yards solid cream for blocks and binding

1¹/₂ yards solid pink for blocks

1¹/₂ yards backing fabric

42×51 inches of quilt batting

Finished quilt top: 36×45 inches

Finished block: 3 inches square

Quantities specified are for 44/45-inch-wide, 100-percent-cotton fabrics. All measurements include a ¹/₄-inch seam allowance. Sew with right sides together unless otherwise stated.

Cut the Fabrics

To make the best use of your fabrics, cut the pieces in the order that follows.

From assorted pink prints, cut:

◆ 180—3¹/₂-inch squares

From solid cream, cut:

◆ 5—2¹/₂×42-inch binding strips

◆ 360—2-inch squares

From solid pink, cut:

◆ 360—2-inch squares

Assemble Block A

1 For one Block A you'll need one assorted pink print 3¹/₂-inch square and four solid pink 2-inch squares.

2 For accurate sewing lines, use a quilter's pencil to mark a diagonal line on the wrong side of each solid pink 2-inch square. (To prevent your fabric from stretching as you draw the lines, place 220-grit sandpaper under the squares.)

3 Align two marked solid pink 2-inch squares with opposite corners of the assorted pink print 3¹/₂-inch square (see Diagram 1; note the placement of the marked diagonal lines). Stitch on the marked lines; trim the seam allowances to ¹/₄-inch. Press the attached triangles open.

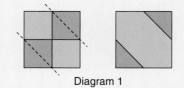

Diagram 1

instructions continued on page 212

4 Align two marked solid pink 2-inch squares with the remaining corners of the pink print square (see Diagram 2; note the placement of the marked diagonal lines). Stitch on the marked lines; trim the seam allowances and press triangles open as before to make a Block A. Pieced Block A should measure $3^1/2$ inches square, including the seam allowances.

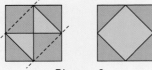

Diagram 2

5 Repeat steps 1–4 to make a total of 90 of Block A.

Assemble Block B

1 For one Block B you'll need one assorted pink print $3^1/2$-inch square and four solid cream 2-inch squares.

2 Mark a diagonal line on the wrong side of the solid cream 2-inch squares as before.

3 Align two marked solid cream 2-inch squares with opposite corners of the assorted pink print $3^1/2$-inch square (see Diagram 3; note the placement of the marked diagonal lines). Stitch, trim, and press as before.

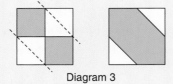

Diagram 3

4 Align two marked solid cream 2-inch squares with the remaining corners of the pink print square (see Diagram 4; note the placement of the marked diagonal lines). Stitch, trim, and press as before to make a Block B. Pieced Block B should measure $3^1/2$ inches square, including the seam allowances.

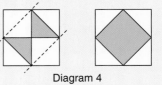

Diagram 4

5 Repeat steps 1 through 4 to make a total of 90 of Block B.

Assemble the Quilt Top

1 Referring to the photograph *opposite* for placement, lay out the 90 A blocks and the 90 B blocks in 15 horizontal rows of 12 blocks each, alternating Blocks A and B as shown.

2 Sew together the blocks in each horizontal row. Press the seam allowances toward the A blocks. Then join the rows to make the quilt top. Press the seam allowances in one direction.

Complete the Quilt

1 Layer the quilt top, batting, and backing. Baste the three layers together (see tips for completing the quilt in Quilter's Workshop beginning on *page 280*).

2 Quilt as desired. The crib quilt shown is hand-quilted by stitching through the center of each block in both directions.

3 Use the solid cream $2^1/2\times42$-inch strips to bind the quilt (see binding tips in Quilter's Workshop beginning on *page 280*).

BACK TO THE '30s

Virtually everyone has a memory of the pastel print fabrics of the 1930s, whether from an old dress or heirloom quilt. With her collection of 1930s reproduction fabrics, designer Judie Rothermel has provided quilters a way to create the looks of their grandmothers' and great-grandmothers' quilts.

Hired as a designer for Marcus Brothers Textiles in 1987, Judie based her first line, The Centennial Collection, on the 1840s to 1880s fabrics that are her first love.

Four years later she introduced the Aunt Grace Collection of charming 1930s prints. Named to honor her great-great aunt Grace with whom Judie quilted, the collection contains all original designs inspired by antique textiles, not remakes of old prints.

tulip garden

1920 – 1950

*Brilliant appliquéd red tulips seem to pop from
the intricately quilted white background of this quilt. The simply
bound edges allow the vine to stand out.*

Materials

7³/₄ yards of solid white fabric
3 yards of solid green fabric
1³/₄ yards of solid red fabric
6 yards of backing fabric
90×108 inches of quilt batting

Finished quilt: 79¹/₂×97 inches
Finished block: 12¹/₂ inches square

Quantities specified are for 44/45-inch-wide,
100-percent-cotton fabrics. All measurements
include a ¹/₄-inch seam allowance. Sew with right
sides together unless otherwise stated.

Quilt Notes

The appliquéd border makes a stunning
framework for this classic red, white, and green
tulip design. The quilt has 12 appliquéd blocks
assembled in an alternate diagonal set.

Cut the Fabrics

To make the best use of your fabrics, cut the
pieces in the order that follows. See tips for
making templates for patchwork and appliqué in
Quilter's Workshop beginning on *page 280*. Make
appliqué templates for Patterns A, B, C, and D
and a patchwork template for Pattern E on the
Pattern Sheet.

When cutting the A, B, and C appliqués from
fabric, add a ³/₁₆-inch seam allowance around

each piece. Add a ¹/₄-inch seam allowance at the
straight ends of each D piece as indicated on the
pattern because D pieces are seamed together.

From solid white fabric, cut:
◆ 1—29×42-inch piece for the binding
◆ 2—14×103-inch border strips
◆ 2—14×84-inch border strips
◆ 5—19-inch squares. Cut each of these squares
   in quarters diagonally to obtain 10 setting
   triangles.
◆ 2—10-inch squares. Cut both squares in half
   diagonally for four corner triangles.
◆ 18—13-inch squares

From solid red fabric, cut:
◆ 12—Pattern A
◆ 76—Pattern B

From solid green fabric, cut:
◆ 5—1×42-inch strips for the tulip stems
◆ 1—32×42-inch piece. From this piece, cut 76 of
   Pattern C and 76 of Pattern C reversed.
◆ 1—63×42-inch piece. From this piece, cut 14 of
   Pattern D and 14 of Pattern D reversed.
◆ 4—Pattern E

Prepare the Stems for Appliqué

1 With right sides together, fold one 1×42-inch
green strip in half lengthwise. Machine-stitch
a scant ¹/₄ inch from the raw edge of the strip.

instructions continued on page 216

tulip garden

1920 – 1950

2 Press the seam allowance open, centering the seam line in the center of the strip. Turn the strip right side out and press again.

3 Stitch the remaining four stem strips in this manner.

4 Cut 2½-inch-long segments from these strips for the tulip stems. Cut 76 stems. It is not necessary to turn under the short ends because these will be covered by other pieces.

Appliqué the Blocks

1 Turn under the seam allowances on one A center piece, including the little square in the center of the fabric. Clip the seam allowance as needed to achieve nicely curved edges.

2 Turn under the edges of four tulips and eight leaves (four of Pattern C and four of Pattern C reversed). Do not turn under the straight edges of the leaves; these will be covered by the stems.

3 Fold one white square in half vertically, horizontally, and diagonally; finger-press each fold to mark placement lines.

4 Pin the appliqué in place. Align the deep indents of the A piece on the horizontal and vertical placement lines and the center of each curved section on the diagonal lines. Tuck a stem under the A piece at each diagonal placement line. Position C and C reversed leaves on opposite sides of each stem. Place a B tulip at the top of each stem.

5 When all the pieces are correctly positioned, appliqué them in place. For the center of the A piece, use your needle to turn back and appliqué the edge of the inner square, revealing the white fabric underneath. Make a total of 12 appliquéd blocks.

Assemble the Quilt Top

1 Referring to the Quilt Assembly Diagram, *opposite*, lay out the appliquéd blocks, the six setting squares, and the setting triangles in diagonal rows.

2 Assemble the blocks and setting pieces in diagonal rows, then join the rows. The assembled quilt top without the border should measure approximately 53×71 inches.

Add the Appliquéd Swag Border

1 Stitch one 14×84-inch border strip to the top and bottom edges of the quilt, matching the center of each strip with the center of the edge of the quilt top. Sew a 14×103-inch border strip onto the side edges of the quilt and miter the corners (see tips for mitering corners in Quilter's Workshop beginning on *page 280*).

Border Appliqué Placement Diagram

Quilt Assembly Diagram

2 Machine-stitch each D piece to one D reversed piece with a 1/4-inch seam allowance. Press the seam allowances open to avoid bulkiness when turning the edges. Each of these pairs is one swag of the border.

3 To make a curved swag border for one short side of the quilt, join three swags end to end. Turn under the curved edges to prepare the border for appliqué.

4 Center and pin the prepared border on one short side of the quilt, matching the center seam of the swag border with the center of the white border strip (see Border Appliqué Placement Diagram, *opposite*). In the same manner, prepare a three-swag border for the opposite side of quilt.

5 Join four swags end to end for each side border. Stitch an E piece onto each end of both four-swag strips. Turn under the edges of each swag strip to prepare it for appliqué.

6 Center a four-swag border on each long side of the quilt, matching centers. If your stitching has been precise, the diamond-shape E piece will straddle the mitered seam of the white borders and align with the swag border on the adjacent side. Some adjustment may be required to align the swag borders.

7 When all four swag borders are correctly positioned, baste them in place. Tuck a stem under the swags at each seam line and at the tip of each E corner piece. The stems at the E corner piece will point to the outside corner of the quilt, and the other stems will alternate directions, half the stems pointing toward the inside of the quilt and half pointing toward the outside edge (see photograph on *page 214*). Pin a tulip and two leaves in place on each stem.

8 Appliqué the swags and the border tulips in place on the white fabric.

Complete the Quilt

1 Layer the quilt top, batting, and backing. Baste the three layers together (see tips for completing the quilt in Quilter's Workshop beginning on *page 280*).

2 Quilt as desired. This quilt has a diagonal grid of 1-inch squares quilted in the white background and outline quilting around the appliqué pieces. Quilting lines for the center pieces and tulips are shown on the A and B patterns. Parallel lines of quilting follow the curves in the appliquéd border swags.

3 Use the remaining white fabric to make approximately 365 inches of binding, either bias or straight-grain (see tips for making and applying binding in Quilter's Workshop).

kaleidoscope

1920 – 1950

Three shapes, eight colors, and ninety-nine blocks
in light and dark fabrics seem to rotate and spin on this vibrant quilt.
Solid borders frame the quilt center.

Materials

2³/₄ yards of muslin

¹/₃ yard of solid gold fabric for the block centers

⁷/₈ yard *each* of solid light peach, red, green, blue, yellow, lavender, dark pink, and light pink for the block patchwork

³/₄ yard of solid dark peach for inner border

1 yard of solid pink for binding

3 yards of 90-inch-wide sheeting for backing

90×108 inches of quilt batting

Finished quilt: 83×99 inches
Finished block: 8 inches square

Quantities specified are for 44/45-inch-wide, 100-percent-cotton fabrics. All measurements include a ¹/₄-inch seam allowance. Sew with right sides together unless otherwise stated.

Quilt Notes

This quilt has 99 Kaleidoscope blocks in a 9×11-block straight set. Each of the eight triangles in the blocks is a different color. The same colors are used, in the same positions, in all the blocks. A gold circle is appliquéd in the center of the blocks where triangle points meet.

Cut the Fabrics

To make the best use of your fabrics, cut the pieces in the order that follows. See tips for making templates for patchwork and appliqué in Quilter's Workshop beginning on *page 280*. Make templates for Patterns A, B, and C on *page 221*. Add a ³/₁₆-inch seam allowance to each C piece when cutting out the traced circles.

From muslin, cut:

- 4—4¹/₂×94-inch borders
- 396—Pattern B

From gold fabric, cut:

- 99—Pattern C, adding the seam allowance

From each of the solid light peach, red, green, blue, yellow, lavender, dark pink, and light pink, cut:

- 99—Pattern A

From solid dark peach fabric, cut:

- 4—2×42-inch strips for the end borders
- 6—2×30-inch strips for the side borders

Make the Kaleidoscope Blocks

Select one A triangle of each color to make one block. Refer to the Block Assembly Diagram for color placement as you make each block.

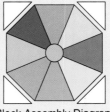

Block Assembly Diagram

instructions continued on page 220

1 Begin by sewing pairs of A triangles together. Stitch the red triangle to the green one and the peach triangle to the lavender one. Press the seam allowances toward the red and the lavender fabrics.

2 Join the two pairs by sewing the red and peach triangles together (see Diagram 1); press the seam allowance toward the peach triangle.

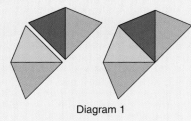

Diagram 1

3 Make the other half of the block in the same manner, stitching the dark pink and yellow triangles together, then joining the blue triangle to the light pink one (see Diagram 2). Press the seam allowances toward the yellow and pink triangles. Join the two pairs to make a half-block.

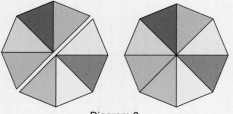

Diagram 2

4 Join the block halves to form an octagon (see Diagram 2). Don't worry if the triangle points don't come together exactly in the center; this will be covered by the C circle.

5 Stitch the long side (hypotenuse) of a muslin B triangle to the edges of the yellow, lavender, light pink, and red edges; press the seam allowances toward the B triangles.

6 Turn under the edge of a gold C circle. Appliqué the circle in place over the center of the block to make one Kaleidoscope block.

7 Repeat steps 1–6 to make a total of 99 Kaleidoscope blocks.

Assemble the Quilt Top

1 Referring to the Quilt Assembly Diagram, join the blocks in 11 horizontal rows of nine blocks each. When piecing a row, join the peach triangle of each block to the blue triangle in the adjacent block to keep all the blocks in the same relative position.

2 Stitch the rows together to complete the quilt top.

Add the Borders

1 For the inner border, stitch three 2×30-inch strips of dark peach fabric together end to end to make a border strip for each long side of the quilt. Match the center of the border strip with the center of one side of the quilt top; stitch borders in place on both sides. Press the seam allowances toward the borders, then trim the excess border fabric even with the top and bottom edges of the quilt top.

2 Join two 2×42-inch strips of dark peach fabric to make a border strip for the top and bottom edges. Add these borders in the same manner as the side borders.

3 For the outer border, stitch a muslin border strip onto each long side of the quilt top. Press the seam allowances toward the inner border. Trim excess border fabric even with the edges of the quilt top.

4 Repeat to add borders to the top and bottom edges.

Complete the Quilt

1 Layer the quilt top, batting, and backing. Baste the three layers together (see tips for completing the quilt in Quilter's Workshop beginning on *page 280*).

2 Quilt as desired. The quilt pictured on *page 218* has outline quilting inside each triangle. It also has a circle of quilting about 2 inches from the gold circle in each block. The borders are quilted with diagonal lines, 1 inch apart.

3 Use the solid pink fabric to make approximately 370 inches of binding, either bias or straight-grain (see tips for making and applying binding in Quilter's Workshop beginning on *page 280*).

Quilt Assembly Diagram

Kaleidoscope
Pattern B

Kaleidoscope
Pattern C

Kaleidoscope
Pattern A

dogwood

1920 – 1950

Pretty pastel fabrics
blanket this dainty pieced quilt.

Materials

4³/₄ yards of solid pink for patchwork, borders, and binding

4¹/₄ yards of muslin for patchwork

3¹/₈ yards of green print for patchwork

¹/₄ yard of yellow print for patchwork

49—7-inch squares of assorted pastel prints

2¹/₂ yards of 90-inch-wide sheeting for backing

90×108 inches of quilt batting

Finished quilt: 83 inches square
Finished block: 11 inches square

Quantities specified are for 44/45-inch-wide, 100-percent-cotton fabrics. All measurements include a ¹/₄-inch seam allowance. Sew with right sides together unless otherwise stated.

Quilt Notes

This quilt is a straight set made in seven rows of seven blocks each. The fabrics in each of the 49 Dogwood blocks are the same except for the B pieces that form the large center flower. Different print fabrics in a rainbow of pastel colors give this quilt a look of spring flowers.

Curved seams and set-in pieces make this block a challenge, and most quilters will prefer to do some or all of the patchwork by hand. Take extra care to ensure accuracy in cutting and piecing.

instructions continued on page 224

Cut the Fabrics

To make the best use of your fabrics, cut the pieces in the order that follows. See tips for making templates for patchwork in Quilter's Workshop beginning on *page 280*. Review the instructions for the patchwork, then decide whether to piece the Dogwood block by hand or by machine. Prepare a template for each of Patterns A–G on the Pattern Sheet.

From solid pink, cut:

◆ 4—3¹/₂×85-inch border strips
◆ 1—27×42-inch piece for binding
◆ 196—Patterns D and D reversed (Dr)

From muslin, cut:

◆ 196—*each* of patterns C, E, F, and F reversed (Fr)

From green print, cut:

◆ 196—Patterns E and G

From yellow print, cut:

◆ 49—Pattern A

From each square of assorted pastel prints, cut:

◆ 4—Pattern B

Make the Dogwood Blocks

Make center and corner units as described below. Use four corner units, each with the same B fabric, and four center units for one block.

1 Join muslin and green print E triangles to form a square; sew a D piece onto the muslin side of the square (see Diagram 1). Press the seam allowances away from the muslin triangle.

Diagram 1

2 Sew a C triangle onto the bottom edge of a D reversed piece (see Diagram 1); press seam allowance toward the D piece. Add a B piece to the long side of the C triangle as shown.

3 Join the EED/BCDr units to complete the corner unit. Make a total of 196 corner units, 4 for each block.

4 For the center units, sew the curved side of one F piece and one F reversed piece to the curved sides of each G piece as shown in Diagram 2. See tips for piecing curved seams in Quilter's Workshop beginning on *page 280*. Press the seam allowances toward the F pieces. Make 196 center units, four for each block.

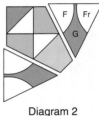

Diagram 2

5 Referring to the Block Assembly Diagram, *opposite*, join two corner blocks in a diagonal row with an A square between them. Leave ¹/₄ inch of the seam allowance unstitched at both ends of each seam. Press seam allowances toward the center square.

6 Stitch a center unit onto both sides of the two remaining corner units. Press the seam allowances toward the corner units.

7 Join the three sections to complete one Dogwood block. Repeat steps 1–6 to make a total of 49 Dogwood blocks.

Assemble the Quilt Top

Join the blocks in seven horizontal rows of seven blocks each. Matching seam lines carefully, stitch the rows together to complete the quilt top.

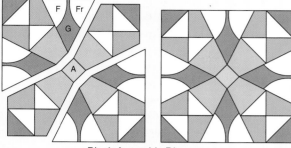

Block Assembly Diagram

Add the Borders

1 Sew a solid pink border strip onto opposite sides of the quilt top. Press the seam allowances toward the borders, then trim the excess border fabric even with the sides of the quilt top.

2 Add the remaining solid pink borders to the sides of the quilt in the same manner.

Complete the Quilt

1 Layer the quilt top, batting, and backing. Baste the three layers together (see tips for completing the quilt in Quilter's Workshop).

2 Quilt as desired. The quilt pictured on *page 223* has outline quilting around the patchwork pieces and a simple cable quilted in the borders.

3 Use the remaining solid pink fabric to make 340 inches of binding, either bias or straight-grain (see tips for making and applying binding in Quilter's Workshop).

Quilt Assembly Diagram

flower garden

1920 – 1950

Thousands of tiny fabric hexagons in a garden of colors make up this classic Depression era quilt.

Materials

5 yards of muslin for patchwork and inner border

2 yards of solid lavender for patchwork, outer border, and binding

1¼ yards *each* of solid light yellow and light green for patchwork and borders

52—6×9-inch scraps of assorted solid fabrics for patchwork

59—9×12-inch scraps of assorted print fabrics for patchwork

3 yards of 90-inch-wide sheeting for backing fabric

90×108 inches of quilt batting

Finished quilt: 85½×91 inches

Quantities specified are for 44/45-inch-wide, 100-percent-cotton fabrics. All measurements include a ¼-inch seam allowance. Sew with right sides together unless otherwise stated.

Quilt Notes

This classic Depression-era quilt has 59 "flowers" set along a pieced "garden path." Each flower has a solid yellow center, enclosed by an inner circle of 6 solid-color hexagons, a ring of 12 print hexagons, and an outer circle of 18 muslin hexagons.

instructions continued on page 228

flower garden
1920 - 1950

When the Flower Blocks are joined, wide paths of muslin separate them. Four borders of hexagons in muslin, light yellow, light green, and lavender complete the quilt with an edge that follows the hexagonal pieces.

This quilt, with its set-in pieces, can be sewn by hand or by machine, but hand-piecing is recommended (see tips for setting in seams in Quilter's Workshop beginning on *page 280*).

Cut the Fabrics

To make the best use of your fabrics, cut the pieces in the order that follows. See tips for making and using templates for patchwork in Quilter's Workshop. Make a template for the hexagon pattern, *opposite. Note:* If you prefer to buy ready-made templates, buy a template for a 1-inch (finished size) hexagon.

From muslin, cut:
- 1,062 hexagons for 59 flower blocks
- 220 hexagons for the first border

From solid light yellow fabric, cut:
- 59 hexagons for flower centers
- 226 hexagons for the second border

From solid light green fabric, cut:
- 6 hexagons for one flower block
- 232 hexagons for the third border

From solid lavender, cut:
- 1—38-inch square for binding
- 36 hexagons for six flower blocks
- 238 hexagons for the outer border

From each solid scrap fabric, cut:
- 6 hexagons for one flower block

From each print scrap fabric, cut:
- 12 hexagons for one flower block

Block Assembly Diagram

Make the Flower Blocks

1 Referring to the Block Assembly Diagram, join 37 hexagons to make one flower block. Using a traditional sewing method (or, if you prefer, you can use an English paper-piecing method), begin by sewing six solid-color hexagons around the yellow center.

2 Add 12 print hexagons in the next ring, then complete the flower blocks with an outer ring of 18 muslin hexagons. Repeat to make a total of 59 flower blocks.

Assemble the Quilt Top

Referring to the Quilt Assembly Diagram, *opposite*, join the 59 flower blocks. Because every seam is set in, you can join the blocks in any order you like. Some quiltmakers prefer to make horizontal rows, others join the blocks in undefined groups.

Add the Borders

For the first border, add a row of muslin hexagons around the outside edge of the quilt top. Add the second border of solid light yellow hexagons, then stitch a border of solid light green hexagons. Complete the quilt top with a row of lavender hexagons.

Complete the Quilt

1 Layer the quilt top, batting, and backing. Baste the three layers together (see tips for completing the quilt in Quilter's Workshop).

2 Quilt as desired. The quilt shown has outline quilting inside each hexagon.

3 Use the 38-inch square of solid lavender to make 375 inches of binding, either bias or straight-grain (see tips for making continuous bias binding in Quilter's Workshop).

Flower Garden Pattern

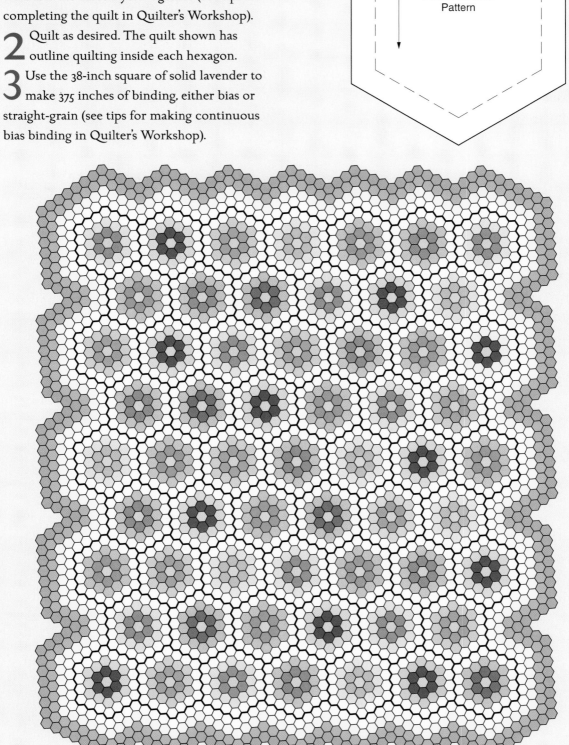

Quilt Assembly Diagram

bride's bouquet

1920 - 1950

A variation of a Star Block, this striking

pattern has several names, including Nosegay and Cornucopia.

Navy blue fabric provides a distinct border.

Materials

5¹/₂ yards of muslin for patchwork and
   inner border

2³/₄ yards of navy blue pindot for patchwork,
   outer border, and binding

2 yards of solid purple fabric

1 yard of solid yellow fabric

2 yards of scraps of assorted print fabrics

6 yards of backing fabric

90×108 inches of quilt batting

Finished quilt: 83¹/₂×98 inches

Finished block: 10¹/₄ inches square

Quantities specified are for 44/45-inch-wide,
100-percent-cotton fabrics. All measurements
include a ¹/₄-inch seam allowance. Sew with right
sides together unless otherwise stated.

Quilt Notes

The Chelsea Station mail-order company sold a
Laura Wheeler pattern for this quilt in the 1930s,
calling it Old-Fashioned Nosegay.

   The quilt shown, *opposite*, has 49 Bride's
Bouquet blocks joined in a diagonal set. The
triangular spaces at the sides are filled with
half-blocks.

   Set-in seams make this block a challenge.
See tips for sewing set-in seams in Quilter's
Workshop beginning on *page 280.*

Cut the Fabrics

To make the best use of your fabrics, cut the
pieces in the order that follows. See tips for
making and using templates for patchwork
Quilter's Workshop. Prepare templates for
Patterns A, C, D, E, and F on the Pattern Sheet.

From muslin, cut:
- 4—4¹/₂×89-inch border strips
- 240—Pattern C
- 180—*each* of Pattern D and D reversed
- 60—*each* of Patterns F and F reversed

From navy pindot, cut:
- 2—2×97-inch border strips
- 2—2×86-inch border strips
- 1—34-inch square for binding
- 120—Pattern A

From solid yellow, cut:
- 16—2×42-inch strips. From these strips, cut
   316 B squares, each 2 inches square.

From solid purple, cut:
- 66—Pattern E

From scrap print fabrics, cut:
- 240—Pattern A

Make the Bride's Bouquet Blocks

Because this block is relatively difficult,
complete one block to gain an understanding of
its construction before you proceed.

instructions continued on page 232

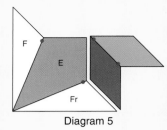
Diagram 5

1 To make each block, use two A diamonds of the navy pindot and four A diamonds of scrap fabrics, five B squares, four C triangles, three each of D and D reversed pieces, and one each of pieces E, F, and F reversed.

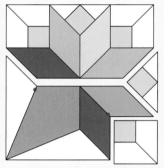
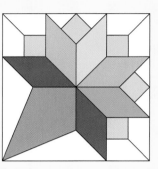
Block Assembly Diagram

2 Referring to the Block Assembly Diagram and Diagram 1, stitch the six A diamonds together into three pairs. Be careful not to stitch into the seam allowance at the ends of each seam so you can set in the side and corner units.

Diagram 1

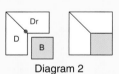
Diagram 2

3 To make each corner unit, join one D and one D reversed piece (see Diagram 2). Set a B square into the angle to complete the corner unit. Make three corner units. Set a corner unit into the angle of each diamond pair.

4 To make the CBC side units, stitch a C triangle onto two adjacent sides of a B square (see Diagram 3).

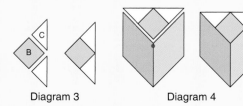
Diagram 3   Diagram 4

5 Join two AA corner units as shown at the top of the Block Assembly Diagram. Set a CBC side unit into the open angle at the top of the joined unit (see Diagram 4).

6 Sew the F and F reversed pieces onto the long sides of the E piece (see Diagram 5). Join the remaining AA corner unit and the FEFr unit.

7 Combine the two halves of the block. Complete the block by setting the remaining CBC side unit into the open angle of the diamonds. Make 49 Bride's Bouquet blocks.

Make the Half Blocks

When the blocks are joined in a diagonal set, triangular spaces are left around the sides. Half blocks fill in these spaces, continuing the repeated pattern of the blocks.

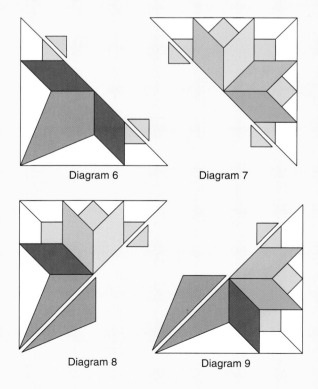
Diagram 6   Diagram 7

Diagram 8   Diagram 9

1 Referring to Diagrams 6–9, *opposite,* assemble the four types of half blocks in the same manner as the full blocks. Make five top half blocks and five bottom half blocks as shown. When these are complete, lay a ruler along the diagonal edge of each half block and trim the excess fabric of the B squares with a rotary cutter.

2 Make six left half blocks and six right half blocks, then trim the excess fabric of the B and E pieces.

Assemble the Quilt Top

1 Using the Quilt Assembly Diagram, *right,* lay out the blocks and half blocks in diagonal rows.

2 Picking up one block at a time, join the blocks in each row. Assemble the rows to complete the quilt top, matching the seam lines of adjoining blocks.

Add the Borders

1 Stitch a 4¹/₂×89-inch muslin border onto each long side of the quilt top. Press the seam allowances toward the border strip. Trim the excess border fabric even with the top and bottom edges of the quilt top.

2 Stitch the remaining muslin border strips onto top and bottom edges.

3 Sew the navy pindot borders onto the quilt top, adding the side borders first and then the top and bottom borders.

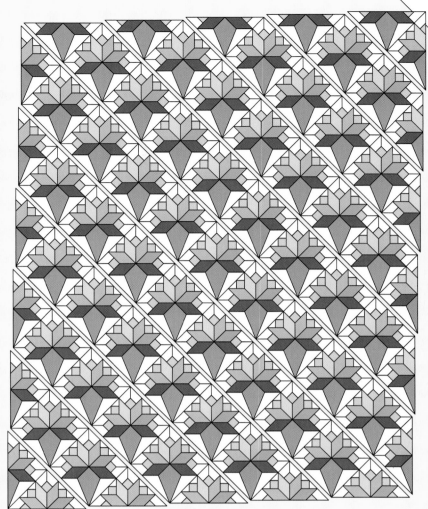

Quilt Assembly Diagram

Complete the Quilt

1 Layer the quilt top, batting, and backing. Baste the three layers together (see tips for completing the quilt in Quilter's Workshop beginning on *page 280*).

2 Quilt as desired. The quilt shown has outline quilting inside each patch. The E pieces are quilted with a heart-and-stem motif that complements the bridal bouquet theme; this quilting motif is shown on the E pattern on the Pattern Sheet.

3 Use the remaining navy pindot to make approximately 360 inches of binding, either bias or straight-grain (see tips for making and applying binding in Quilter's Workshop).

schoolhouse

1920 – 1950

Quilted with scrolling leaf designs, bright yellow sashing and green setting squares frame the pieced Schoolhouse Blocks on this twin-size quilt.

Materials

3 yards of solid yellow for sashing and binding

$2^5/8$ yards of muslin for background of Schoolhouse Blocks

35 assorted prints, *each* 10 inches square, for schoolhouses; or $2^3/4$ yards of a single fabric

$^1/2$ yard of solid green fabric for sashing squares

$5^1/2$ yards of backing fabric or 3 yards of 90-inch-wide sheeting

81×96 inches of quilt batting

Finished quilt: 68×94 inches
Finished Schoolhouse block: 10 inches square

Quantities specified are for 44/45-inch-wide, 100-percent-cotton fabrics. All measurements include a $^1/4$-inch seam allowance. Sew with right sides together unless otherwise stated.

Quilt Notes

Blue, navy, and black schoolhouses alternate with bright-color schoolhouse blocks in this twin-size quilt. The thirty-five 10-inch blocks are separated by 3-inch-wide sashing strips in a 5×7-block straight set.

Cut the Fabrics

To make the best use of your fabrics, cut the pieces in the order that follows. The horizontal and vertical sashing strips are the same size, but are cut on the crosswise and length-wise grains,

respectively. To avoid confusion, cut and sew the vertical sashing strips first, and then cut the horizontal sashing to assemble the quilt.

Make templates for Patterns D, E, F, and G on the Pattern Sheet; all other pieces are rectangular and can be measured using a ruler. Refer to the Block Assembly Diagram on *page 236* to identify the pieces for which patterns are not given.

Cutting requirements for blocks are given for one block, with the number required for the entire quilt shown in parentheses. Make a single block to test the accuracy of your templates before cutting the remaining fabric.

From solid green fabric, cut:
- 48—$3^1/2$-inch sashing squares

From each assorted print, cut:
- 2—$1^3/4$×2-inch pieces for Patch B (70)
- 1—*each* of Patterns E and G (35)
- 2—$1^3/4$×$4^1/4$-inch pieces for Patch H (70)
- 2—$1^3/4$×$3^3/4$-inch pieces for Patch I (70)
- 2—$1^3/4$×$5^3/4$-inch pieces for Patch L (70)
- 2—$1^1/2$×$2^3/4$-inch pieces for Patch M (70)
- 1—$1^3/4$×$2^3/4$-inch piece for Patch N (35)

From muslin, cut:
- 8—2×42-inch strips. From these strips, cut two (70) 2×$2^3/8$-inch pieces for Patch A and one (35) 2×$4^1/4$-inch piece for Patch C.
- 7—$3^1/4$×42-inch strips. From these strips, cut one (35) each of Patterns D, D reversed, and F.

instructions continued on page 236

- 4—1³/₄×42-inch strips. From these strips, cut one (35) 1³/₄×3³/₄-inch piece for patch I.
- 16—1¹/₂×42-inch strips. From these strips, cut one (35) 1¹/₂×6¹/₄-inch piece for patch J; one (35) 1¹/₂×5³/₄-inch piece for patch K; and two (70) 1¹/₂×2³/₄-inch pieces for patch M.

From solid yellow, cut:

- ³/₄ yard for binding
- 4—10¹/₂×42-inch strips. Cut each strip into twelve 3¹/₂×10¹/₂-inch pieces to obtain 42 vertical sashing strips.
- 10—3¹/₂×42-inch strips. Cut forty 10¹/₂-inch pieces for horizontal sashing strips.

Make the Schoolhouse Blocks

Refer to the Block Assembly Diagram to identify the pieces in each unit.

1 To make Unit 1, sew together two pairs of A and B pieces; complete the unit by stitching both B pieces to opposite ends of a C piece.

2 When making Unit 2, handle the bias edges carefully to avoid distorting the pieces. Sew a D triangle onto the right edge of G piece as illustrated; press seam allowance toward G. Sew the D reversed triangle onto the left side of E triangle, and stitch F piece onto the right side; press both seams away from E piece. Complete the unit by sewing the FG seam; press seam allowance toward F.

3 For Unit 3, sew the muslin I piece between two I pieces of print fabric; press seams toward the center. Complete the unit with H pieces at the top and bottom of the unit; press seams away from center.

4 To begin Unit 4, join two pairs of muslin and print M pieces, then complete the strip with the N piece in the center. Add L pieces to the top and bottom, then complete the unit with a muslin K piece at the top. Press all seams toward the print fabric.

5 Join Units 1 and 2, matching the seam lines carefully.

6 Sew Unit 3 to one side of the J piece, then sew Unit 4 to the opposite side. Press seams toward the J piece.

7 Matching seam lines carefully, sew the two pieces together. Make 35 Schoolhouse blocks.

Join the Horizontal Rows

1 Sew one vertical sashing strip to the left side of each Schoolhouse block; press seam allowances toward the sashing.

2 On the floor or a table, lay out the blocks in a pleasing arrangement; separate the blocks into seven rows with five blocks in each row.

3 Join the blocks for Row 1, sewing each block to the sashing strip of the adjacent block.

4 End the row by sewing a vertical sashing strip to the right side of the last block in the row. Press all sashing seam allowances toward the sashing.

5 Repeat steps 1–4 to complete Rows 2 through 7.

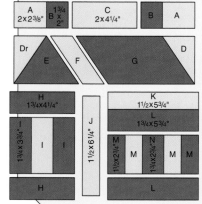

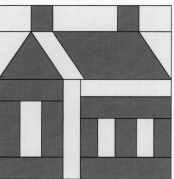

Block Assembly Diagram

Quilt Assembly Diagram

Assemble the Quilt Top

1 Each row of horizontal sashing is made by alternating solid green sashing squares with solid yellow sashing strips (see Quilt Assembly Diagram). Starting with a square, sew five sashing strips and six squares together to make a row; make eight rows of horizontal sashing.

2 Matching seam lines carefully, sew a row of horizontal sashing to the top of each of the seven block rows. Press seams toward horizontal sashing.

3 Join the rows, sewing the top of the sashing row to the bottom of the adjacent block row. Press seam allowances toward sashing.

4 Complete the quilt top by sewing the remaining row of sashing to the bottom of the seventh block row.

Complete the Quilt

1 Layer the quilt top, batting, and backing. Baste the three layers together (see tips for completing the quilt in Quilter's Workshop beginning on *page 280*).

2 Quilt as desired. The quilt shown on *page 234* has a vine and leaf quilting design in all the sashing strips. A full-size pattern for this quilting design is given on the Pattern Sheet. A leaf motif is repeated in the sashing squares. The blocks are outline-quilted, with diagonal lines quilted on the roof pieces (E and G).

3 Use the ³⁄₄ yard of solid yellow to make approximately 324 inches of binding, either bias or straight-grain (see tips for making and applying binding in Quilter's Workshop).

Make a Larger Quilt

Adding more rows, vertically and/or horizontally, easily makes this quilt larger. When making a larger quilt, carefully adjust the required yardage for the muslin, the solid yellow and green sashing fabrics, and the backing fabric. A larger piece of batting also is necessary.

For a full-size quilt, make seven more blocks for another vertical row. The finished size is 81×94 inches.

For a queen-size quilt, make 12 extra blocks for one more vertical row and one more horizontal row. The finished size is 94×107 inches.

To make a king-size quilt, you need 19 more blocks for two additional vertical rows and one more horizontal row. The finished size is 107×107 inches.

new york beauty

1920 – 1950

Triangles and diamonds give this

quilt energy. The pieced components and the open background

are embellished with fanciful quilted designs.

Materials

7¼ yards of solid white

3½ yards of solid green

3 yards of solid lavender

6 yards of backing fabric

76×98 inches of quilt batting

Finished quilt: 70×92 inches

Finished block: 16 inches square

Sashing: 5½ inches wide

Quantities specified are for 44/45-inch-wide, 100-percent-cotton fabrics. All measurements include a ¼-inch seam allowance. Sew with right sides together unless otherwise stated.

Quilt Notes

Trace and make templates for pattern pieces A–I, DD, and FF on the Pattern Sheet. Patterns are full size; add ¼-inch seam allowances when cutting the pieces from fabric. (*Note:* Because there are so many small pieces, and accurate cutting is essential, use plastic template material.)

Take care to transfer the dots on curved pattern pieces.

Cut the Fabrics

To make the best use of your fabrics, cut the pieces in the order that follows. Cutting requirements for blocks are given for one block,

with the number required for the entire quilt shown in parentheses.

From solid white, cut:

◆ 1—Pattern A (12)

◆ 4—Pattern H triangles (80)

◆ 4—Pattern I squares (80)

◆ 26—Pattern F sashing triangles (806)

◆ 6—Pattern D curved triangles (288)

◆ 4—*each* of patterns DD and DD reversed (48)

From solid green, cut:

◆ 24—Pattern F triangles (744)

◆ 2—*each* of patterns FF triangles and FF reversed triangles (62)

◆ 28—Pattern C (336)

◆ 10—2½×42-inch binding strips

From solid lavender, cut:

◆ 1—Pattern E strips (31)

◆ 4—Pattern B quarter-circles (48)

◆ 8—Pattern G diamonds (160)

Make the Blocks

1 Referring to Diagram 1, piece seven green C triangles and six white D triangles together to form an arc. Sew a DD and a reversed DD piece to each end of the arc.

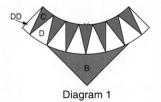

Diagram 1

instructions continued on page 240

2 Ease this arc to Piece B, matching dots on the curve to the middle of center C pieces (see Diagrams 2 and 3). Make four fan units.

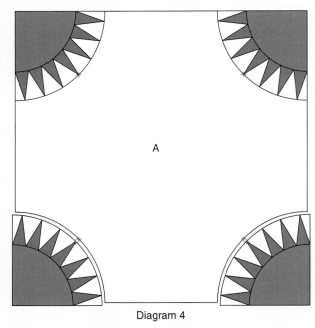

Diagram 2

Diagram 3

3 Set the fans into Piece A, matching dots to point of center C pieces and easing fullness at the curve (see Diagram 4). Make 12 blocks.

A

Diagram 4

Make the Sashing Strips

1 Referring to Diagram 5, *above right*, alternate 13 white F triangles and 12 green F triangles; stitch together along long sides to form a strip. Stitch an FF and a reversed FF piece to each end of the strip. Make two strips.

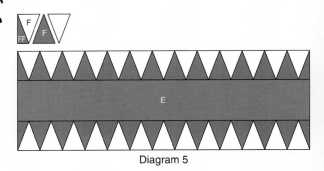

E

Diagram 5

2 Stitch a strip to each long side of the E rectangle, with green triangles adjacent to the lavender rectangle. Make 31 sashing strips.

Make the Star Blocks

Referring to Diagrams 6 and 7, join eight G diamonds to form a star. Set in H triangles and I squares to make a square (see tips for setting in seams in Quilter's Workshop beginning on *page 280*). Make a total of 20 corner blocks.

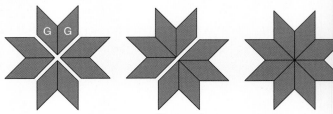

G G

Diagram 6

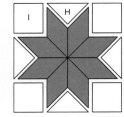

I H

Diagram 7

Assemble the Quilt Top

1 Arrange the quilt blocks in four rows of three blocks. Place a sashing strip between each block and along outer edges. Place a star block at the ends of each sashing strip.

2 Sew the units into rows; sew the rows together.

Quilt Assembly Diagram

Complete the Quilt

1 Enlarge the quilting patterns on the Pattern Sheet and transfer to the A and E pieces. Fill in center of A pieces and B pieces with a grid of 3/4-inch squares.

2 Layer the quilt top, batting, and backing. Baste the three layers together (see tips for completing the quilt in Quilter's Workshop).

3 Quilt as desired. Quilt marked designs and outline-quilt 1/4 inch from seams.

4 Use the solid green 2 1/2 ×42-inch strips to bind quilt (see binding tips in Quilter's Workshop).

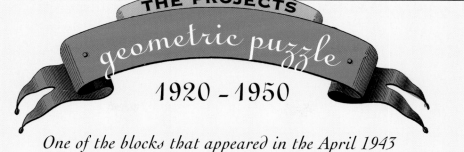

geometric puzzle

1920 – 1950

One of the blocks that appeared in the April 1943

issue of Successful Farming *makes a dramatic statement in this quilt.*

At that time patterns were sold by mail order.

Materials

5 yards of muslin for blocks, setting squares and
   triangles, and outer border
2 yards of solid orange for blocks and binding
1 yard of orange print for blocks and inner border
5 yards of backing fabric
67×86 inches of quilt batting

Finished quilt top: 60⁷/₈×80 inches
Geometric Puzzle block: 13¹/₂ inches square

Quantities specified are for 44/45-inch-wide,
100-percent-cotton fabrics. All measurements
include a ¹/₄-inch seam allowance. Sew with right
sides together unless otherwise stated.

Cut the Fabrics

To make the best use of your fabrics, cut the
pieces in the order that follows.

From muslin, cut:

- 7—3×42-inch strips for outer border
- 12—2×42-inch strips
- 3—20³/₈-inch squares, cutting each diagonally
   twice in an X for a total of 12 side setting
   triangles (you'll have 2 leftover triangles)
- 6—14-inch setting squares
- 2—10¹/₂-inch squares, cutting each in half
   diagonally for a total of four corner triangles
- 216—2³/₈-inch squares, cutting each in half
   diagonally for a total of 432 small triangles
- 12—3¹/₂-inch squares
- 4—4-inch squares for border corners

From solid orange, cut:

- 8—2¹/₂×42-inch binding strips
- 216—2³/₈-inch squares, cutting each in half
   diagonally for a total of 432 small triangles
- 24—1¹/₄×5-inch rectangles
- 24—1¹/₄×3¹/₂-inch rectangles

From orange print, cut:

- 6—2×42-inch strips
- 7—1¹/₂×42-inch strips for inner border

Assemble the Units

TRIANGLE UNITS:

1 Sew together one small muslin triangle
and one small solid orange triangle to make
a triangle-square (see Diagram 1 on *page 244*).
Press the seam allowance toward the solid orange
triangle. The pieced triangle-square should

instructions continued on page 244

measure 2 inches square, including the seam allowances. Repeat to make a total of 432 triangle-squares.

Diagram 1

Diagram 2

2 Referring to Diagram 2, sew together nine triangle-squares in three horizontal rows. Press the seam allowances in each row in one direction, alternating the direction with each row. Then join the rows to make a triangle unit. Press the seam allowances away from the center row. The pieced unit should measure 5 inches square, including the seam allowances. Repeat to make a total of 48 triangle units.

RECTANGLE UNITS:

1 Aligning long edges, sew two muslin 2×42-inch strips to an orange print 2×42-inch strip to make a strip set (see Diagram 3). Press the seam allowances toward the orange print strip. Repeat to make a total of six strip sets.

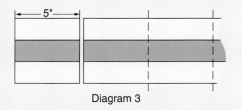

Diagram 3

2 Cut the strip sets into 5-inch-wide segments for a total of 48 rectangle units.

CENTER UNITS:

1 Referring to Diagram 4, sew a solid orange 1¼×3½-inch rectangle to opposite edges of a muslin 3½-inch square. Press the seam allowances toward the solid orange rectangles.

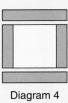

Diagram 4

2 Join a solid orange 1¼×5-inch rectangle to the remaining edges of the muslin 3½-inch square to make a center unit. Press the seam allowances toward the solid orange rectangles. The pieced center unit should measure 5 inches square, including seam allowances. Repeat to make a total of 12 center units.

Assemble the Blocks

1 Referring to Diagram 5, lay out four triangle units, four rectangle units, and one center unit in three horizontal rows. Sew together the pieces in each row. Press the seam allowances toward the rectangle units.

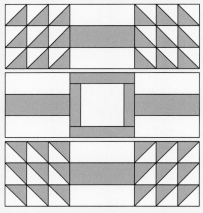

Diagram 5

2 Join the rows to make a Geometric Puzzle block. The finished block should measure 14 inches square, including the seam allowances.

3 Repeat Steps 1 and 2 to make a total of 12 Geometric Puzzle blocks.

Assemble the Quilt Center

1 Referring to the photograph, *above*, for placement, lay out the 12 pieced blocks, the six muslin 14-inch setting squares, 10 side setting triangles, and the four corner triangles in diagonal rows.

2 Sew together the pieces in each diagonal row, except for the corner triangles. Press the seam allowances toward the setting squares and setting triangles. Join the rows. Press the seam allowances in one direction.

3 Add the corner triangles to complete the quilt center. The pieced quilt center should measure $57^7/8\times77$ inches, including the seam allowances.

Add the Borders

1 Cut and piece the orange print $1^1/2\times42$-inch strips to make the following:
- 2—$1^1/2\times77$-inch inner border strips
- 2—$1^1/2\times57^7/8$-inch inner border strips

2 Cut and piece the muslin 3×42-inch strips to make the following:
- 2—3×77-inch outer border strips
- 2—3×$57^7/8$-inch outer border strips

3 Join one orange print $1^1/2\times77$-inch inner border strip and one muslin 3×77-inch outer border strip along a pair of long edges to make a side border unit. Press the seam allowances toward the orange print strip. Repeat to make a second side border unit.

4 Join a side border unit to each side edge of the quilt center. Press the seam allowances toward the border unit.

5 Sew together one orange print $1^1/2\times57^7/8$-inch inner border strip and one muslin 3×$57^7/8$-inch outer border strip along long edges. Press the seam allowances toward the orange print strip. Sew a muslin 4-inch square to each end of the pieced strip to make the top border unit. Join the top border to the top edge of the pieced quilt center. Press the seam allowances toward the pieced border.

6 Repeat step 5 to make the bottom border unit. Join it to the bottom edge of the pieced quilt center to complete the quilt top.

Complete the Quilt

1 Layer the quilt top, batting, and backing. Baste the three layers together (see tips for completing the quilt in Quilter's Workshop beginning on *page 280*).

2 Quilt as desired. The quilt shown has machine-quilted muslin setting squares and triangles, and the centers of the puzzle blocks have quilted feather motifs.

3 Use the solid orange $2^1/2\times42$-inch strips to bind the quilt (see binding tips in Quilter's Workshop).

1950-present

Unlimited fabrics, innovative tools, and updated technology unleash quilting possibilities.

By the late 1950s, many Americans had enjoyed a decade of relative prosperity. The Korean War was over and the Cold War had begun. Americans savored their status as citizens of the world's first superpower.

The hopeful era included the election of a youthful president, John F. Kennedy, in 1960. Causes such as the Civil Rights movement, equal rights for women, and the environmental movement captured the spirit of young and old alike. The space program, including a moon walk, drew people to their television sets. Other events, though—the Cuban Missile Crisis, the Vietnam War, antiwar demonstrations, and a string of assassinations—cast a pall over the time period.

War and Fabric Design

The United States participated in three wars between 1940 and 1969. Those situations often affected fabric design, usage, and availability. World War II, for example, cut deeply into domestic textile production. At the same time it led to rising patriotism. Red, white, and blue designs were popular and included stars, military insignia, nautical images, and Uncle Sam.

Postwar fabric designs decorated the baby boom that followed. Children's prints with colorful characters, cowboys, and baby animals were popular for children's rooms. Cottons for home decorating often carried such designs as flowers, fruits, or kitchen and garden tools. Popular colors were terra-cotta and moss green, often used with pale butter yellow. A generation of nonquilters preferred purchased rather than homemade decorating and clothing items in the prosperous postwar years.

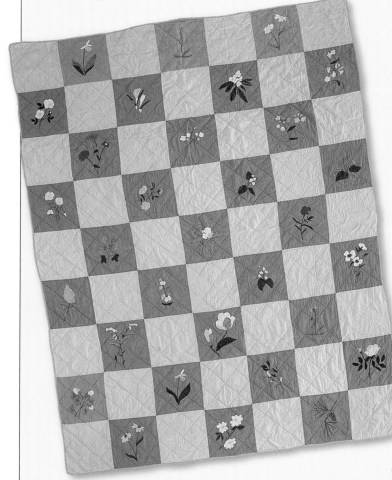

STATE FLOWER QUILT c. 1955
This quilt was designed by Marion Cheever Whiteside and was featured in Ladies' Home Journal *in 1955.*

continued on page 250

Fabric of the Time

The 1900s yielded a revolution in fabrics. The three wars in which the United States participated between 1940 and 1969 affected what fabrics looked like, how they were used, and where they could be purchased.

As women went to war or to work outside their homes, they often wore job-related uniforms rather than dresses, reducing their sewing needs. Home sewing was directed toward remaking old garments in updated styles, rather than the construction of clothing from new fabrics.

As women turned away from quiltmaking, the market for cotton fabrics declined. In the 1940s and 1950s, "miracle" fabrics appeared. Synthetics and fabrics with permanent pleats and crease-resistant finishes emerged.

In the early 1960s, the back-to-nature movement led to widespread interest in home sewing and quiltmaking. Preferred fabric colors were earth tones. During the Vietnam War, counterculture movements wore fabrics in bright colors and large flower-power motifs.

The late '60s brought easy-care polyester double-knits. Women quickly adopted double-knit for its versatility in garment construction and quiltmaking. Quilters used it to fashion such solid-color designs as "Giant Dahlia" and "Grandmother's Flower Garden," making colorful and durable quilts.

The last three decades of the century brought about the second major quilt revival of the 20th century. The textile industry began to answer the need for appropriate fabrics. Focus on the Bicentennial directed public attention to the quilts that were a part of America's heritage. Red, white, and blue fabrics and eagle, star, and other Bicentennial designs rose in popularity, as did Colonial and Early American images. Soon fabric manufacturers turned to early textiles to see how they might be reproduced.

(LEFT) *In the 1950s with the population booming, novelty or conversation prints that depicted make-believe and cartoon characters appealed to families with young children.*

Synthetics, such as nylon, rayon, acetate, Celanese, Dacron, and fabrics with crease-resistant finishes promised relief from ironing. For dedicated quilters, however, in the 1950s and 1960s there were a few calicoes in pink, blue, green, yellow, or lavender prints. The launch of Sputnik in 1957 inspired fabrics printed with rockets, ringed planets, and satellites. Favored colors during the 1950s were lime green or chartreuse, aqua, pink, and brown.

A back-to-nature movement in the early 1960s caused a turn to fabric colors in copper, rust, beige, dark gold, and olive green. And during the Vietnam War, counterculture movements were associated with fabrics in hot psychedelic colors (such as lime green and shocking pink) and oversize stylized floral motifs, as well as fabrics printed with peace signs and pacifist images.

Late in the period, polyester double-knit fabrics, which were washable, wrinkle-free, and seemingly indestructible, caught on with the public for clothing and crafts. Despite its weight and thickness, some quilters used it for solid-color quilt designs.

In the 1960s, *Better Homes and Gardens* published some of designer and author Jean Ray Laury's patterns. She is credited as one of the first contemporary quilting teachers who encouraged beginners to reinvent quiltmaking for themselves by experimenting with old techniques and new ideas. (In 1999 one of her quilts was chosen among the top 100 quilts of the 20th century.) Her inspiration helped to spark a new interest in the time-honored art form of quiltmaking.

America Celebrates

A magical spirit of pride seemed to blanket the nation as Americans prepared for the country's Bicentennial in 1976. From stenciling to basketmaking and from tole painting to quilting, Americans looked back to the crafts and skills that had withstood the country's growing pains.

ERA TIMELINE

1950 North Korea invades South Korea; cartoonist Charles Schulz's comic strip "Peanuts" debuts in seven newspapers. **1951** Color television has first telecast. **1952** Coronation of Elizabeth II takes place. **1953** Sir Edmund Hillary reaches the summit of Mount Everest; the Korean War ends. **1954** Jonas Salk creates the polio vaccine. **1955** Ray Kroc opens the first McDonald's restaurant; Disneyland opens. **1957** *American Bandstand* debuts on national television with host Dick Clark. **1959** Alaska and Hawaii become the 49th and 50th states. **1962** John Glenn is first American to orbit the Earth. **1963** Betty Friedan writes *The Feminine Mystique*, galvanizing the new feminist movement; November 22: President John F. Kennedy is assassinated in Dallas. **1964** The Civil Rights Act passes. **1965** The United States enters the Vietnam conflict; the St. Louis Gateway Arch is completed; the first countertop microwave oven for the home is produced by Amana. **1967** Dr. Christiaan Barnard performs the first heart transplant. **1969** Neil Armstrong becomes the first man to walk on the moon's

Traditional-style quilts continued to appeal to magazine readers through the '50s. With the dawning of the '60s, quilt design was destined for a new direction.

While the technique was, at its heart, basically the same, the invention of quilting tools made efficient work of projects. Tools included rotary cutters, cutting mats, transparent rulers in various sizes, sewing machines with integrated computers, software for desktop computers to help in color and setting selections, plastic-coated freezer paper, and template vinyl and plastic.

At the same time, early quilting bees evolved into classes at the growing number of colorful quilt shops around the country. Groups of quilters formed local, regional, and nationwide guilds. Around the country there were retreats, workshops, and all-night quilting sessions that promoted art and fun.

Local and national quilt shows developed to showcase quilts, share ideas, display techniques, and give vendors a venue for marketing tools. County and state fairs found room to display growing numbers of quilted items, from bedding to clothing.

Magazines, including *Better Homes and Gardens American Patchwork & Quilting*, and numerous books shared new ideas, color suggestions, and techniques for successful quilting. Television shows focused on sharing quilting tips and ideas for completing projects.

All these years later, quilting continues to serve its original purpose—to create warmth and beauty for those we love.

surface. 1972 *M*A*S*H*, the popular television series based on a mobile surgical unit during the Korean War, begins an 11-season run. 1974 Richard Nixon resigns as president. 1976 The United States celebrates its Bicentennial. 1979 OLFA develops the first rotary cutter. 1980 The American Quilt Study Group (AQSG) is founded. 1981 IBM introduces the personal computer; Sandra Day O'Connor becomes the first woman Supreme Court justice. 1982 The blockbuster movie *E.T.: The Extraterrestrial* opens in theaters. 1987 The AIDS Memorial Quilt is displayed on the National Mall in Washington, D.C. 1989 The Berlin Wall comes down. 1992 The World Wide Web is born. 1993 *The Bridges of Madison County* by Robert James Waller is a fictional best seller. 1997 *Harry Potter and the Sorcerer's Stone*, the first in a series of popular children's books, is published; *Titanic* is the most successful movie ever. 2000 At age 24, Tiger Woods is the youngest golfer to win the U.S. Open, British Open, PGA, and Masters tournaments. 2001 September 11: World Trade Center towers in New York City collapse in terrorist attacks.

posy patch

1950-present

Blooms borrowed from Jean Ray Laury's
appliquéd headboard in a 1964 issue of Better Homes and Gardens
magazine make a cheery accent pillow.

Materials

½ yard of tan batik for appliqué foundation
  and pillow backing
Scraps of assorted green batiks for leaf and
  stem appliqués
Scraps of yellow, red, orange, pink, peach,
  gold, and blue batiks for leaf, flower, and
  butterfly appliqués
12×16-inch pillow form
¼ yard of lightweight fusible web
Machine embroidery thread in

Finished pillow: 12×16 inches

Quantities specified are for 44/45-inch-wide,
100-percent-cotton fabrics. All measurements
include a ¼-inch seam allowance. Sew with
right sides together unless otherwise stated.

Cut the Fabrics

To make the best use of your fabrics, cut
the pieces in the order that follows. The
patterns are on the Pattern Sheet.

To use fusible web for appliqué, as
was done in this project, complete the
following steps.

1 Lay the fusible web, paper side up,
  over the patterns. Use a pencil to
trace each pattern the specified number
of times, leaving ½-inch between
tracings. Cut out the pieces roughly
¼-inch outside of the traced lines.

2 Following the manufacturer's instructions, press the fusible web shapes onto the backs of the designated fabrics; let cool. Cut out the fabric shapes on the drawn lines. Peel off the paper backings.

From tan batik, cut:
- 1—14×18-inch rectangle for appliqué foundation
- 1—13×17-inch rectangle for pillow backing

From assorted green batiks, cut:
- 1 *each of patterns A, B, C, D, E, F, L, and M*
- 3—Pattern H
- 2—Pattern I
- 3—Pattern K

From assorted yellow, red, orange, pink, peach, gold, and blue batiks, cut:
- 1—*each of patterns G, G reversed, I, J, L, N, O, P, Q, and R*
- 5—Pattern H

Appliqué the Pillow Top

1 Referring to the photograph, *opposite,* and the full-size patterns on the Pattern Sheet, position the prepared flower and leaf appliqué pieces on the tan batik 14×18-inch rectangle. When pleased with the arrangement, fuse them in place.

2 Use matching or contrasting machine embroidery thread to appliqué the pieces to the foundation. The pillow shown *opposite* has a dense satin stitch holding the flower and leaf shapes in place.

3 Centering the appliquéd design, trim the appliquéd pillow top to measure 13×17 inches, including the seam allowances.

Complete the Pillow

1 Stitch together the appliquéd pillow top and the tan batik pillow backing, using a ½-inch seam allowance and leaving a 5- to 6-inch opening at the bottom (see Diagram 1).

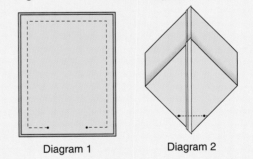

Diagram 1   Diagram 2

2 To shape the corners, match seams on adjacent sides of pillow top, creating a flattened triangle (see Diagram 2). Measure and mark a dot 2½ inches from the point of the corner on the two folded edges. Draw a line between the dots, then stitch across the drawn line. Repeat at each corner; press. Turn the pillow right side out.

3 Insert the pillow form through the opening. Whipstitch the opening closed.

star spangled

1950–present

More than 25 years have passed since

this quilt—created for America's Bicentennial—graced the cover of

Better Homes and Gardens *magazine. The color scheme remains the same,*

though our current fabrics carry star and flag motifs.

Materials

5¼ yards of red print for blocks, sashing, outer border, and binding

1½ yards of blue print for blocks

4½ yards of solid white for blocks, sashing, and inner border

⅜ yard of patriotic print for sashing squares

7½ yards of backing fabric

89×103 inches of quilt batting

Finished quilt top: 82½×97 inches

Finished block: 12 inches square

Quantities specified are for 44/45-inch-wide, 100-percent-cotton fabrics. All measurements include a ¼-inch seam allowance. Sew with right sides together unless otherwise stated.

Cut the Fabrics

To make the best use of your fabrics, cut the pieces in the order that follows. The patterns are on the Pattern Sheet. (See tips for making templates in Quilter's Workshop beginning on *page 280*).

Cut the border strips the length of the fabric (parallel to the selvage). The measurements are mathematically correct. You may wish to cut the border strips longer than specified to allow for possible sewing differences.

From red print, cut:

♦ 2—2½×93½-inch outer border strips

♦ 2—2½×83-inch outer border strips

♦ 9—2½×42-inch binding strips

♦ 142—1¼×12½-inch sashing strips

♦ 120—Pattern A

From blue print, cut:

♦ 120—Pattern A reversed

From solid white, cut:

♦ 2—2¼×90-inch inner border strips

♦ 2—2¼×79-inch inner border strips

♦ 71—1½×12½-inch sashing strips

♦ 120—4-inch squares, or 120 of Pattern C

♦ 120—Pattern B

From patriotic print, cut:

♦ 42—3-inch sashing squares

instructions continued on page 256

star spangled

1950–present

Assemble the Blocks

1 For one Star block, you will need four of red print Pattern A, four of blue print Pattern A reversed, four white B triangles, and four white C squares.

2 Pin together one red print A and one blue print A reversed diamond. Carefully align the matching points (see Diagram 1). A matching point is where the seam should begin or end, $\frac{1}{4}$ inch from the end of each piece, so you do not sew into a seam allowance needed for a future piece. Sew together diamonds, stopping precisely at the matching points, to make a diamond pair. Repeat to make a total of four diamond pairs.

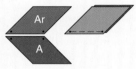

Diagram 1

3 With right sides together, pin one piece of the diamond pair to one short side of the B triangle. (See Diagram 2 for placement of the B triangle and diamond pair.)

Diagram 2   Diagram 3

4 Match the seam's matching points, pushing a pin through both fabric layers to check the alignment. Machine-stitch the seam, backstitching to secure ends and stopping at the matching points (see Diagram 3). Do not stitch into the $\frac{1}{4}$-inch seam allowances. Remove the unit from the sewing machine. Bring the adjacent edge of the angled unit up and align it with the other short edge of the triangle. Insert a pin in each corner to align matching points, then pin the remainder of the seam.

Machine-stitch between matching points as before. Press seam allowances of the set-in piece away from it. Repeat to make a total of four double-diamond subunits.

5 Sew together two of the double-diamond subunits as shown in Diagram 4 to form one partial-star unit. Align the matching points as before and do not sew into the $\frac{1}{4}$-inch seam allowances at each end. Attach a solid white square to one of the partial-star units, following the directions for attaching the triangles. Repeat with the remaining two double-diamond subunits. Sew together the two partial-star units (see Diagram 5), making sure not to sew into the $\frac{1}{4}$-inch seam allowance.

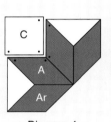
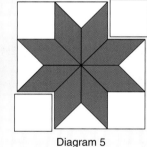

Diagram 4   Diagram 5

6 Set in the remaining two solid white C squares to complete a Star block. The pieced Star block should measure $12\frac{1}{2}$ inches square, including the seam allowances.

7 Repeat steps 2–6 to make a total of 30 Star blocks.

Assemble the Striped Sashing Strips

1 For each striped sashing strip, you will need two red print $1\frac{1}{4} \times 12\frac{1}{2}$-inch sashing strips and one solid white $1\frac{1}{2} \times 12\frac{1}{2}$-inch sashing strip.

2 Referring to Diagram 6, join a red print strip to each long side of the solid white strip.

Diagram 6

Press the seam allowances toward the red print strips. The striped sashing strip should measure 3×12$\frac{1}{2}$ inches, including the seam allowances.

3 Repeat step 2 to make a total of 71 striped sashing strips.

Assemble the Quilt Center

1 Referring to the photograph, *below right,* lay out the 30 Star blocks, the 71 striped sashing strips, and the forty-two 3-inch patriotic print sashing squares in 13 horizontal rows.

2 Sew together the pieces in each row. Press the seam allowances in one direction, alternating the direction with each row. Join the rows to make the quilt center. Press the seam allowances in one direction. The pieced quilt center should measure 75$\frac{1}{2}$×90 inches, including the seam allowances.

Add the Borders

1 Sew one solid white 2$\frac{1}{4}$×90-inch inner border strip to each side edge of the pieced quilt center. Then add one solid white 2$\frac{1}{4}$×79-inch inner border strip to the top and bottom edges of the pieced quilt center. Press all seam allowances toward the solid white border.

2 Join one red print 2$\frac{1}{2}$×93$\frac{1}{2}$-inch outer border strip to each side edge of the quilt center. Then add one red print 2$\frac{1}{2}$×83-inch outer border strip to the top and bottom edges of the pieced quilt center to complete the quilt top. Press all seam allowances toward the red print border.

Complete the Quilt

1 Layer the quilt top, batting, and backing. Baste the three layers together (see tips for completing the quilt in Quilter's Workshop beginning on *page 280*).

2 Quilt as desired. The quilt shown is machine-stitched through the center of each diamond in each Star block and in the middle of each sashing unit.

3 Use the red print 2$\frac{1}{2}$×42-inch strips to bind the quilt (see binding tips in Quilter's Workshop).

star spangled

1950–present

Materials for One Pillow Sham

$^{1}/_{4}$ yard of red print for block and border

$1^{1}/_{2}$ yards of blue print for block, border, and pillow sham back

$^{1}/_{4}$ yard of solid white for block and border

$^{3}/_{4}$ yard of muslin for lining

26×31 inches of quilt batting

Finished size: Fits one standard bed pillow

Cut the Fabrics

To make the best use of your fabrics, cut the pieces in the order that follows.

From red print, cut:

- 2—$2^{1}/_{2}$×$12^{1}/_{2}$-inch inner border strips
- 2—$2^{1}/_{2}$×$16^{1}/_{2}$-inch inner border strips
- 4—Pattern A

From blue print, cut:

- 2—21×32-inch rectangles for pillow sham back
- 2—$4^{1}/_{2}$×$20^{1}/_{2}$-inch outer border strips
- 2—2×$28^{1}/_{2}$-inch outer border strips
- 4—Pattern A reversed

From solid white, cut:

- 2—$2^{1}/_{2}$×$16^{1}/_{2}$-inch middle border strips
- 2—$21^{1}/_{2}$×$20^{1}/_{2}$-inch middle border strips
- 4—Pattern B
- 4—4-inch squares, or 4 of Pattern C

Assemble the Pillow Top

1 Piece one Star block as for quilt. See "Assemble the Blocks" on *page 256*.

2 Referring to Diagram 1, sew the red print $2^{1}/_{2}$×$12^{1}/_{2}$-inch inner border strips to opposite edges of the pieced Star block. Sew the red print $2^{1}/_{2}$×$16^{1}/_{2}$-inch inner border strips to remaining edges of block. Press the seam allowances toward the red print border.

3 Referring to Diagram 1, sew the solid white $2^{1}/_{2}$×$16^{1}/_{2}$-inch middle border strips to opposite edges of the block. Sew the solid white $2^{1}/_{2}$×$20^{1}/_{2}$-inch middle border strips to remaining edges of the block. Press the seam allowances toward the red print border.

4 Referring to Diagram 1, sew the blue print $4^{1}/_{2}$×$20^{1}/_{2}$-inch outer border strips to

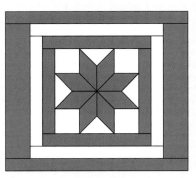

Diagram 1

opposite edges of the block. Sew the blue print 2×28½-inch outer border strips to remaining edges to complete the pillow sham top. Press the seam allowances toward the blue print border.

5 Layer the pillow sham top, batting, and lining according to tips in Quilter's Workshop beginning on *page 280*. Quilt as desired. The pillow sham shown is machine-quilted through the center of each diamond of the Star block and outline-quilted on the borders of the pillow sham.

6 Centering the Star block, trim the quilted pillow sham top to measure 21×27 inches, including the seam allowances.

Assemble the Pillow Sham

1 With wrong sides together, fold the two blue print 21×32-inch rectangles in half to form two 21×16-inch double-thick pillow sham back pieces.

2 Overlap the two folded edges by about 4 inches. Using a ½-inch seam allowance, stitch the pieces along the long edges and across the folds to create a single pillow sham back.

3 With right sides together, layer and pin the edges of the pillow sham top and back together; join. Trim the pillow sham back and corner seam allowances as needed. Turn the sham right side out. Insert the pillow.

THE STARS BEHIND THE QUILT

In celebration of America's 200th birthday, *Better Homes and Gardens* magazine featured a star-studded quilt on the cover of the February 1976 issue. Mrs. Arthur "Willie" Woodburn of Texas, who pieced the quilt, and Mabel Metcalf of Oklahoma, inset *right,* who quilted it, were two of seven quilters featured in the magazine as the "Southwest Quilters."

Having grown up in the early part of the 20th century, the women and their quilting memories created a charming American story rooted in heritage and love. They spoke of times when, as Willie explained, "everything was precious." As a young girl, she would pick up fabric

pieces that her mother dropped on the floor and stash them away in her scrap box. "They taught us not to waste," said a featured quilter from New Mexico.

While some of the women quilted in order to pay for food and keep warm, others quilted to keep memories alive. "I quilted for all my babies and grandbabies," said Mabel. "Keeps me busy, quiltin' for all of 'em."

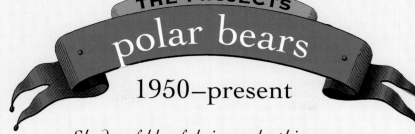

polar bears

1950–present

Shades of blue fabrics make this square

quilt composed of blocks resembling bear paw print, a cabin-style favorite.

Appliquéd bears and snowflakes embellish two opposite corners.

Materials

$7/8$ yard of light blue print for blocks

$1/2$ yard of white print for blocks and appliqués

$7/8$ yard of solid navy for blocks and binding

$5/8$ yard of blue print for sashing and inner border

$7/8$ yard of navy winter print for outer border

3 yards of backing fabric

53-inch square of quilt batting

$1/2$ yard lightweight fusible web

Finished quilt top: $46^{1}/_{2}$ inches square

Finished block: $10^{1}/_{2}$ inches square

Quantities specified are for 44/45-inch-wide, 100-percent-cotton fabrics. All measurements include a $1/4$-inch seam allowance. Sew with right sides together unless otherwise stated.

Cut the Fabrics

To make the best use of your fabrics, cut the pieces in the order that follows. Cut the sashing and border strips the length of the fabric (parallel to the selvage). The measurements are mathematically correct. You may wish to cut sashing and border strips longer than specified to allow for possible sewing differences. The appliqué border patterns A and B are on the Pattern Sheet.

From light blue print, cut:

- ♦ 36—2×5-inch rectangles
- ♦ 36—2-inch squares
- ♦ 72—$2^{3}/_{8}$-inch squares, cutting each in half diagonally to make a total of 144 triangles

From white print, cut:

- ♦ 36—$3^{1}/_{2}$-inch squares for Patterns A and B

From solid navy, cut:

- ♦ 72—$2^{3}/_{8}$-inch squares, cutting each in half diagonally to make a total of 144 triangles
- ♦ 9—2-inch squares
- ♦ 5—$2^{1}/_{4}$×42-inch binding strips

From blue print, cut:

- ♦ 4—2×35-inch strips for sashing and inner border
- ♦ 2—2×38-inch inner border strips
- ♦ 6—2×11-inch sashing strips

From navy winter print, cut:

- ♦ 5—5×42-inch strips for outer border

Assemble the Blocks

1 Sew together a solid navy triangle and a light blue print triangle to make a triangle-square (see Diagram 1). Press the seam allowance toward

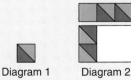

Diagram 1   Diagram 2

instructions continued on page 262

square should measure 2 inches square, including the seam allowances. Repeat to make a total of 16 triangle-squares.

2 Referring to Diagram 2 on *page 261* for placement, sew together two rows of two triangle-squares. Press the seam allowances in one direction.

3 Sew one triangle-square row to the left edge of a white print 3½-inch square. Press the seam allowance toward the white print square. Join a light blue print 2-inch square to the remaining triangle-square row. Press the seam allowance toward the light blue print square. Sew this row to the top edge of the white print 3½-inch square to make a Bear's Paw unit. Press the seam allowance in one direction. The pieced Bear's Paw unit should measure 5 inches square, including the seam allowances.

4 Repeat steps 2 and 3 to make a total of four Bear's Paw units.

5 Referring to Diagram 3, lay out the four Bear's Paw units, four light blue print 2×5-inch rectangles, and one solid navy 2-inch square in three horizontal rows.

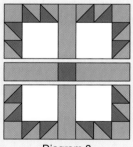
Diagram 3

6 Sew together the pieces in each row. Press the seam allowances in each row toward the light blue print rectangles. Join the rows to make a Bear's Paw block. Press the seam allowances toward the center row. The pieced Bear's Paw

block should measure 11 inches square, including the seam allowances.

7 Repeat steps 1 through 6 to make a total of nine Bear's Paw blocks.

Assemble the Quilt Center

1 Referring to the photograph *opposite* for placement, lay out the nine Bear's Paw blocks and the six blue print 2×11-inch sashing strips in three horizontal rows, alternating blocks and strips. Sew together the blocks and sashing strips in each row to make three block rows.

2 Lay out the three block rows and two blue print 2×35-inch sashing strips; join to make the quilt center. The pieced quilt center should measure 35 inches square, including the seam allowances.

Add the Borders

1 Sew a blue print 2×35-inch inner border strip to the top and bottom edges of the pieced quilt center. Then add a blue print 2×38-inch inner border strip to each side edge of the pieced quilt center. Press all seam allowances toward the blue print border.

2 Cut and piece the navy winter print 5×42-inch strips to measure the following:
- 2—5×47-inch outer border strips
- 2—5×38-inch outer border strips

3 Sew one navy winter print 5×38-inch outer border strip to each the top and bottom edges of the pieced quilt center. Then add a navy winter print 5×47-inch outer border strip to each side edge of the quilt center to complete the quilt top. Press all seam allowances toward the navy winter print outer border.

Appliqué the Quilt Border

1 Lay the lightweight fusible web, paper side up, over the patterns found on the Pattern Sheet. With a pencil, trace Pattern A twice, Pattern A reversed twice, and Pattern B twice. Cut out the pieces roughly ¼ inch outside the traced lines.

2 Following the manufacturer's instructions, press the fusible web patterns onto the back of the white print. Let the fabric cool. Cut out the shapes on the drawn lines. Peel the paper from the fabric.

3 Referring to the photograph, *above*, for placement, place the appliqué shapes on the outer border of the quilt top. Fuse in place with a hot, dry iron.

4 Machine-blanket-stitch the fused shapes in place.

Complete the Quilt

1 Layer the quilt top, batting, and backing. Baste the three layers together (see tips for completing the quilt in Quilter's Workshop beginning on *page 280*). Quilt as desired.

2 Use the solid navy 2½×42-inch strips to bind the quilt (see binding tips in Quilter's Workshop).

under the sea

1950–present

Pieced in two sizes, each fish on this quilt is created in shades of yellow and gold and detailed with a button eye. Subtle blue prints and wavy quilting lend the appearance of water to the background.

Materials

$^1/_3$ yard total of assorted dark gold prints for fish

$^1/_8$ yard of yellow print for fish

$1^1/_4$ yards total of assorted blue prints
for background

$^1/_8$ yard of dark gold print for inner border

$^3/_4$ yard of dark blue print for outer border
and binding

$1^1/_4$ yards of backing fabric

45×38 inches of quilt batting

14 small buttons for fish eyes

Finished quilt top: 39×$32^1/_2$ inches

Finished small fish block: 4 inches square

Finished large fish block: 6 inches square

Quantities specified are for 44/45-inch-wide, 100-percent-cotton fabrics. All measurements include a $^1/_4$-inch seam allowance. Sew with right sides together unless otherwise stated.

Cut the Fabrics

To make the best use of your fabrics, cut the pieces in the order that follows. To make templates of the patterns, which are found on the Pattern Sheet, see tips for making templates in Quilter's Workshop beginning on *page 280*. The setting and corner triangles initially are cut larger than necessary; they will be trimmed before the borders are added.

From assorted dark gold prints, cut:

- 3—$3^7/_8$-inch squares, cutting each in half diagonally for a total of six A triangles, or six of Pattern A
- 4—$2^7/_8$-inch squares, cutting each in half diagonally for a total of eight C triangles, or eight of Pattern C
- 12—2-inch squares
- 16—$1^1/_2$-inch squares
- 6—*each* of patterns B and B reversed
- 8—*each* of patterns D and D reversed

From yellow print, cut:

- 3—$3^7/_8$-inch squares, cutting each in half diagonally for a total of six A triangles, or six of Pattern A
- 4—$2^7/_8$-inch squares, cutting each in half diagonally for a total of eight C triangles, or eight of Pattern C

From assorted blue prints, cut:

- 3—$9^3/_4$-inch squares, cutting each diagonally twice in an X for a total of 12 setting triangles
- 2—$5^1/_2$-inch squares, cutting each in half diagonally for a total of 4 corner triangles (you'll have 1 leftover triangle)
- 1—$4^1/_2$-inch square
- 6—$3^1/_2$-inch squares
- 1—$2^1/_2$×$11^1/_2$-inch rectangle
- 3—$2^1/_2$×$8^1/_2$-inch rectangles
- 7—$2^1/_2$×$6^1/_2$-inch rectangles
- 1—$2^1/_2$×$5^1/_2$-inch rectangle
- 2—$2^1/_2$×$4^1/_2$-inch rectangles

instructions continued on page 266

- 8—2¹/₂-inch squares
- 12—2×3¹/₂-inch rectangles
- 6—*each* of patterns B and B reversed
- 8—*each* of patterns D and D reversed
- 2—1¹/₂×10¹/₂-inch rectangles
- 7—1¹/₂×8¹/₂-inch rectangles
- 12—1¹/₂×7¹/₂-inch rectangles
- 4—1¹/₂×6¹/₂-inch rectangles
- 2—1¹/₂×5¹/₂-inch rectangles
- 5—1¹/₂×4¹/₂-inch rectangles
- 16—1¹/₂×2¹/₂-inch rectangles

From gold print, cut:

- 2—1×33¹/₂-inch inner border strips
- 2—1×28-inch inner border strips

From dark blue print, cut:

- 2—3×34¹/₂-inch outer border strips
- 2—3×33-inch outer border strips
- 4—2¹/₂×42-inch binding strips

Assemble the Large Fish Blocks

1 Sew together one dark gold print A triangle and one yellow print A triangle to make a triangle-square (see Diagram 1). Press the seam allowance toward the dark gold print triangle. The pieced triangle-square should measure 3¹/₂ inches square, including the seam allowances.

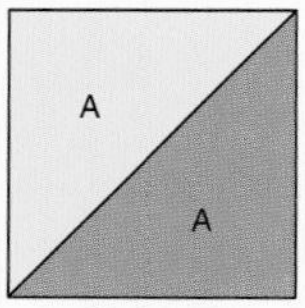

Diagram 1

2 Use a quilter's pencil to mark a diagonal line on the wrong side of two dark gold print 2-inch squares for accurate sewing lines. (To prevent your fabric from stretching as you draw the lines, place 220-grit sandpaper under the squares.)

3 With right sides together, align a marked dark gold print 2-inch square with the left end of an blue print 2×3¹/₂-inch rectangle (see Diagram 2, noting the direction of the marked diagonal line). Stitch on the marked line; trim the seam allowance to ¹/₄ inch. Press the attached triangle open.

Diagram 2

4 Repeat Step 3, except run the diagonal sewing line in the opposite direction (see Diagram 3).

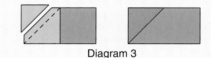

Diagram 3

5 Sew together one dark gold print B triangle and one blue print B triangle (see Diagram 4). Press the seam allowance toward the dark gold print triangle.

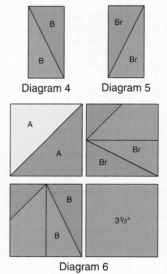

Diagram 4   Diagram 5

Diagram 6

6 Repeat Step 5 using one dark gold print B reversed triangle and one blue print B reversed triangle (see Diagram 5). Press the seam allowance toward the dark gold print triangle.

Diagram 8

7 Referring to Diagram 6, *opposite*, for placement, lay out the pieced units and one blue print 3$\frac{1}{2}$-inch square in four sections. Sew together the pieces in each section.

8 Lay out the sections in two rows. Sew each row together. Press the seam allowances in opposite directions. Then join the rows to make a large fish block. Press the seam allowance in one direction. The pieced large fish block should measure 6$\frac{1}{2}$ inches square, including seam allowances.

9 Repeat steps 1–8 to make a total of six large fish blocks.

Assemble the Small Fish Blocks

1 Sew together one dark gold print C triangle and one yellow print C triangle to make a triangle-square (see Diagram 7). Press the seam allowance toward the dark gold triangle. The pieced triangle-square should measure 2$\frac{1}{2}$ inches square, including the seam allowances.

Diagram 7

2 Use a quilter's pencil to mark a diagonal line on the wrong side of two dark gold print 1$\frac{1}{2}$-inch squares for accurate sewing lines. (To prevent your fabric from stretching as you draw the lines, place 220-grit sandpaper under the squares.)

3 With right sides together, align a marked dark gold print 1$\frac{1}{2}$-inch square with the left end of a blue print 1$\frac{1}{2}$×2$\frac{1}{2}$-inch rectangle (see Diagram 8). Stitch on the marked line; trim the seam allowance to $\frac{1}{4}$ inch. Press the attached triangle open.

4 Repeat Step 3, except run the diagonal sewing line in the opposite direction (see Diagram 9).

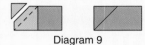

Diagram 9

5 Sew together one dark gold print D triangle and one blue print D triangle (see Diagram 10). Press the seam allowance toward the dark gold print triangle.

Diagram 10   Diagram 11

6 Repeat Step 5 using one dark gold print D reversed triangle and one blue print D reversed triangle (see Diagram 11). Press the seam allowance toward the dark gold print triangle.

7 Referring to Diagram 12 for placement, lay out the pieced units and one blue print 2$\frac{1}{2}$-inch square in four sections. Sew together the pieces in each section.

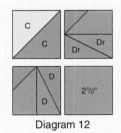

Diagram 12

8 Lay the sections in two rows. Sew each row together. Press seam allowances in opposite directions. Join the rows to make a small fish block. The pieced small fish block should measure 4$\frac{1}{2}$ inches square, including the seam allowances.

9 Repeat steps 1–8 to make a total of eight small fish blocks.

instructions continued on page 268

under the sea

1950–present

Assemble the Quilt Center

1 Referring to the Quilt Assembly Diagram *opposite,* lay out the pieced large fish blocks, pieced small fish blocks, the blue print 4½-inch square, the remaining blue print rectangles, and the blue print setting triangles in diagonal rows.

2 Sew together the pieces in each diagonal row. Press the seam allowances in one direction, alternating the direction with each row. Then join the rows.

3 Add the three blue print corner triangles to complete the quilt center. Press the seam allowances toward the corner triangles.

4 Leaving ¼-inch seam allowances beyond the block corners, trim the edges of the pieced quilt center to measure 33½×27 inches, including the seam allowances.

Add the Borders

The following border strip measurements are mathematically correct. Before cutting, measure your pieced quilt center and adjust the border strip lengths accordingly.

1 Sew one gold print 1×33½-inch inner border strip to the top and bottom edges of the pieced quilt center. Then add a gold print 1×28-inch inner border strip to each side edge of the pieced quilt center. Press all seam allowances toward the gold print border.

2 Sew one dark blue print 3×34½-inch outer border strip to the top and bottom edges of the pieced quilt center. Then add a dark blue print 3×33-inch outer border strip to each side edge of the pieced quilt center to complete the quilt top. Press all seam allowances toward the dark blue print border.

Complete the Quilt

1 Layer the quilt top, batting, and backing. Baste the three layers together (see tips for completing the quilt in Quilter's Workshop beginning on *page 280*). Quilt as desired.

2 Use the dark blue print 2½×42-inch strips to bind the quilt (see binding tips in Quilter's Workshop). Sew buttons on fish blocks for eyes.

Note: To view this quilt using alternate fabrics, see *pages 246–247.*

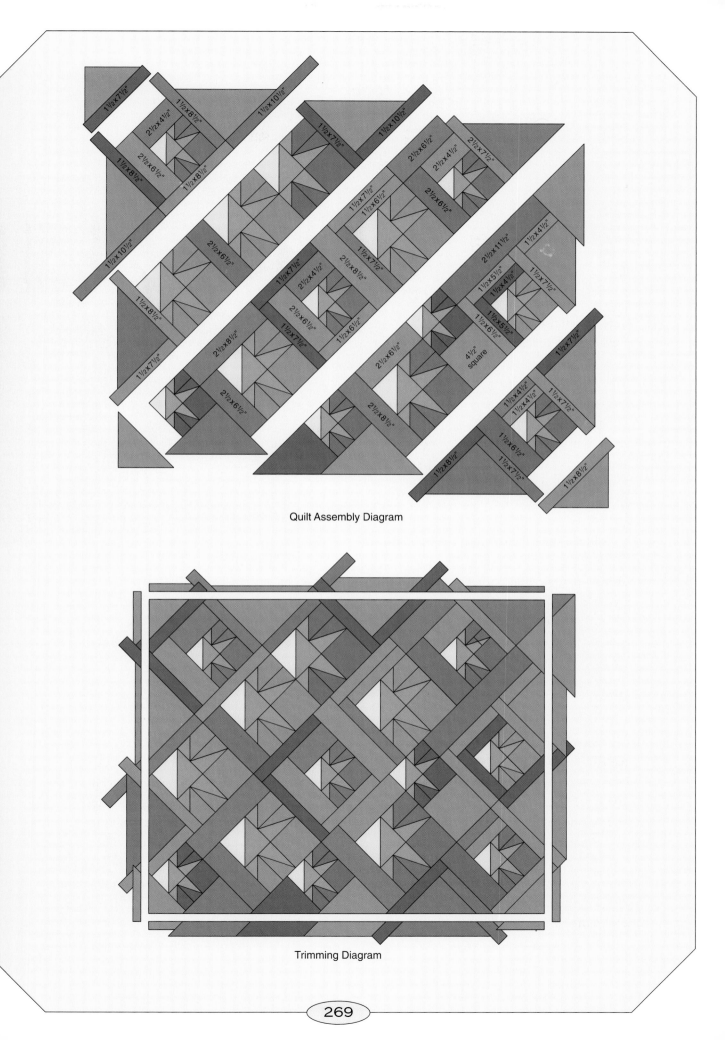

Quilt Assembly Diagram

Trimming Diagram

vines & roses

1950–present

Contemporary flowers, fabrics, and borders

make this bed quilt playfully sweet. Pink, purple, and green accent

the gold and tan backgrounds.

Materials

1 yard total of assorted gold and tan prints for
blocks and borders

¼ yard of tan print for outer border

¼ yard of pink print for flower appliqués
and borders

¼ yard of pink plaid for sashing and borders

¼ yard of purple-and-green plaid for sashing
squares and borders

¼ yard of lavender print for flower center
appliqués and borders

½ yard total of assorted green prints for leaf and
vine appliqués and borders

⅔ yard of green plaid for scalloped edging

2 yards of fusible web

1 yard of backing fabric

36×44 inches of quilt batting

No. 8 black perle cotton

Finished quilt: 30×38 inches

Quantities specified are for 44/45-inch-wide,
100-percent-cotton fabrics. All measurements
include a ¼-inch seam allowance. Sew with right
sides together unless otherwise stated.

Cut the Fabrics

The appliqué patterns A–G are on the Pattern
Sheet. To make the best use of your fabrics, cut
the pieces in the order that follows.

From assorted gold and tan prints, cut:

◆ 9—4½-inch squares for appliqué foundations

◆ 2—4½×16½-inch rectangles for appliqué border

◆ 2—4½×14½-inch rectangles for appliqué border

◆ 1—4½×9½-inch rectangle for appliqué border

◆ 1—4½×8½-inch rectangle for appliqué border

◆ 1—4½×7½-inch rectangle for appliqué border

◆ 1—4½×6½-inch rectangle for appliqué border

◆ 1—4½×5½-inch rectangle for appliqué border

◆ 1—4½-inch square for appliqué border

◆ 1—4½×3½-inch rectangle for appliqué border

◆ 9—2×4¾-inch rectangles for inner border

◆ 21—2½×2-inch rectangles for outer border

From tan print, cut:

◆ 2—3×30½-inch outer border strips

From pink print, cut:

◆ 4—2×4¾-inch rectangles for inner border

◆ 6—2½×2-inch rectangles for outer border

From pink plaid, cut:

◆ 1—2×4¾-inch rectangle for inner border

◆ 21—2×4½-inch rectangles for slashing

◆ 2—2½×2-inch rectangles for outer border

From purple-and-green plaid, cut:

◆ 3—2×4¾-inch rectangles for inner border

◆ 4—2½×2-inch rectangles for outer border

◆ 12—2-inch squares for sashing

From lavender print, cut:

◆ 4—2×4¾-inch rectangles for inner border

◆ 5—2½×2-inch rectangles for outer border

From assorted green prints, cut:

◆ 3—2×4¾-inch rectangles for inner border

◆ 6—2½×2-inch rectangles for outer border

instructions continued on page 272

From green plaid, cut:

- 2—5×38½-inch strips for scalloped edging
- 2—5×30½-inch strips for scalloped edging

Assemble the Quilt Center

1 Sew a purple-and-green plaid 2-inch square to a pink plaid 2×4½-inch rectangle to make a sashing unit (see Diagram 1). Press the seam allowance toward the pink plaid rectangle. Repeat to make a total of 12 sashing units.

Diagram 1

2 Sew one of the remaining pink plaid 2×4½-inch rectangles to a gold or tan print 4½-inch square to make a pieced appliqué foundation (see Diagram 2). Press the seam allowance toward the pink plaid rectangle. Repeat to make a total of nine pieced appliqué foundations.

Diagram 2

3 Referring to Diagram 3 for placement, lay out four sashing units and three pieced appliqué foundations in a horizontal row. Sew together to make a block row. Press the seam allowances in one direction. Repeat to make a total of three block rows, pressing the seam allowances in alternate directions.

Diagram 3

4 Referring to the Quilt Assembly Diagram for placement, lay out the block rows. Join the rows to make the quilt center. Press the seam allowances in one direction. The pieced quilt center should measure 18½×17 inches, including the seam allowances.

Assemble and Add the Borders

1 Aligning long edges, join 12 assorted gold or tan print, pink print, pink plaid, purple-and-green plaid, lavender print, and green print 2×4¾-inch rectangles to make an inner border strip that measures 4¾×18½ inches including the seam allowances (see Quilt Assembly Diagram). Press the seam allowances in one direction. Repeat to make a second inner border strip.

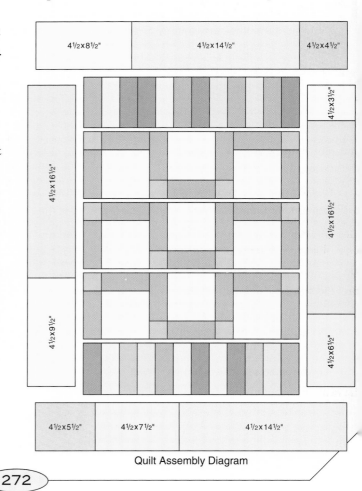

Quilt Assembly Diagram

2 Sew an inner border strip to the top and bottom edges of the pieced quilt center. Press the seam allowances toward the quilt center.

3 Sew together the gold or tan print $4\frac{1}{2}\times9\frac{1}{2}$-inch rectangle and a gold or tan print $4\frac{1}{2}\times16\frac{1}{2}$-inch rectangle to make the left-hand appliqué border strip (see Quilt Assembly Diagram). The border strip should measure $4\frac{1}{2}\times25\frac{1}{2}$ inches, including the seam allowances. Sew the appliqué border strip to the left-hand edge of the quilt center. Press the seam allowance toward the border.

4 Sew together the gold or tan print $4\frac{1}{2}\times6\frac{1}{2}$-inch rectangle, the remaining gold or tan print $4\frac{1}{2}\times16\frac{1}{2}$-inch rectangle, and the gold or tan print $4\frac{1}{2}\times3\frac{1}{2}$-inch rectangle to make the right-hand appliqué border strip (see Quilt Assembly Diagram). The border strip should measure $4\frac{1}{2}\times25\frac{1}{2}$ inches, including the seam allowances. Sew the appliqué border strip to the right-hand edge of the quilt center. Press the seam allowance toward the border.

5 Sew together the gold or tan print $4\frac{1}{2}\times8\frac{1}{2}$-inch rectangle, a gold or tan print $4\frac{1}{2}\times14\frac{1}{2}$-inch rectangle, and the gold or tan print $4\frac{1}{2}$-inch square to make the top appliqué border strip (see Quilt Assembly Diagram). The border strip should measure $4\frac{1}{2}\times26\frac{1}{2}$ inches, including the seam allowances. Sew the appliqué border strip to the top edge of the quilt center. Press the seam allowance toward the border.

6 Sew together the gold or tan print $4\frac{1}{2}\times5\frac{1}{2}$-inch rectangle, the gold or tan print $4\frac{1}{2}\times7\frac{1}{2}$-inch rectangle, and the remaining $4\frac{1}{2}\times14\frac{1}{2}$-inch rectangle to make the bottom appliqué border strip (see Quilt Assembly Diagram, *opposite*). The border strip should measure $4\frac{1}{2}\times26\frac{1}{2}$ inches including the seam allowances. Sew the appliqué border strip to the bottom edge of the quilt center. Press the seam allowance toward the border.

7 Aligning long edges, join 22 assorted gold or tan print, pink print, pink plaid, purple-and-green plaid, lavender print, and green print $2\frac{1}{2}\times2$-inch rectangles to make an outer border strip that measures $2\frac{1}{2}\times33\frac{1}{2}$ inches, including seam allowances. Press the seam allowances in one direction. Repeat to make a second outer border strip. Sew an outer border strip to each side edge of the quilt center. Press the seam allowances toward the quilt center.

8 Sew a tan print $3\times30\frac{1}{2}$-inch outer border strip to the top and bottom edges of the quilt center to complete the quilt top. Press the seam allowances toward the border. The pieced quilt top should measure $30\frac{1}{2}\times38\frac{1}{2}$ inches, including the seam allowances.

Appliqué the Quilt Top

1 Place the fusible web paper side up on the flower, leaf, and vine appliqué patterns on the Pattern Sheet. With a pencil, trace the patterns the following number of times, leaving $\frac{1}{2}$ inch between tracings. Cut out the pieces roughly $\frac{1}{4}$ inch outside the traced lines.

From pink print, cut:
- 11—Pattern A

From lavender print, cut:
- 11—Pattern B

From assorted green prints, cut:
- 26—*each* of patterns C and D
- 5—*each* of patterns E and E reversed
- 4—Pattern F

2 Following the manufacturer's instructions, press fusible web shapes onto the back of

instructions continued on page 274

the designated fabrics. Let the fabrics cool. Cut out the shapes on the drawn lines. Peel the paper off the fabrics.

3 Place nine flower appliqué pieces on the quilt top pieced appliqué foundations, overlapping the shapes as needed (refer to the photograph *opposite* for placement). Tuck the ends of the leaf shapes under the flowers. Fuse the pieces in place.

4 Using one strand of black perle cotton and working from the bottom layer to the top, blanket-stitch around each appliqué shape. To blanket-stitch, pull the needle up at A (see diagram *below*), form a reverse L shape with the thread, and hold the angle of the L shape in place with your thumb. Push the needle down at B and come up at C to secure the stitch.

If your sewing machine has a blanket stitch function, you may prefer to machine-stitch around the shapes with black sewing thread.

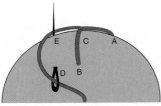

Blanket Stitch Diagram

5 Referring to the photograph *opposite*, place three E vine appliqué pieces on the top appliqué border, three E reversed vine pieces on the bottom appliqué border, and one E and one E reversed vine piece on both the left-hand and right-hand appliqué borders. Place an F vine appliqué piece in each appliqué border corner. Overlap the vine shapes roughly $^{1}/_{4}$ inch to form a continuous vine around the entire border, except at the center of the right- and left-hand appliqué borders where the vine ends, which will be covered by a flower.

6 Place the remaining flower appliqué pieces at the center of the right- and left-hand

borders where the vine appliqués end. Tuck the ends of two leaf shapes under each flower. Place the remaining leaves along the vine, overlapping the appliqué shapes as needed. Fuse the pieces in place.

7 Using black perle cotton, blanket-stitch around each appliqué shape as before.

Make the Scalloped Edging

1 Fold the four green plaid 5-inch-wide strips in half lengthwise with the right sides inside; press.

2 Align the straight edge of Pattern G with the raw edges of a folded $30^{1}/_{2}$-inch-long strip, allowing a $^{1}/_{2}$-inch margin at the left end. Trace the scallops, reverse Pattern G, and trace the scallops again for a total of nine (see Diagram 5). Repeat with the second folded $30^{1}/_{2}$-inch-long strip.

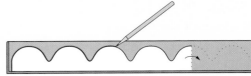

Diagram 5

3 In the same manner, use Pattern G to trace 11 scallops on the two green plaid $38^{1}/_{2}$-inch-long strips.

4 Machine-stitch along the traced lines (see Diagram 6). Trim along the stitching, leaving a $^{1}/_{4}$-inch seam allowance. Clip the curves. Turn the scalloped strips right side out, gently push out and smooth the curves, and press to create the scalloped edging strips.

Diagram 6

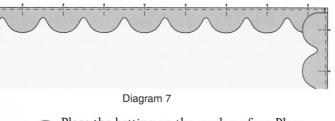

Complete the Quilt

From backing fabric, cut:

◆ 1—30½×38½-inch rectangle

1 Place the backing rectangle right side up on a flat work surface. Center a scalloped edging strip along each edge of the backing with raw edges aligned, a ½-inch margin at each end, and the scallops facing in; pin in place (see Diagram 7). Stitch the scalloped strips to the backing's right side with a scant ¼-inch seam allowance.

Diagram 7

2 Place the batting on the work surface. Place the backing right side up on the batting. (Make sure the scallops face toward the quilt center.) Trim the batting to the same size as the backing rectangle. Place the pieced quilt top, right side down, on the backing. Pin through all layers around the outer edges.

3 Sew through all layers ¼ inch from the raw edges, leaving a 10-inch opening along one edge. Turn the quilt right side out through the opening; gently push the corners of the quilt top out. Hand-stitch the opening closed.

4 Smooth the quilt on a work surface; baste the layers. Quilt as desired. The quilt shown is machine-quilted in the ditch around each of the gold or tan square appliqué foundations, between the quilt center and the vine-covered border, and between the vine-covered and outer borders. It is quilted diagonally in the rectangles of the inner border to create a zigzag design and also quilted ¼-inch in from the outer edge of the quilt top.

colorful cakes

1950—present

A fabric designer and a quilt shop owner joined creative forces to design this cheerful wall hanging. Using more than 70 fabrics, they transformed the traditional Cake Stand block into a contemporary work of art.

Materials

70—18×22-inch pieces (fat quarters) of assorted light, medium, and dark prints for blocks and binding

³/₄ yard of gold print for setting and corner triangles

2⁷/₈ yards of backing fabric

51×63 inches of quilt batting

Finished quilt top: 45×56¹/₄ inches
Finished block: 8 inches square

Quantities specified are for 44/45-inch-wide, 100-percent-cotton fabrics. All measurements include a ¹/₄-inch seam allowance. Sew with right sides together unless otherwise stated.

Quilt Notes

The traditional way to make the Cake Stand block is to use two fabrics—one for the Cake Stand pieces and one for the background. Although the designer used only two fabrics in several blocks, she was inspired to mix and match both the Cake Stand pieces and the background pieces to add interest to the finished project.

Cut the Fabrics

To make the best use of your fabrics, cut the pieces in the order that follows.

The setting triangles and corner triangles are cut slightly larger than necessary. Trim them to the correct size after piecing the quilt top.

From assorted light and medium prints, cut:

- 16—4⁷/₈-inch squares, cutting each in half diagonally for a total of 32 large triangles
- 96—2⁷/₈-inch squares, cutting each in half diagonally for a total of 192 small triangles
- 192—2¹/₂-inch squares
- 6—2¹/₂×18-inch binding strips

From assorted medium and dark prints, cut:

- 16—4⁷/₈-inch squares, cutting each in half diagonally for a total of 32 large triangles
- 96—2⁷/₈-inch squares, cutting each in half diagonally for a total of 192 small triangles
- 6—2¹/₂×18-inch binding strips

From gold print, cut:

- 4—12³/₄-inch squares, cutting each diagonally twice in an X for a total of 16 setting triangles (you'll have 2 triangles left over)
- 2—6³/₄-inch squares, cutting each in half diagonally for a total of four corner triangles

Assemble the Blocks

1 For one Cake Stand block, you'll need six light or medium print small triangles, six medium or dark print small triangles, one light

instructions continued on page 278

or medium print large triangle, one medium or dark print large triangle, and six light or medium print 2½-inch squares.

2 Join one light or medium print small triangle and one medium or dark print small triangle to make a small triangle-square (see Diagram 1). Press the seam allowance toward the darker triangle. The pieced small triangle-square should measure 2½ inches square, including the seam allowances. Repeat to make a total of six small triangle-squares.

Diagram 1

3 Sew together one light or medium print large triangle and one medium or dark print large triangle to make a large triangle-square. Press the seam allowance toward the darker triangle. The pieced large triangle-square should measure 4½ inches square, including the seam allowances.

4 Referring to Diagram 2 for placement, sew together two pairs of small triangle-squares. Press the seam allowances in one direction.

Diagram 2

Sew one small triangle-square pair to the top edge of the large triangle-square. Press the seam allowance toward the large triangle-square. Join a light or medium print 2½-inch square to a dark edge of the remaining small triangle-square pair to make a vertical row. Press the seam

allowances toward the light or medium print square. Then add the vertical row to the right edge of the large triangle-square. Press the seam allowance toward the large triangle-square.

5 Referring to Diagram 3, sew together one small triangle-square and two light or medium print 2½-inch squares to make a horizontal row. Press the seam allowances in one direction. Sew the row to the bottom edge of the large triangle-square. Press the seam allowance toward the large triangle-square.

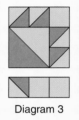

Diagram 3

6 Referring to Diagram 4, lay out the remaining three light or medium print 2½-inch squares and the remaining small triangle-square in a vertical row; join. Press the seam allowances in one direction. Then sew the vertical row to the left edge of the large triangle-square to complete a Cake Stand block. Press the seam allowance toward the large triangle-square. The pieced Cake Stand block should measure 8½ inches square, including the seam allowances.

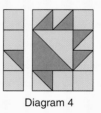

Diagram 4

7 Repeat steps 1–6 to make a total of 32 Cake Stand blocks.

Quilt Assembly Diagram

Assemble the Quilt Top

Referring to the Quilt Assembly Diagram, lay out the 32 pieced Cake Stand blocks and 14 gold print setting triangles in diagonal rows.

Sew together the pieces in each diagonal row. Press the seam allowances in one direction in each row, alternating the direction with each row. Then join the rows. Press the seam allowances in one direction. Add the gold print corner triangles to complete the quilt top. Press the seam allowances toward the gold print corner triangles.

Complete the Quilt

1 Layer the quilt top, batting, and backing. Baste the three layers together (see tips for completing the quilt in Quilter's Workshop beginning on *page 280*). Quilt as desired.

2 Use the assorted light, medium, and dark print 2¹/₂×18-inch strips to bind the quilt (see binding tips in Quilter's Workshop).

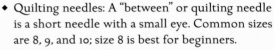

QUILTING

quilter's workshop

Before beginning any project, read through these general quilting instructions to ensure you'll properly cut and assemble your quilt. Accuracy in each step guarantees a successful quiltmaking experience.

TOOLS

The following list includes basic supplies that you may need to make the projects in this book. If a project requires a special tool or piece of equipment, it will be listed in that project's materials list.

- Acrylic ruler: Choose a ruler of thick, clear plastic that can be used with a rotary cutter. Many sizes are available.
- Pencils and marking tools: Marks made with special quilt markers are easy to remove after sewing and quilting.
- Rotary cutter and mat: A rotary cutter's round, sharp blade can cut through several layers of fabric at one time. Use it to cut strips, squares, triangles, and diamonds more quickly, efficiently, and accurately than scissors. A rotary cutter should always be used with a self-healing mat designed specifically for it. In addition to protecting the table, the mat helps keep the fabric from shifting while you cut.
- Scissors: You'll need one pair to cut curved and irregularly shaped fabric pieces and another to cut paper and plastic.
- Template plastic: This slightly frosted plastic comes in thin, sturdy sheets.

PIECING EQUIPMENT

- Iron and ironing board
- Sewing machine: Any machine with well-adjusted tension will produce pucker-free patchwork seams.
- Sewing thread: Use 100-percent-cotton or cotton-covered polyester sewing thread.

HAND QUILTING

- Frame or hoop: For small, tight stitches, stretch your quilt for stitching. A frame supports the quilt's weight, ensures even tension, and frees both hands for quilting. Hoops are portable and inexpensive. Quilting hoops are deeper than embroidery hoops to hold the thickness of quilt layers.

- Quilting needles: A "between" or quilting needle is a short needle with a small eye. Common sizes are 8, 9, and 10; size 8 is best for beginners.
- Quilting thread: Choose 100-percent-cotton quilting thread.
- Thimble: This finger cover relieves the pressure required to push a needle through several layers of fabric and batting.

MACHINE QUILTING

- Darning foot: A darning, or hopper, foot is used for free-motion stitching. You may find it in your sewing machine accessory kit. If not, have the machine brand and model available when you purchase one.
- Quilting thread: Choose from 100-percent-cotton, cotton-covered polyester, or very fine nylon quilting thread.
- Safety pins: These clasps hold the layers together during quilting.
- Table or other large work surface: Use a surface that is level with your machine bed.
- Walking foot: This sewing-machine accessory helps keep long, straight quilting lines smooth.

FABRICS

We specify all quantities for 44/45-inch-wide, 100-percent-cotton fabrics unless otherwise noted. Narrow widths and shrinkage are allowed by figuring yardage based on a 42-inch width, with additional yardage in length for minor errors. If the fabric you work with measures less than 42 inches wide, you'll need more than the specified amount.

MAKE THE TEMPLATES

For some quilts, you'll need to cut out the same shape as many as 200 times. For accurate piecing, each individual piece should be identical to the others.

A template is a pattern made from extra-sturdy material so you can trace around it many times without wearing away the edges. Acrylic templates for many common shapes are available at quilt shops. You can make templates by duplicating the patterns on the Pattern Sheet. Then transfer the patterns to fabric by tracing around the templates.

To make a template, use easy-to-cut template plastic available at crafts supply stores. Lay the plastic over a printed pattern. Trace the pattern onto the plastic using a ruler and a permanent marker to ensure straight lines, accurate corners, and permanency.

For hand piecing and appliquéing, make templates the exact size of the finished pieces, without seam allowances, by tracing the patterns' dashed lines. For machine piecing, make templates with 1/4-inch seam allowances included.

For easy reference, mark each template with its letter designation, grain line, and block name. Verify a template's size by placing it over the printed pattern. To check the template's accuracy, make a test block before cutting the pieces for an entire quilt.

PLAN FOR CUTTING

All dimensions in cutting instructions include a 1/4-inch seam allowance. Patchwork patterns are full size, include a 1/4-inch seam allowance, and show both the seam (dashed) and cutting (solid) lines. Appliqué patterns do not include a seam allowance.

Consider the fabric grain before cutting fabric pieces. The arrow on a pattern piece indicates which direction the fabric grain should run. One or more straight sides of the fabric piece should follow the fabric's lengthwise or crosswise grain. The lengthwise grain, parallel to the selvage (the tightly finished edge), has the least amount of stretch. Crosswise grain, perpendicular to the selvage, has a little more give. Cut the edge of any fabric piece that will be on the outside of a block on the lengthwise grain.

Cut strips for meandering vines and other curved appliqué pattern pieces on the bias (diagonally across the grain of a woven fabric), which runs at a 45-degree angle to the selvage and has the most give or stretch.

TRACE THE TEMPLATES

To mark on fabric, use a pencil, white dressmaker's pencil, chalk, or a special quilt marker that makes a narrow, accurate line. Do not use a ballpoint or ink pen that may bleed when washed. Test all marking tools on a fabric scrap before using them.

To trace pieces that will be used for hand piecing or appliqué, place templates facedown on the wrong side of the fabric; position the tracings at least 1/2 inch apart (see Diagram 1).

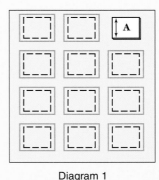

Diagram 1

The lines traced on the fabric are the sewing lines. Mark a seam allowance (cutting lines) around each piece and cut out. Or when cutting out the pieces, estimate a seam allowance by eye. For hand piecing, add a 1/4-inch seam allowance; for hand appliquéing, add a 3/16-inch seam allowance.

Templates used to make pieces for machine piecing have seam allowances included so you can use common lines for efficient cutting. To trace, place the templates facedown on the wrong side of the fabric; position them without space in between (see Diagram 2). Cut out precisely on the drawn (cutting) lines.

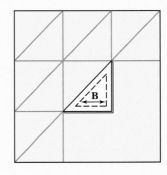

Diagram 2

APPLIQUÉ

In some quilt patterns, especially those with rounded shapes, one layer of fabric is appliquéd, or sewn on another. The most used methods of appliqué are as follows.

- Traditional: Trace the template on the right side of the fabric, then cut out 3/16 inch beyond the traced line. Press the 3/16-inch seam allowance to the wrong side along the traced line. Pin, then slip-stitch the shape on the foundation fabric.
- Fusible appliqué: This method uses paper-backed fusible web material to permanently bond the appliqué shape to the foundation fabric. Depending on the pattern, trace the template (omitting seam allowances) onto the material's paper side before or after it is bonded to the appliqué fabric. After it is bonded, finish the edges with decorative hand or machine stitches.

BIAS STRIPS

Strips for curved appliqué pattern pieces and for binding curved edges should be cut on the bias (diagonally across the grain of a woven fabric), which runs at a 45-degree angle to the selvage and has the most stretch.

To cut bias strips, begin with a fabric square or rectangle. Use a large acrylic ruler to square the left edge and make a 45-degree-angle cut (see Diagram 3). Cut the fabric on the drawn lines. Handle the edges carefully to avoid distorting the bias. Cut enough strips to total the length needed. Seam the strips together for the length needed.

Diagram 3

TRIANGLE-SQUARE

The triangle-square is a basic unit used in making many quilts. Use this simply pieced unit on its own or as a part of a pieced quilt block. Two different methods of making triangle-squares are outlined here. Choose the method that works best for you.

METHOD 1: USING TWO SAME-SIZE TRIANGLES OF CONTRASTING FABRICS

This method eliminates waste but requires careful handling of the fabric to avoid distortion as you join bias edges. To determine what size half-square triangles to cut, add $7/8$ inch to the desired finished size of the triangle-square. For example, for a 2-inch finished triangle-square, cut a $2^7/8$-inch square, cutting it diagonally in half to yield two triangles.

1 With right sides together, sew the triangles together along the long edges using a $1/4$-inch seam allowance. (Photo A)

2 Press the seam allowance toward the darker fabric to make one triangle-square. *Note:* If the seam allowance must be pressed toward the lighter fabric, trim the edge of the darker seam by $1/16$ inch so it won't show through on the right side of the block. (Photo B)

3 Trim the dog-ears of the seam allowance (the fabric that extends beyond the block edges) to make a square. (Photo C)

A
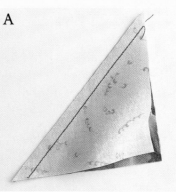

B

C
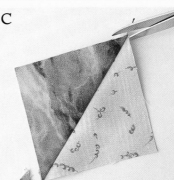

D

E
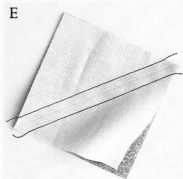

F

G

H

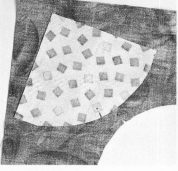

I

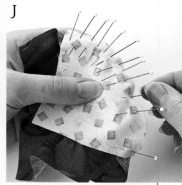

J

K

L

METHOD 2: USING TWO SAME-SIZE SQUARES OF CONTRASTING FABRICS (TO MAKE TWO TRIANGLE-SQUARES)

This method eliminates fabric waste but requires precise marking and stitching. To determine what size squares to cut, add $7/8$ inch to the desired finished size of the triangle-square. For example, for a 3-inch finished triangle-square, cut $3^7/8$-inch squares.

1 Use a quilter's pencil to mark a diagonal line on the wrong side of one square. To prevent the fabric from stretching as you draw the lines, place 220-grit sandpaper under the square. (Photo D)

2 Layer the marked square on the second square, right sides together. Sew the squares together with two seams, stitching $1/4$ inch on each side of the drawn line. (Photo E)

3 Cut the squares apart on the drawn line to make two triangle units. (Photo F)

4 Press each triangle unit open to make two triangle-squares. (Photo G)

5 Trim the dog-ears of the seam allowance to make a square. (Photo H)

CURVED SEAMS

Joining pieces with curved edges presents challenges. Cutting a small notch in the center of a curved edge makes it easier. (Photo I)

1 With right sides together match the center notches of curved edges. Pin together at the center point, at seam ends, and liberally in between, gently easing the edges as needed to align. (Photo J)

2 Sew together the curved edges. Clip into the seam allowance of the edge that curves in (concave) as needed, but do not cut into or beyond the seam lines. Do not clip the convex edge. (Photo K)

3 Press the seam allowance toward the piece that has the inner (concave) curve. (Photo L)

SETTING IN SEAMS

To sew angled pieces together, align marked matching points carefully. Whether you stitch by machine or hand, start and stop sewing precisely at the matching points (see dots in Diagram 4, *top right*) and backstitch to secure seam ends. This prepares the angle for the next piece to be set in.

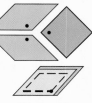

Diagram 4

Join two diamond pieces, sewing between matching points to make an angled unit (see Diagram 5). Follow the specific instructions for either machine or hand piecing to complete the set-in seam.

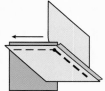

Diagram 5

MACHINE PIECING

With right sides together, pin one piece of the angled unit to one edge of the square. Match the seam's matching points, pushing a pin through both fabric layers to check the alignment. Machine-stitch the seam between the matching points. Backstitch to secure the seam ends; don't stitch into the $1/4$-inch seam allowance. Remove the unit from the sewing machine.

Bring the adjacent edge of the angled unit up and align it with the next edge of the square (see Diagram 6). Insert a pin in each corner to align matching points as before. Machine-stitch between the seam's matching points. Press the seam allowances of the set-in piece away from it.

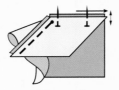

Diagram 6

HAND PIECING

Pin one piece of the angled unit to one edge of the square with right sides together (see Diagram 7). Use pins to align matching points at the corners.

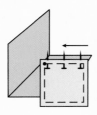

Diagram 7

Hand-sew the seam from the open end of the angle into the corner. Remove pins as you sew between matching points. Backstitch at the corner to secure stitches. Do not sew into the $\frac{1}{4}$-inch seam allowance and do not cut your thread.

Bring the adjacent edge of the square up and align it with the other edge of the angled unit. Insert a pin in each corner to align matching points, then pin the remainder of the seam (see Diagram 8). Hand-sew the seam from the corner to the open end of the angle, removing pins as you sew. Press the seam allowances of the set-in piece away from it.

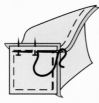

Diagram 8

MARKING THE QUILT TOP

Quilting designs generally are marked on a quilt top before it is layered with batting and backing. First select a marking method according to your project; several options follow. Then select the appropriate marking tool, keeping in mind that some marking tools are more permanent than others.

Secure your quilt top to a large, flat work surface with tape or clips to prevent shifting. Position your quilting design in the center of your quilt top. Reposition your design and quilt top as needed to mark the entire quilt center or quilt top.

USING A TRACING METHOD

Choose from several tracing methods to transfer a quilting design to a quilt top. Because these methods involve placing a light source behind the layered quilting design and quilt top, tracing works best on small- to medium-size projects.

Lightbulb and Glass-Top Table

1 Place a bright light beneath a glass-top table. Or pull apart a table that accommodates leaves and place a piece of glass or clear acrylic over the opening.

2 Tape the quilting design to the top of the glass. Secure the quilt top over the design and trace the design onto the fabric. (Photo M)

Light Box

1 Tape the quilting design to a light box. Turn on the light source.

2 Secure the quilt top over the design, and trace the design onto the fabric. (Photo N)

Sunny Window

1 Tape the quilting design to a clean, dry window on a sunny day.

2 Tape the quilt top over the design and trace the design onto the fabric. (Photo O)

USING STENCIL AND TEMPLATE METHODS

1 To transfer a quilting design using a stencil or template, place the pattern on the quilt top and secure it in place with tape or weights.

2 Mark the pattern on the fabric.

MITERING BORDERS

To add a border with mitered corners, pin a border strip to a quilt top edge, matching the center of the strip and the center of the quilt top edge. Sew together, beginning and ending the seam $1/4$ inch from the quilt top corners (see Diagram 9). Allow excess border fabric to extend beyond the edges. Repeat with remaining border strips. Press the seam allowances toward the border strips.

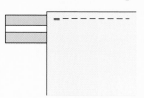

Diagram 9

At one corner, lap one border strip over the other (see Diagram 10).

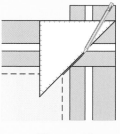

Diagram 10

Align the edge of a 90-degree right triangle with the raw edge of the top strip so the long edge of the triangle intersects the border seam in the corner. With a pencil, draw along the edge of the triangle from the seam out to the raw edge. Place the bottom border strip on top and repeat marking process.

With the right sides together, match the marked seam lines and pin (see Diagram 11).

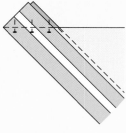

Diagram 11

Beginning with a backstitch at the inside corner, sew together the strips, stitching exactly on the marked lines. Check the right side to see that the corner lies flat. Trim the excess fabric, leaving a $1/4$-inch seam allowance. Press the seam open. Mark and sew the remaining corners in the same manner.

BIAS BINDING

When binding a quilt that has curved edges, cut your strips on the bias to help the binding lie flat.

CUTTING BIAS STRIPS

1 Begin with a fabric square or rectangle. Use a large acrylic ruler to square up the edge of the fabric and find the 45-degree angle.

2 Cut enough strips to total the length needed, handling the edges carefully to avoid stretching and distorting the strips. (Photo P)

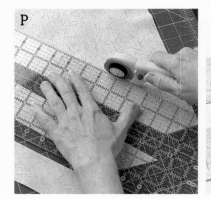

3 Position and pin the strips perpendicular to one another with the raw edges aligned and right sides together. Mark, then join the strips with diagonal seams to make one continuous binding strip. (Photo Q on *page 285*)

4 Trim the excess fabric, leaving $\frac{1}{4}$-inch seam allowances. Press the seam allowances open. Trim the dog-ears.

MAKING CONTINUOUS BIAS FROM A SQUARE

Rather than individual bias strips, you can cut and seam a square to make a continuous bias strip.

1 Cut a square from your binding fabric on the straight grain.

2 Cut the square in half diagonally to form two triangles. (Photo R)

3 With right sides together, align two short triangle edges (see Diagram 12). Sew the triangles together with a $\frac{1}{4}$-inch seam allowance to make a parallelogram. Press the seam allowances open. (Photo S)

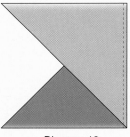

Diagram 12

4 Use a quilt marker or pencil and a ruler to draw lines parallel to the long bias edges, spacing the lines the desired width of the binding strip (see Diagram 13). For example, space the lines $1\frac{1}{2}$ inch apart for a $1\frac{1}{2}$-inch-wide binding strip. (Photo T)

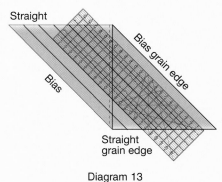

Straight

Bias grain edge

Bias

Straight grain edge

Diagram 13

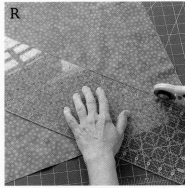
R

S

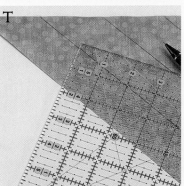
T

U

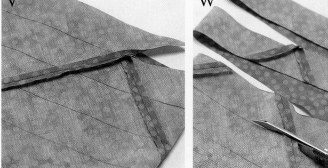
V

W

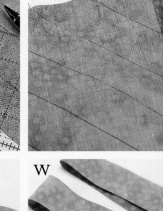

5 With right sides together, bring the straight-grain edges together and align the raw edges. Shift one straight-grain edge so the top corner is offset by the width of one drawn line. (Photo U)

6 Sew the offset edges together using a $\frac{1}{4}$-inch seam allowance. Press the seam allowances open. (Photo V)

7 At the extended edge, begin cutting on the drawn lines to make one continuous bias strip. Trim the strip ends so they are square. (Photo W)

COMPLETE THE QUILT

Cut and piece the backing fabric to measure at least 3 inches larger on all sides than the quilt top. Press all seam allowances open. With wrong sides together, layer the quilt top and backing with the batting in between; baste. Quilt as desired.

The binding for most quilts is cut on the straight grain of the fabric. The cutting instructions specify the number of binding strips needed to finish the quilt with a French-fold, or double-layer, binding, which is the easiest type to apply and adds durability.

Join the strips with diagonal seams (see Diagram 14) to make one continuous binding strip. Trim the excess fabric, leaving $1/4$-inch seam allowances. Press the seam allowances open. Then, with the wrong side inside, fold under 1 inch on one end of the binding strip (see Diagram 15); press. Fold the strip in half lengthwise, again with the wrong side inside (see Diagram 16); press.

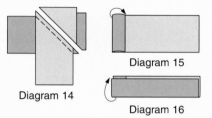

Diagram 15

Diagram 14

Diagram 16

Beginning at the center of one side, place the prepared binding strip against the right side of the quilt top, aligning the binding strip raw edges with the quilt top raw edge (see Diagram 17).

Diagram 17

Sew through all layers, stopping $1/4$ inch from the corner. Backstitch, then clip the threads. Remove the quilt from under the sewing-machine presser foot.

Fold the binding strip upward (see Diagram 18), creating a diagonal fold, and finger-press.

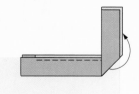

Diagram 18

Holding the diagonal fold in place with your finger, bring down the binding strip in line with the next edge, making a horizontal fold that aligns with the first edge of the quilt (see Diagram 19).

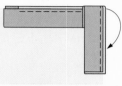

Diagram 19

Start sewing again at the top of the horizontal fold, stitching through all layers. Sew around the quilt, turning each corner in the same manner.

When you return to the starting point, lap the binding strip inside the beginning fold (see Diagram 20).

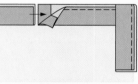

Diagram 20

Finish sewing to the starting point (see Diagram 21). Trim the batting and backing fabric even with the quilt top edges.

Diagram 21

Turn the binding over the edge of the quilt to the back. Hand-stitch the binding to the backing, making sure to cover any machine stitching.

To make mitered corners on the back, hand-stitch the binding up to a corner; fold a miter in the binding; take a stitch or two in the fold to secure it. Then stitch the binding in place up to the next corner. Finish each corner in the same manner.

QUILTING index

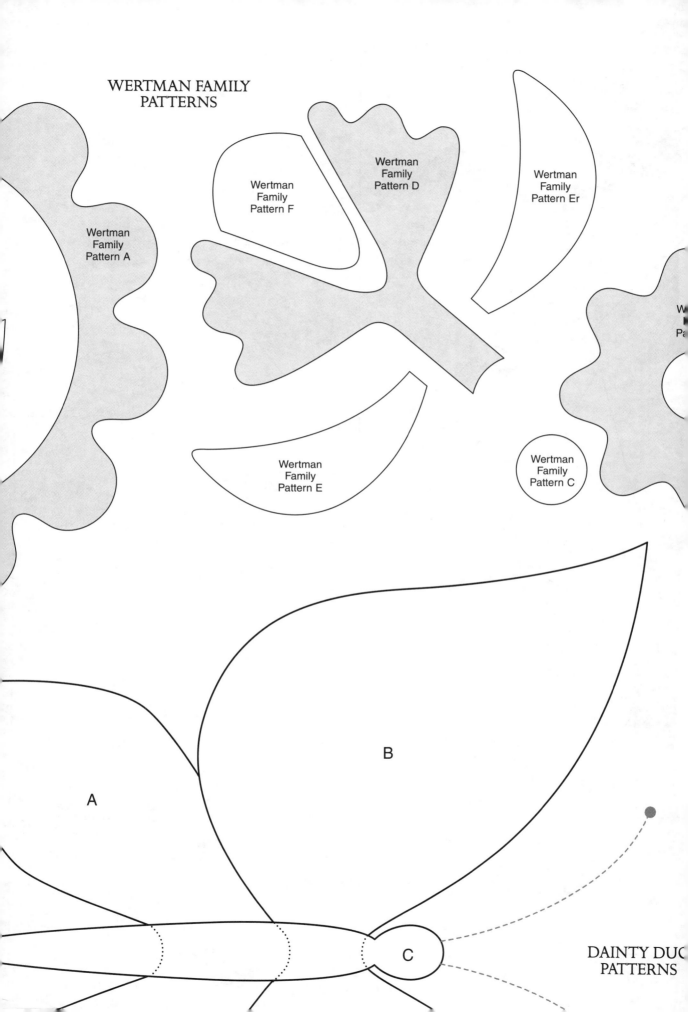

WERTMAN FAMILY
PATTERNS

Wertman
Family
Pattern A

Wertman
Family
Pattern F

Wertman
Family
Pattern D

Wertman
Family
Pattern Er

Wertman
Family
Pattern E

Wertman
Family
Pattern C

B

A

C

DAINTY DUC
PATTERNS

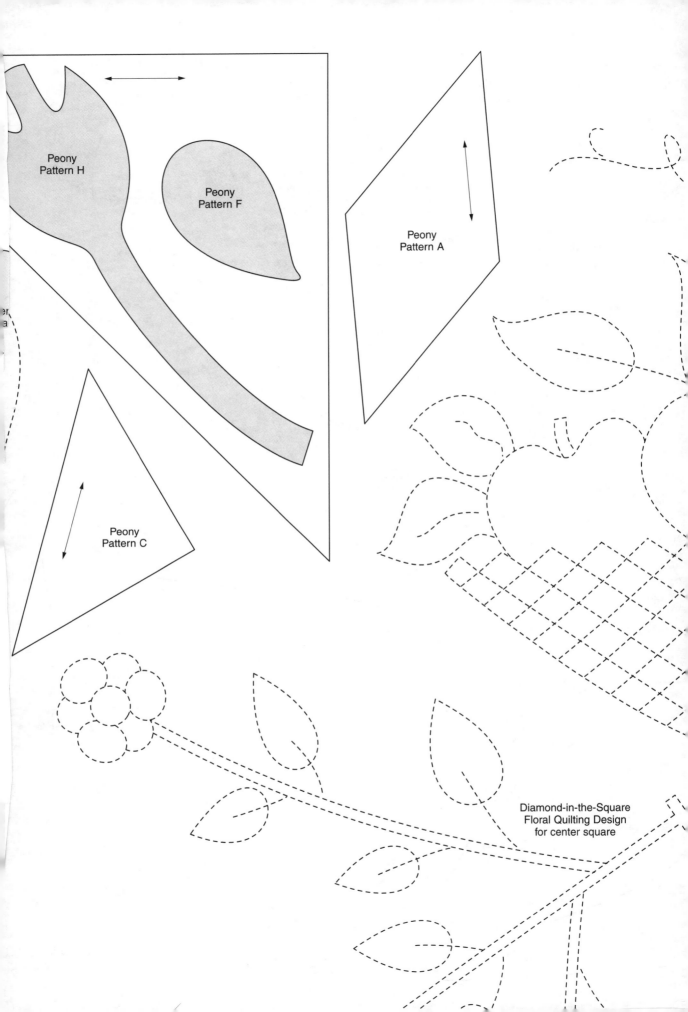

Peony
Pattern H

Peony
Pattern F

Peony
Pattern A

Peony
Pattern C

Diamond-in-the-Square
Floral Quilting Design
for center square

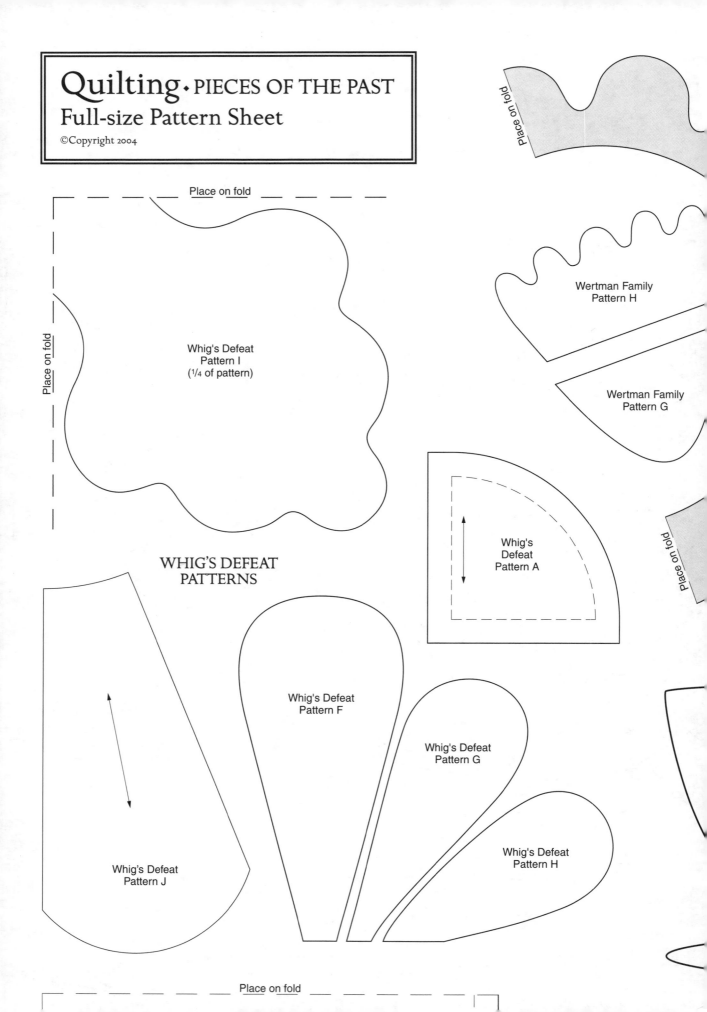

Quilting · PIECES OF THE PAST
Full-size Pattern Sheet
©Copyright 2004

Place on fold

Place on fold

Whig's Defeat
Pattern I
(¼ of pattern)

Wertman Family
Pattern H

Wertman Family
Pattern G

Place on fold

Whig's
Defeat
Pattern A

WHIG'S DEFEAT PATTERNS

Whig's Defeat
Pattern F

Whig's Defeat
Pattern G

Whig's Defeat
Pattern J

Whig's Defeat
Pattern H

Place on fold

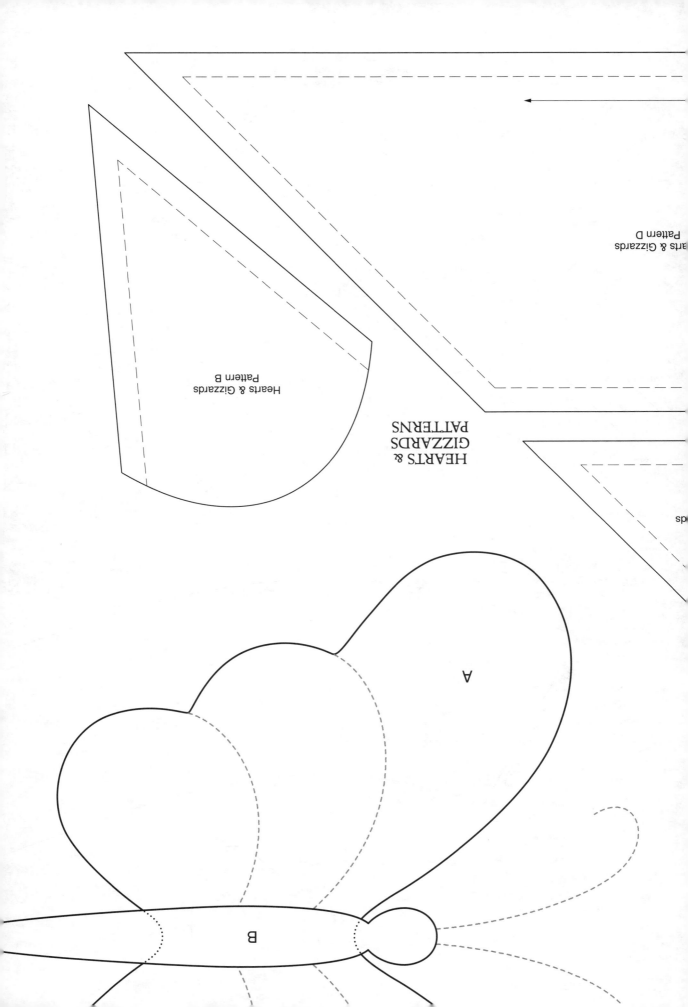

HEARTS &
GIZZARDS
PATTERNS

Hearts & Gizzards
Pattern B

Hearts & Gizzards
Pattern D

A

B

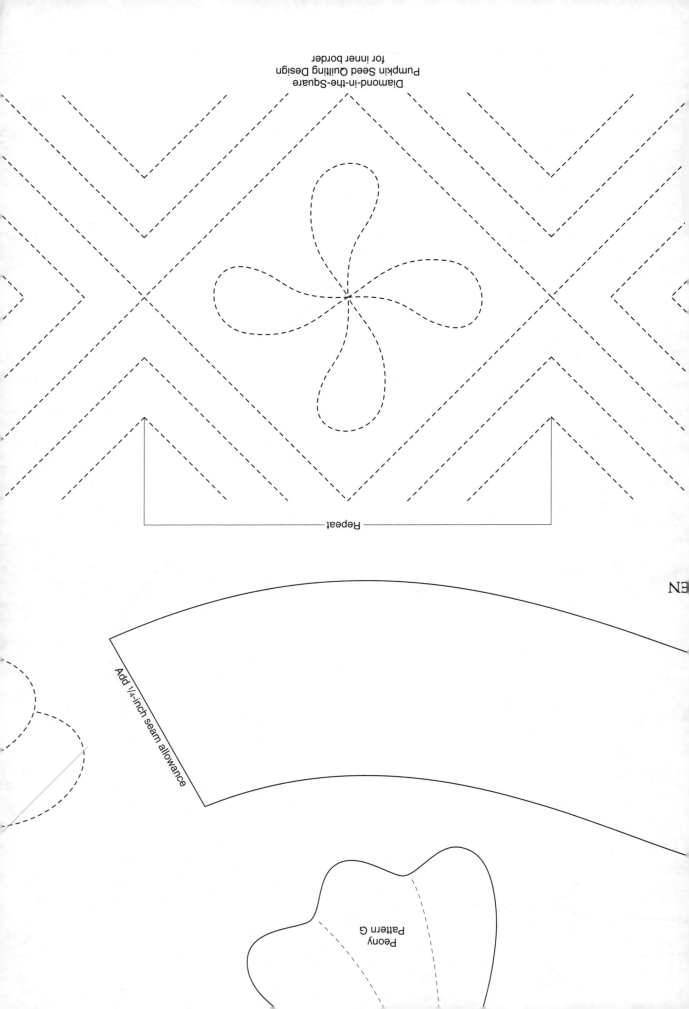

Diamond-in-the-Square
Pumpkin Seed Quilting Design
for inner border

Repeat

Add 1/4-inch seam allowance

Peony
Pattern G

EN

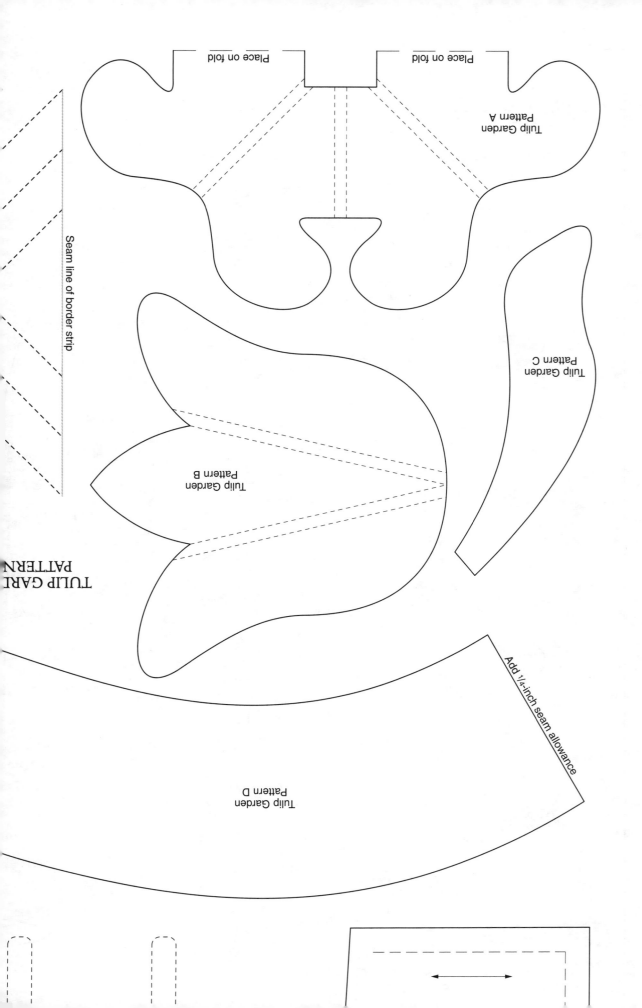

TULIP GARDEN PATTERN

Place on fold

Place on fold

Tulip Garden
Pattern A

Seam line of border strip

Tulip Garden
Pattern C

Tulip Garden
Pattern B

Add ¼-inch seam allowance

Tulip Garden
Pattern D

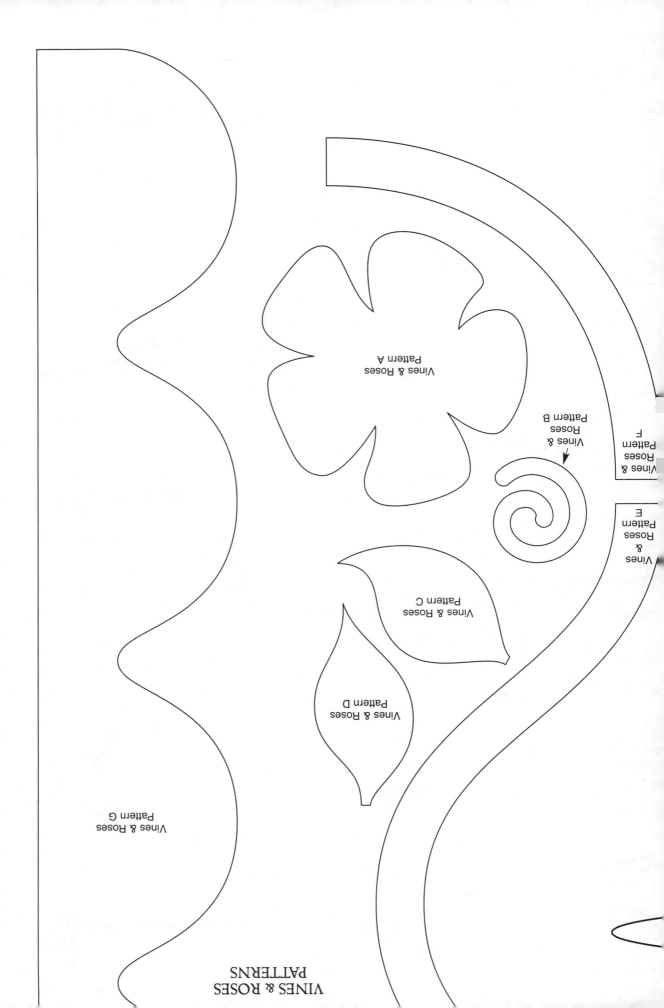

Vines & Roses
Pattern A

Vines &
Roses
Pattern B

Vines &
Roses
Pattern F

Vines &
Roses
Pattern E

Vines & Roses
Pattern C

Vines & Roses
Pattern D

Vines & Roses
Pattern G

VINES & ROSES
PATTERNS

PEONY PATTERNS

Peony Pattern B

Peony Pattern D

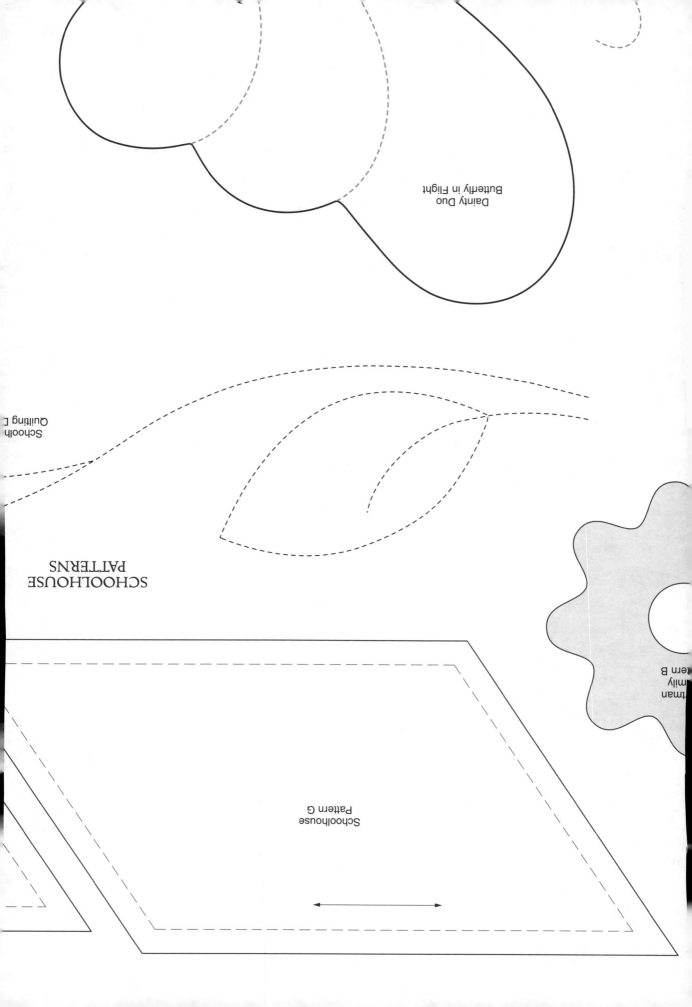

Dainty Duo
Butterfly in Flight

Schoolh
Quilting [

SCHOOLHOUSE PATTERNS

tman
mily
tern B

Schoolhouse
Pattern G

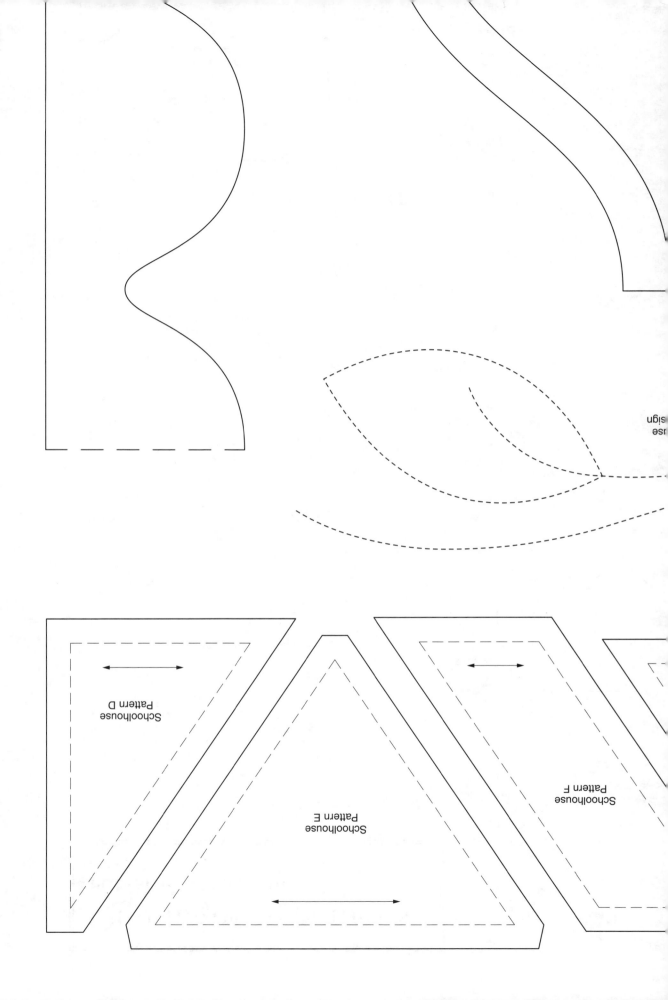

Schoolhouse Pattern D

Schoolhouse Pattern E

Schoolhouse Pattern F

Tulip Garden
Pattern E

Peony
Quilting Patterns

Quilting · PIECES OF THE PAST
Full-size Pattern Sheet

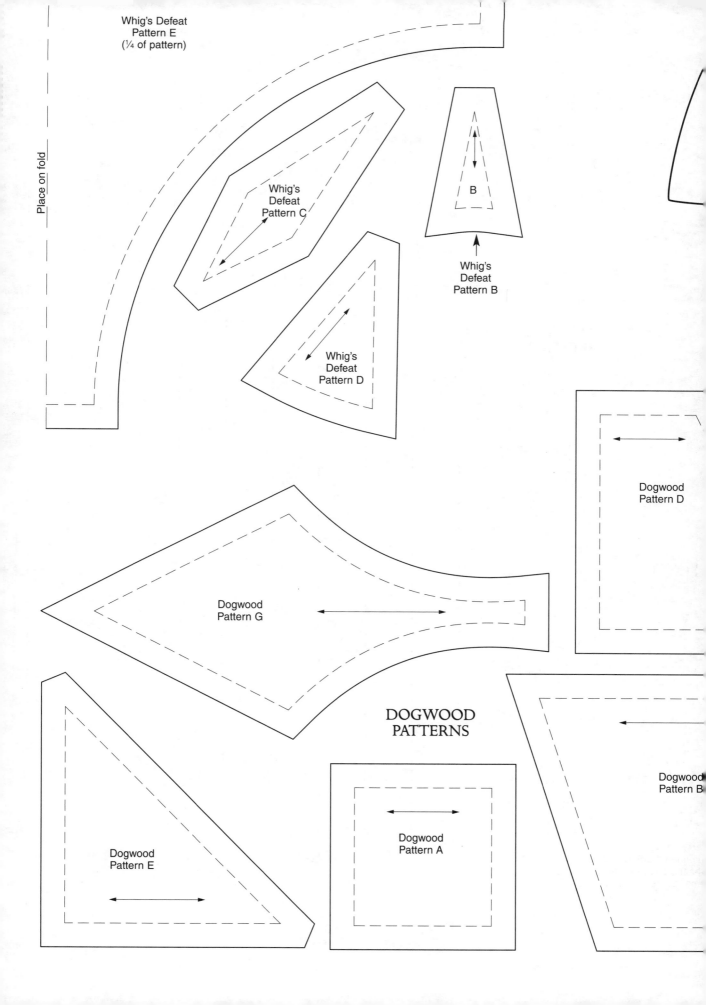

Whig's Defeat
Pattern E
(¼ of pattern)

Place on fold

Whig's
Defeat
Pattern C

B

Whig's
Defeat
Pattern B

Whig's
Defeat
Pattern D

Dogwood
Pattern D

Dogwood
Pattern G

DOGWOOD
PATTERNS

Dogwood
Pattern B

Dogwood
Pattern E

Dogwood
Pattern A

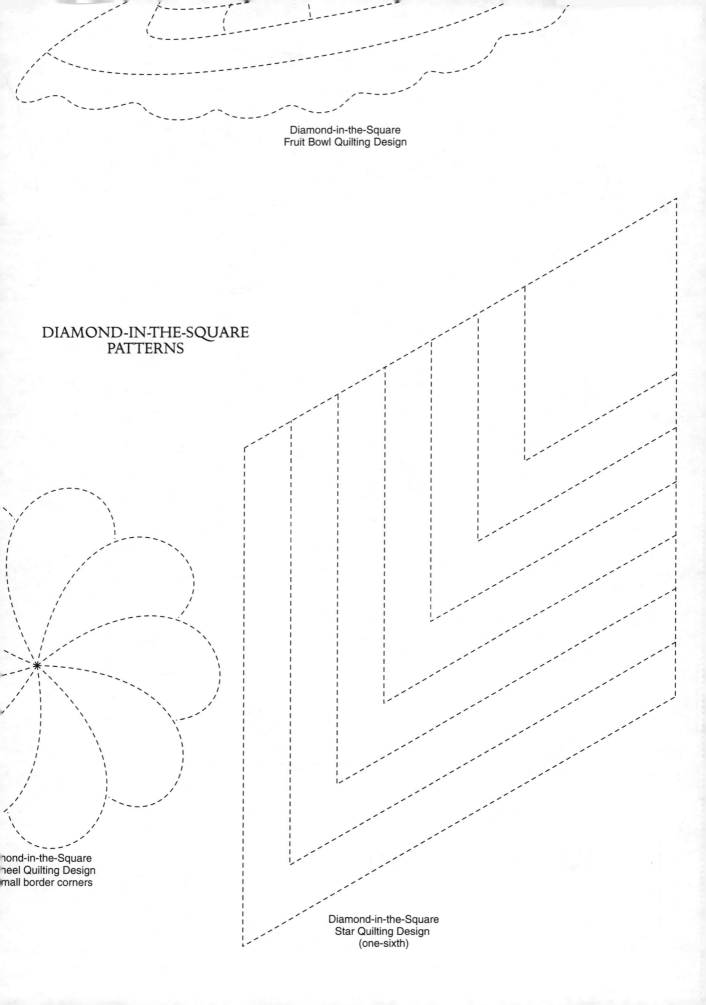

Diamond-in-the-Square
Fruit Bowl Quilting Design

DIAMOND-IN-THE-SQUARE
PATTERNS

Diamond-in-the-Square
Wheel Quilting Design
small border corners

Diamond-in-the-Square
Star Quilting Design
(one-sixth)

Seam line of border strip

Diamond-in-the-Square
Feather Wreath
Quilting Design (one-eighth)

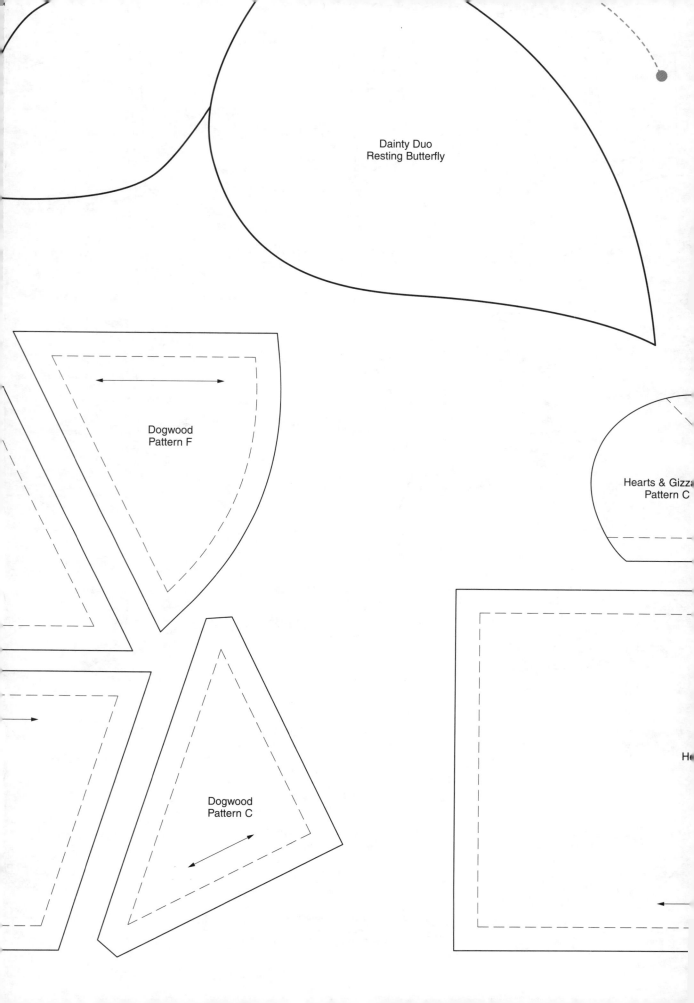

Dainty Duo
Resting Butterfly

Dogwood
Pattern F

Hearts & Gizz
Pattern C

Dogwood
Pattern C

He

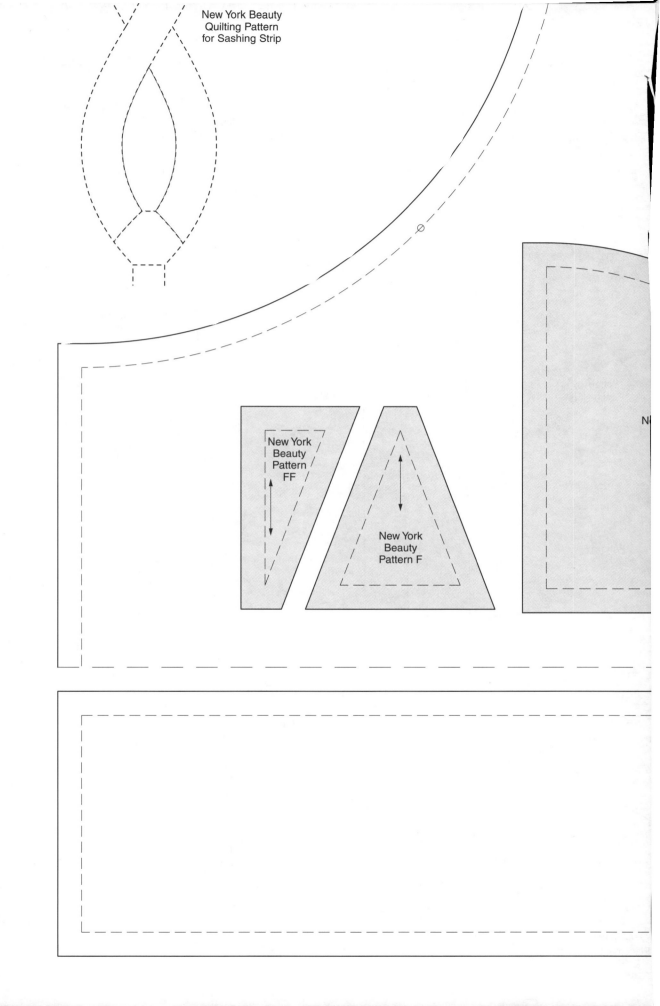

New York Beauty
Quilting Pattern
for Sashing Strip

New York
Beauty
Pattern
FF

New York
Beauty
Pattern F

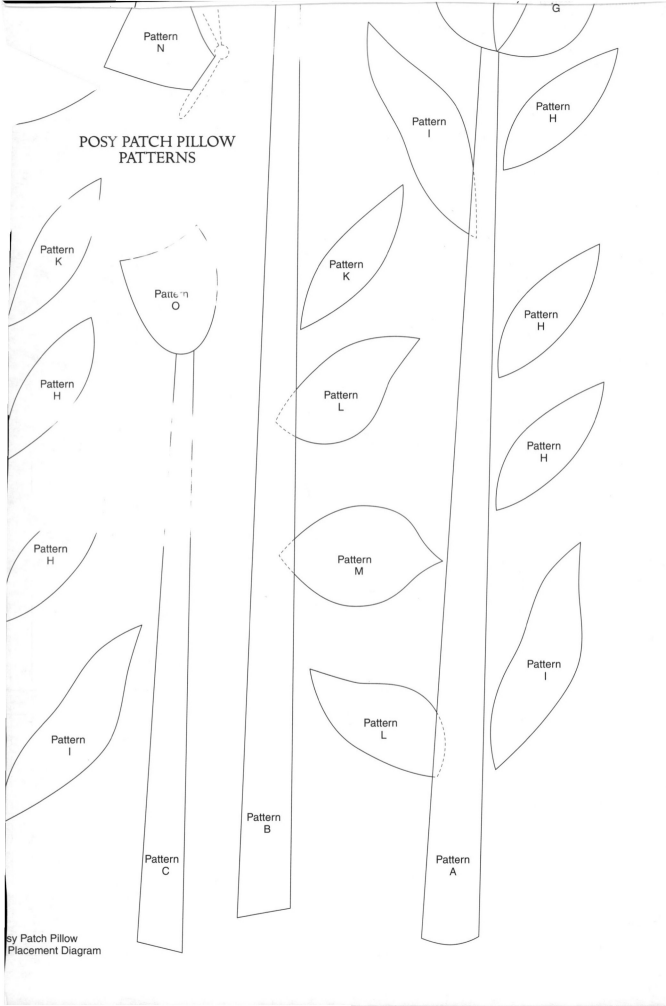

POSY PATCH PILLOW
PATTERNS

Pattern N

Pattern K

Pattern O

Pattern H

Pattern H

Pattern H

Pattern I

Pattern C

Pattern K

Pattern L

Pattern M

Pattern L

Pattern B

Pattern I

Pattern H

Pattern H

Pattern H

Pattern I

Pattern A

G

Pattern D

Posy Patch Pillow
Pattern R

Posy Patch
Pattern

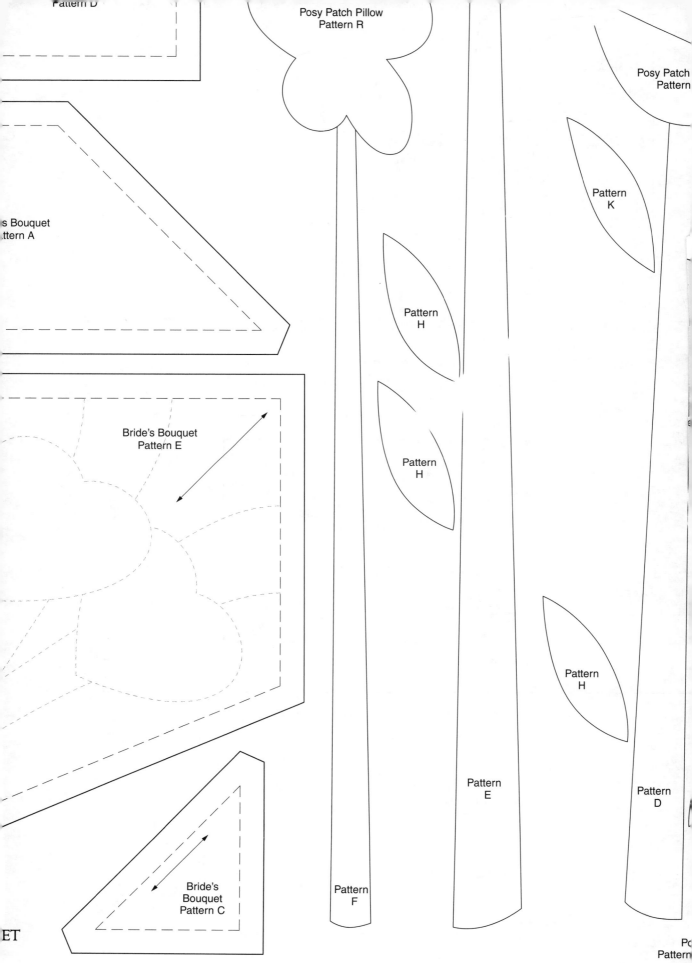

Bouquet
Pattern A

Pattern K

Pattern
H

Bride's Bouquet
Pattern E

Pattern
H

Pattern
H

Pattern
E

Pattern
D

Bride's
Bouquet
Pattern C

Pattern
F

ET

Po
Pattern

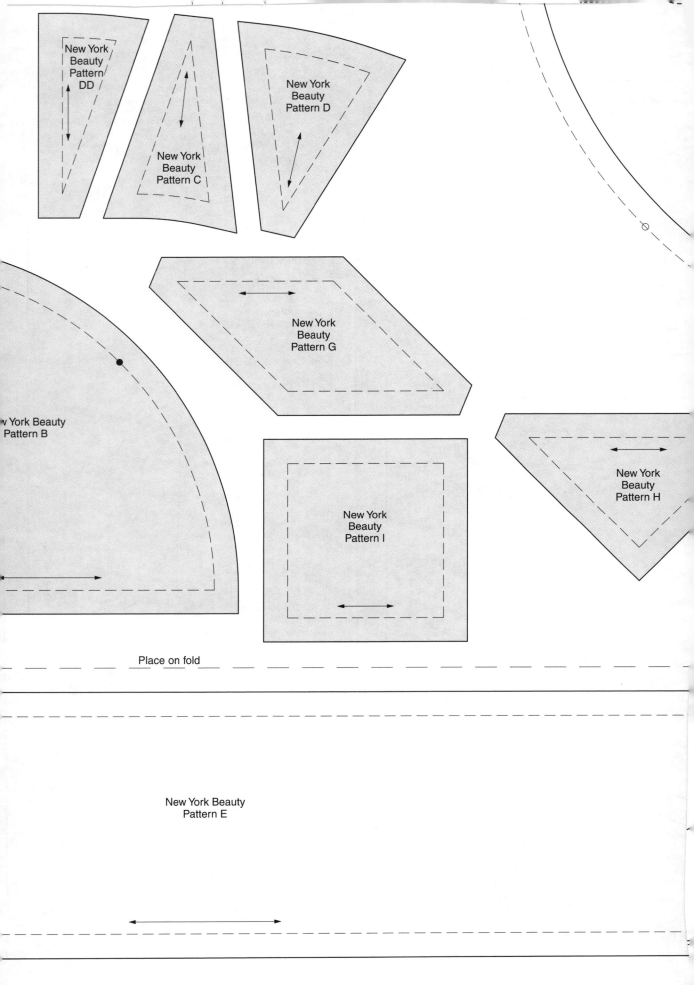

New York
Beauty
Pattern
DD

New York
Beauty
Pattern C

New York
Beauty
Pattern D

New York
Beauty
Pattern G

New York Beauty
Pattern B

New York
Beauty
Pattern I

New York
Beauty
Pattern H

Place on fold

New York Beauty
Pattern E

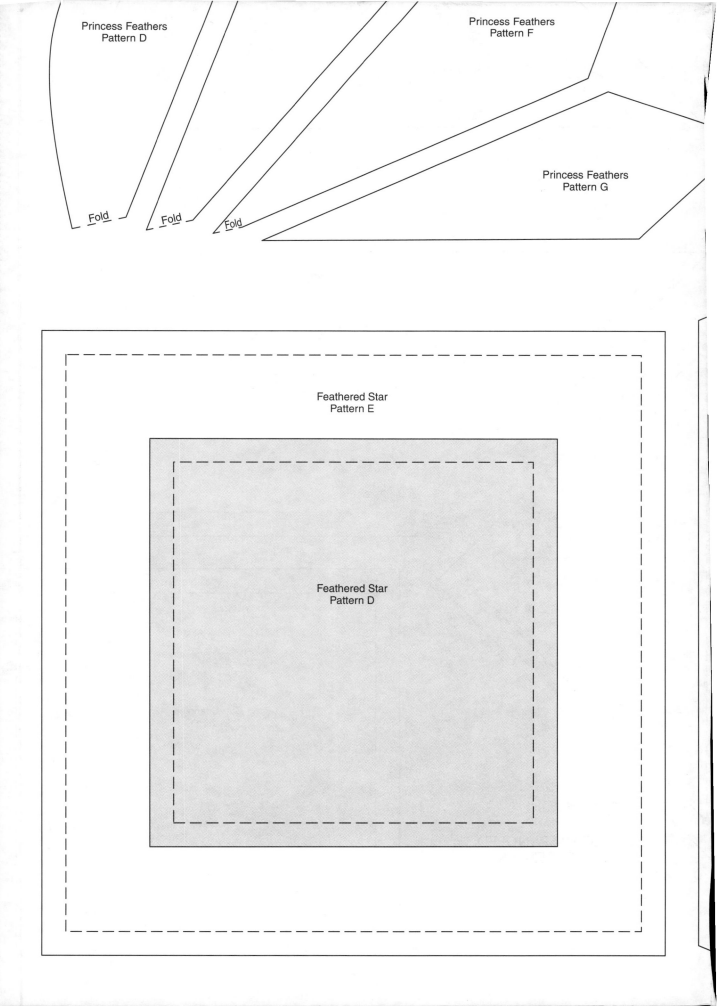

Princess Feathers
Pattern D

Princess Feathers
Pattern F

Fold

Fold

Fold

Princess Feathers
Pattern G

Feathered Star
Pattern E

Feathered Star
Pattern D

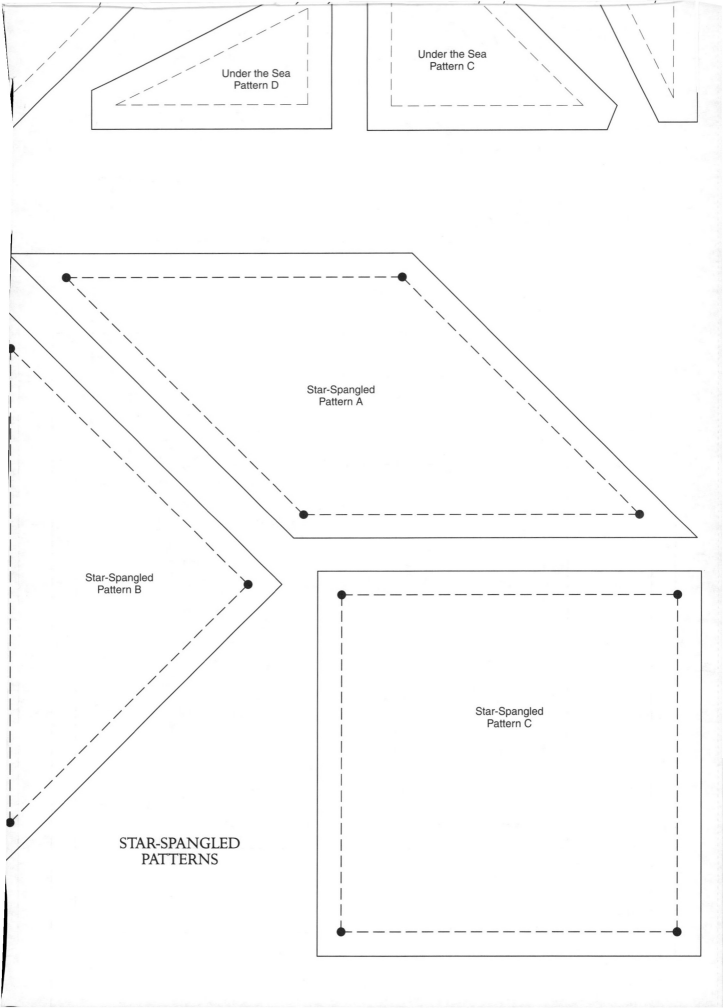

Under the Sea
Pattern D

Under the Sea
Pattern C

Star-Spangled
Pattern A

Star-Spangled
Pattern B

Star-Spangled
Pattern C

STAR-SPANGLED
PATTERNS

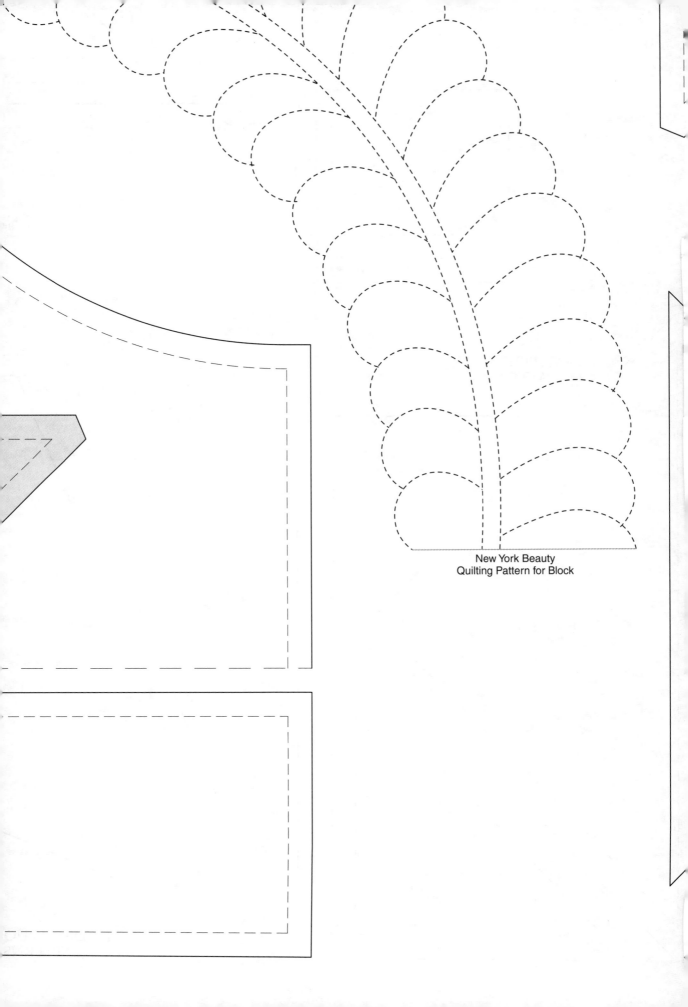

New York Beauty
Quilting Pattern for Block

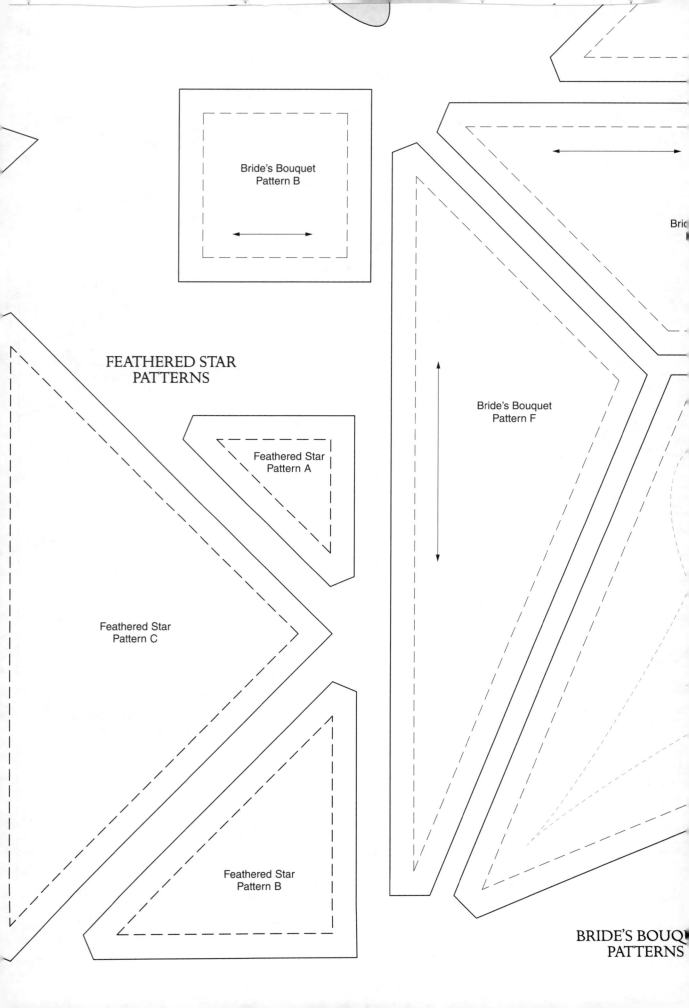

Bride's Bouquet
Pattern B

FEATHERED STAR
PATTERNS

Feathered Star
Pattern A

Bride's Bouquet
Pattern F

Feathered Star
Pattern C

Feathered Star
Pattern B

Bri

BRIDE'S BOUQ
PATTERNS

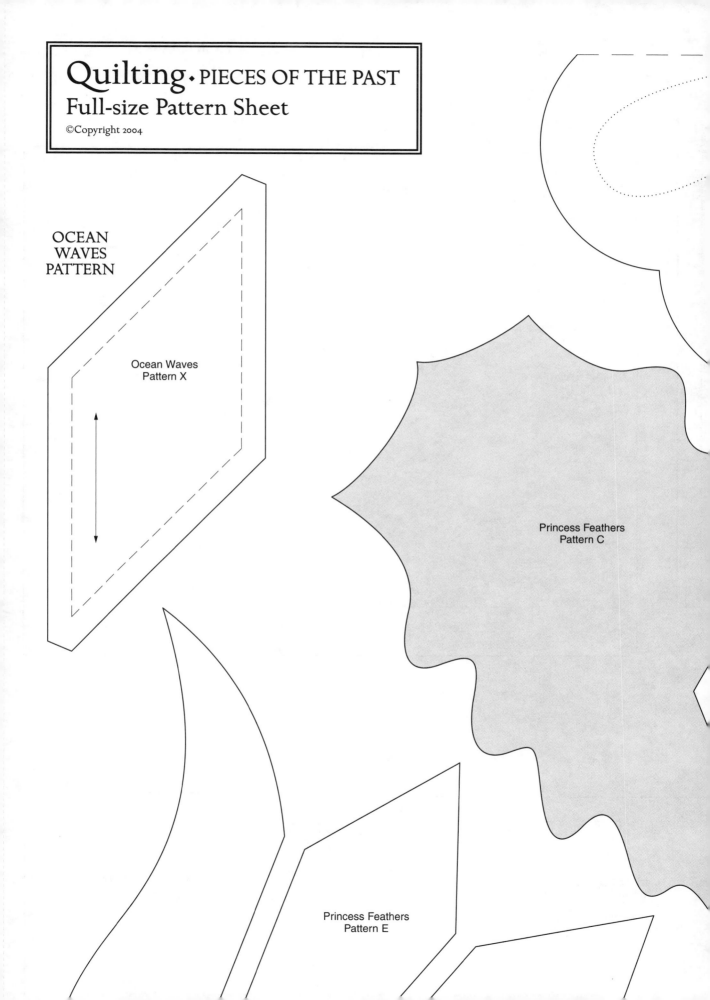

Quilting · PIECES OF THE PAST
Full-size Pattern Sheet

OCEAN
WAVES
PATTERN

Ocean Waves
Pattern X

Princess Feathers
Pattern C

Princess Feathers
Pattern E

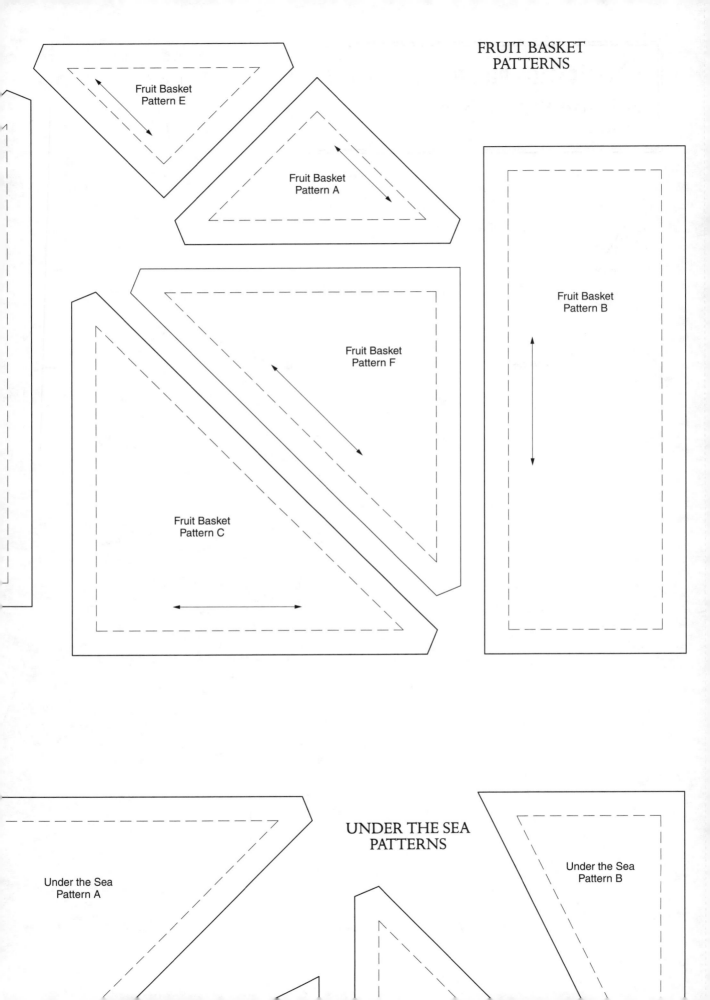

FRUIT BASKET
PATTERNS

Fruit Basket
Pattern E

Fruit Basket
Pattern A

Fruit Basket
Pattern B

Fruit Basket
Pattern F

Fruit Basket
Pattern C

UNDER THE SEA
PATTERNS

Under the Sea
Pattern A

Under the Sea
Pattern B

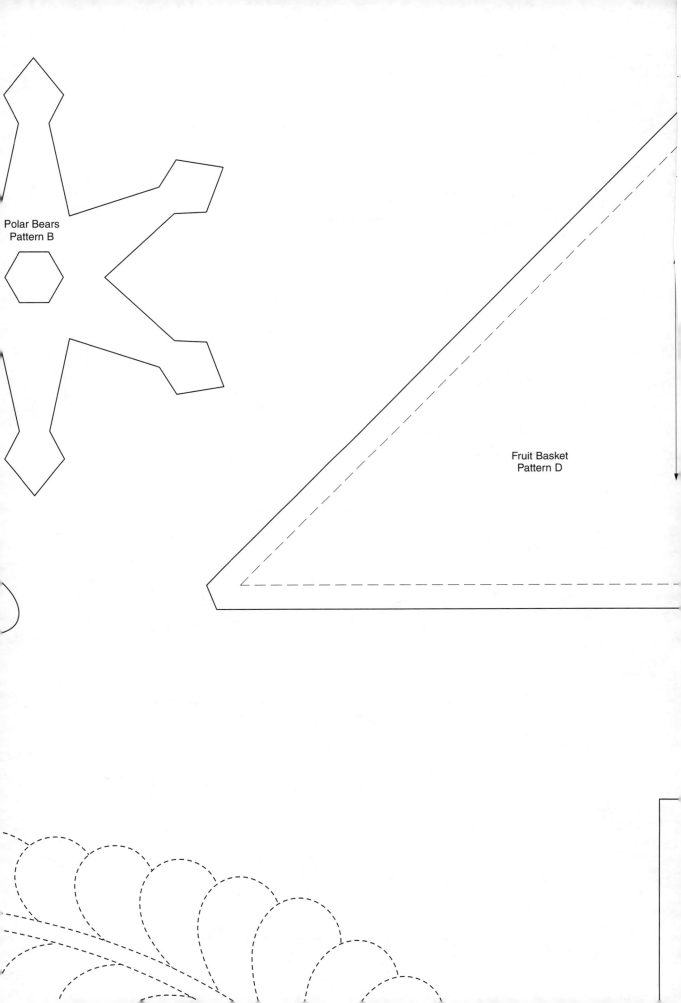

Polar Bears
Pattern B

Fruit Basket
Pattern D

Place on fold

Princess Feathers
Pattern A

PRINCESS FEATHERS
PATTERNS

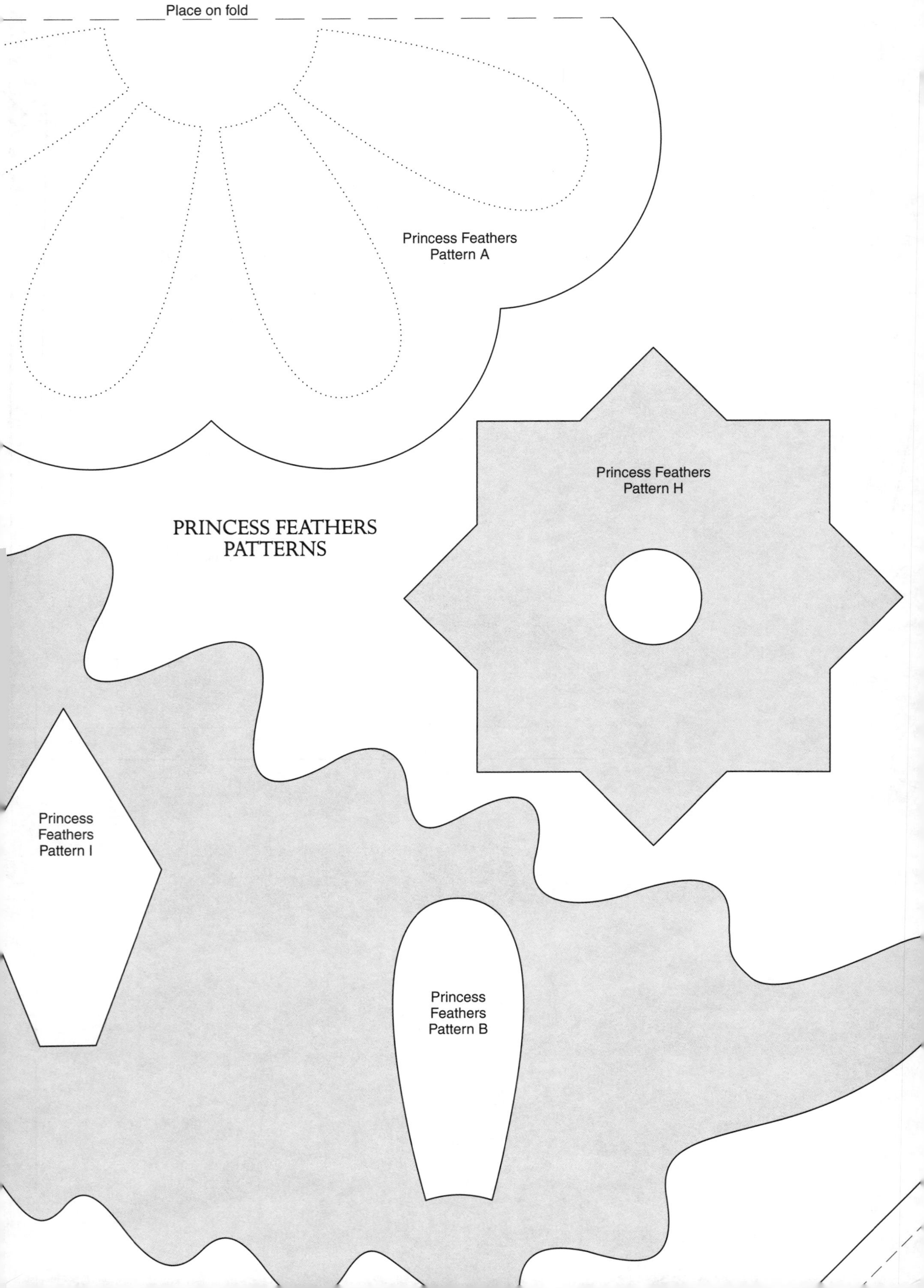

Princess Feathers
Pattern H

Princess
Feathers
Pattern I

Princess
Feathers
Pattern B

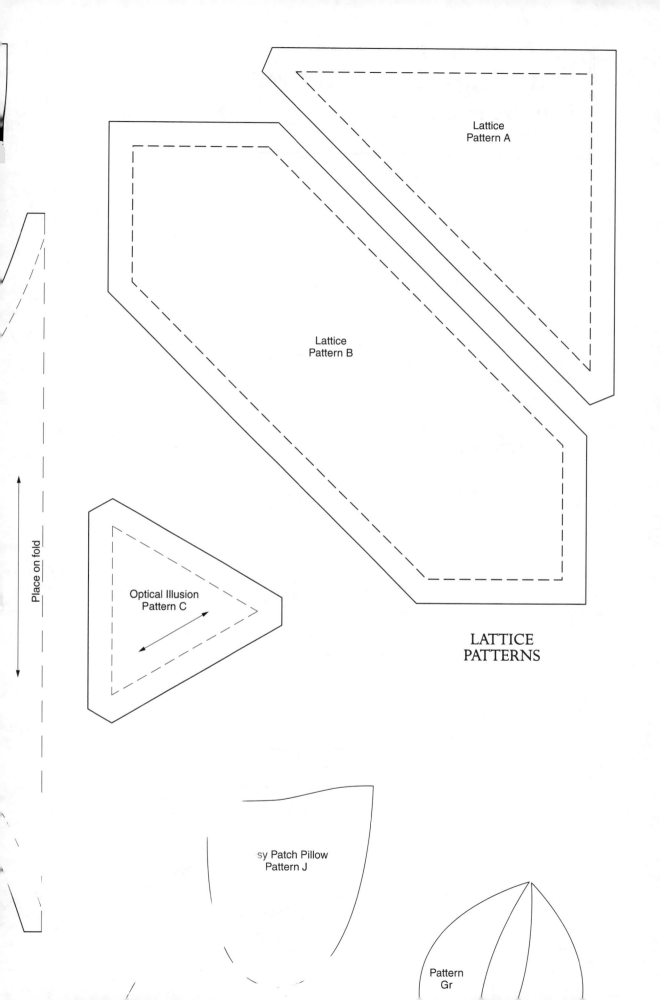

Lattice
Pattern A

Lattice
Pattern B

Place on fold

Optical Illusion
Pattern C

LATTICE
PATTERNS

sy Patch Pillow
Pattern J

Pattern
Gr

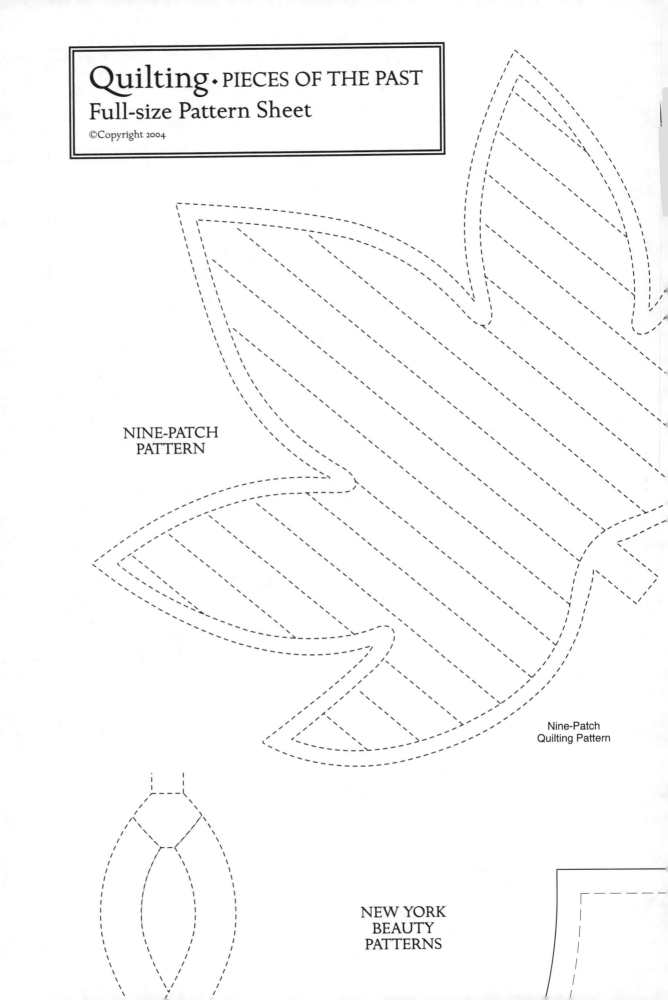

Quilting · PIECES OF THE PAST
Full-size Pattern Sheet
©Copyright 2004

NINE-PATCH
PATTERN

Nine-Patch
Quilting Pattern

NEW YORK
BEAUTY
PATTERNS

POLAR BEARS
PATTERNS

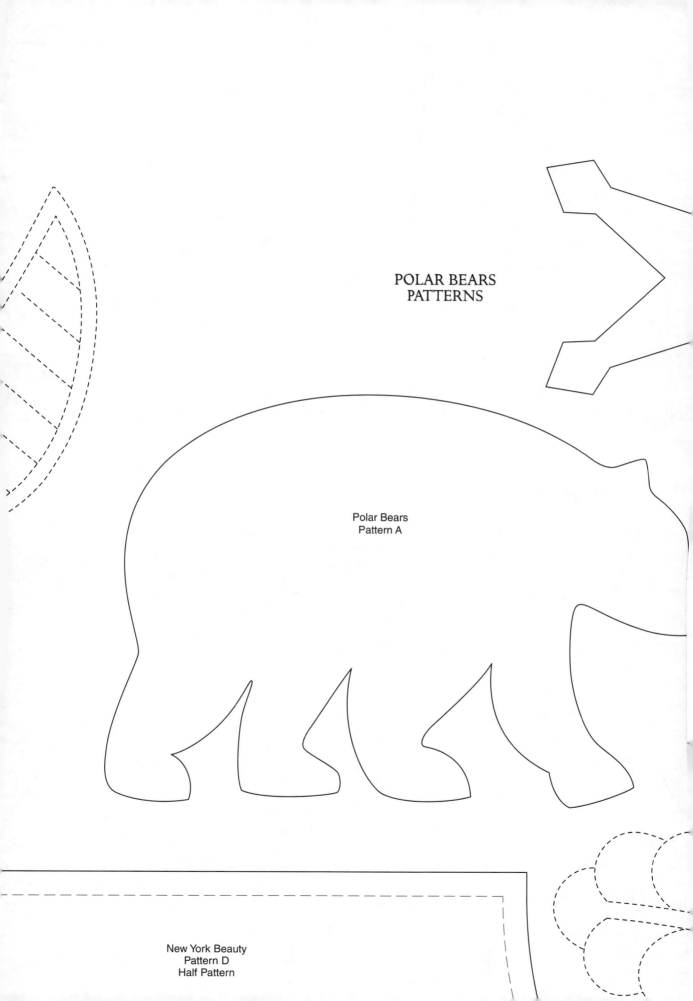

Polar Bears
Pattern A

New York Beauty
Pattern D
Half Pattern

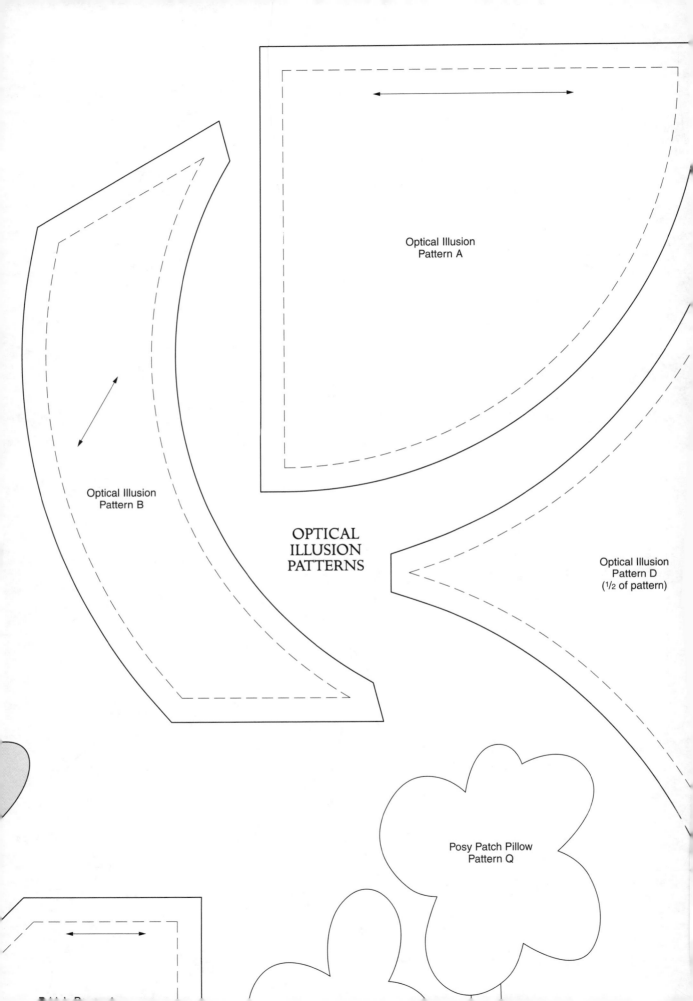

Optical Illusion
Pattern A

Optical Illusion
Pattern B

OPTICAL
ILLUSION
PATTERNS

Optical Illusion
Pattern D
(1/2 of pattern)

Posy Patch Pillow
Pattern Q